Challenges and Opportunities for Deep Learning Applications in Industry 4.0

Edited by

Vaishali Mehta
*School of Computer Science and Engineering, Geeta
University, Panipat, Haryana, India*

Dolly Sharma
*Department of Computer Science
Amity University
Noida
India*

Monika Mangla
*Department of Information Technology
Dwarkadas J. Sanghvi College of Engineering
Mumbai
India*

Anita Gehlot
*Uttaranchal Institute of Technology
Uttaranchal University
Dehradun
India*

Rajesh Singh
*Uttaranchal Institute of Technology
Uttaranchal University
Dehradun
India*

&

Sergio Marquez Sanchez
*University of Salamanca
Salamanca
Spain*

Challenges and Opportunities for Deep Learning Applications in Industry 4.0

Editors: Vaishali Mehta, Dolly Sharma, Monika Mangla, Anita Gehlot,
Rajesh Singh and Sergio Marquez Sanchez

ISBN (Online): 978-981-5036-06-0

ISBN (Print): 978-981-5036-07-7

ISBN (Paperback): 978-981-5036-08-4

© 2022, Bentham Books imprint.

Published by Bentham Science Publishers Pte. Ltd. Singapore. All Rights Reserved.

First published in 2022.

need for a court order if at any point you breach any terms of this License Agreement. In no event will any delay or failure by Bentham Science Publishers in enforcing your compliance with this License Agreement constitute a waiver of any of its rights.

3. You acknowledge that you have read this License Agreement, and agree to be bound by its terms and conditions. To the extent that any other terms and conditions presented on any website of Bentham Science Publishers conflict with, or are inconsistent with, the terms and conditions set out in this License Agreement, you acknowledge that the terms and conditions set out in this License Agreement shall prevail.

Bentham Science Publishers Pte. Ltd.
80 Robinson Road #02-00
Singapore 068898
Singapore
Email: subscriptions@benthamscience.net

CONTENTS

PREFACE

The book aims to take the reader on a technological voyage of deep learning (DL) highlighting the associated challenges and opportunities in Industry 4.0. The competence of DL for automation and manufacturing sector has received astonishing attention during past decade. The manufacturing industry has recently experienced a revolutionary advancement despite several issues. One of the prime hindrances is enormous increase in the data comprising of various formats, semantics, qualities and features. DL enables detection of meaningful features that were far difficult to perform through traditional methods so far. The goal of this book *"Challenges and Opportunities for Deep Learning Applications in Industry 4.0"* is to present the challenges and opportunities in smart industry. The book also discusses the prospective research directions that focus on the theory and practical applications of DL in industrial automation. Hence, the book aims to serve as a complete handbook and research guide to the readers working in this domain. The target audience of this book will include Researchers, IT Industry, Research Agencies, and industrialists *etc*.

ORGANIZATION OF THE BOOK

The book is organized so as to include related rudiments and applications of deep learning in various industries *viz*. healthcare, transportation and agriculture *etc*. The book comprises of nine chapters. A brief description of each of the chapters of this book is as follows:

Chapter 1 discusses the Machine Learning Approaches to Industry 4.0. Inclusion of this chapter in the book augments the belief that Manufacturing plays a prominent role in the development and economic growth of countries. However, transformation in the Industry 4.0 also faces several challenges. Fortunately, Machine Learning can prove to be the essential tool and optimize the production process owing to its capability to respond quickly to the changes and market demand. Hence, it can predict certain aspects to improve performance and thus Machine Learning can prove its effectiveness by enabling 'Predictive quality and yield' and 'Predictive maintenance.'

Chapter 2 provides a comprehensive survey of IOT in Industry 4.0. IoT becomes a topic of paramount importance as we are entering into the new generation of computing technology where IOT plays a crucial role impacting the life around us in homes, healthcare, education, and transportation *etc*. There are more than 14 billion digital devices which are interconnected in the world in IOT which is more than twice the population of the world. IoT makes our lives more comfortable as it does not require any physical interaction between the machine and humans. IoT is widely used to exchange information either remotely or locally with the help of sensors. These IoT devices, then process the information according to their needs. The chapter provides an overview about the recent technologies in the field of IOT and discusses some of its very relevant applications. It also provides an opportunity for the young researchers to gather more and more information in this domain.

Chapter 3 discusses the scope of cloud computing in Industry 4.0 as it has transformed the traditional mass production model to mass customization model. The vision of Industry 4.0 is to make machines that have the capability of self- learning and self-awareness for improving the planning, performance, operations and maintenance of manufacturing units. This chapter discusses the fundamental technologies behind success of cloud computing in great detail. The chapter additionally presents numerous applications along with various issues and challenges.

Chapter 4 presents the Deep Learning Models for Covid19 Diagnosis and Prediction, a current pandemic that has shaken the entire world. The motive behind employing deep learning is its competence to improve the advanced computing power across the globe in various industries. In this chapter, authors provide a review of existing deep learning models to study the impact of artificial intelligent techniques on the development of intelligent models in healthcare sector specifically in dealing with SARS-CoV-2 coronavirus. Additionally, authors also highlight major challenges and open issues.

Chapter 5 presents a model for Air Pollution Analysis using Machine Learning and Artificial Intelligence. Here, authors focus on discovering patterns and trends, making forecasts, finding relationships and possible explanations, mapping different causes of Air Pollution in Delhi with various demographics and detecting patterns. During the implementation, some interesting results have been obtained related to COVID-19 pandemic.

Chapter 6 predicts the current trend using machine learning. The release of cryptocurrency like Bitcoin has started a new era in the financial sector. Here, authors examine the prediction of prices and the model predicts prices of Bitcoin using machine learning. The current work is described in detail in the chapter.

Chapter 7 performs a Bibliometric Analysis of Fault Prediction System using Machine Learning Techniques. Software fault prediction (SFP) is crucial for the software quality assurance process and is applied to identify the faulty modules of the software. Software metric based fault prediction reflects several aspects of the software. Several Machine Learning (ML) techniques have been implemented to eliminate faulty and unnecessary data from faulty modules. This chapter gives a brief introduction to SFP and includes a bibliometric analysis. This chapter can be beneficial for young researchers to locate attractive and relevant research insights within SFP.

Chapter 8 presents a COVID-19 Forecasting model using machine learning. The epidemiological dataset of coronavirus is used to forecast a future number of cases using various machine learning models. This chapter presents a comparative study of the existing forecasting machine models used on the COVID-19 dataset to predict worldwide growth cases. The machine learning models, namely polynomial regression, linear regression, support vector regression (SVR), were applied on the dataset that was outperformed by Holt's linear and winter model in predicting the worldwide cases.

Chapter 9 discusses the application of AI in agriculture as it has the potential to boost the social and economic wellbeing of farmers within the medium to long run. The study highlights that AI-based farm advisory systems play an immense role in solving the farmers' problems by enabling them to require proactive decisions in their respective farms. Various applications of Artificial Intelligence (AI in harvesting, plant disease detection, pesticide usage, AI-based mobile applications for farmer support *etc.*) have been discussed in this survey in detail.

Thus, the aim of this book is to familiarize researchers with the latest trends in deep learning ranging from rudiments to its applications in Industry 4.0.

Vaishali Mehta
Panipat Institute of Engineering & Technology
Samalkha, Panipat, Haryana
India

Dolly Sharma
Department of Computer Science
Amity University
Noida
India

Monika Mangla
Department of Information Technology
Dwarkadas J Sanghvi College of Engineering
Mumbai
India

Anita Gehlot
Uttaranchal Institute of Technology
Uttaranchal University
Dehradun
India

Rajesh Singh
Uttaranchal Institute of Technology
Uttaranchal University
Dehradun
India

&

Sergio Marquez Sanchez
University of Salamanca
Salamanca
Spain

List of Contributors

Abhikriti Narwal	Department of Computer Science & Engineering, University Institute of Engineering & Technology, Maharshi Dayanand University, Rohtak Haryana, India
Achyuth Sarkar	Department of Computer Engineering, National Institute of Technology, Arunachal Pradesh, India
Aditi Sakalle	USICT, Gautam Buddha University, Greater Noida, India
Akashdeep Sharma	University Institute of Engineering and Technology, Panjab University, Chandigarh, India
Arpit Bhardwaj	Bennett University, Greater Noida, India
Deepak Yadav	Department of Computer Science, Amity University, Noida, India
Deepali Gupta	Chitkara University Institute of Engineering and Technology, Chitkara University, Punjab, India
Devendra Singh	IFTM University, Moradabad, India
Dolly Sharma	Department of Computer Science, Amity University, Noida, India
Gurleen Kaur	Dronacharya Group of Institutions, Greater Noida, Uttar Pradesh, India
Harshit Bhadwaj	Mangalmay Institute of Engineering and Technology, Greater Noida, Uttar Pradesh, India
Indu Malik	Galgotias University, Greater Noida, Uttar Pradesh, India
Lalita Verma	Mangalmay Institute of Engineering and Technology, Greater Noida, India
Monika Mangla	Department of Information Technology, Dwarkadas J Sanghvi College of Engineering, Mumbai, India
Mudita Uppal	Chitkara University Institute of Engineering and Technology, Chitkara University, Punjab, India
Mukesh Chawla	Department of Information Technology, Panipat Institute of Engineering and Technology, Panipat, India
Nipun R. Navadia	Dronacharya Group of Institutions, Greater Noida, Uttar Pradesh, India
Rattandeep Aneja	Department of Information Technology, Panipat Institute of Engineering and Technology, Panipat, India
Richa Mishra	Department of Computer Science & Engineering, Amity University, Noida, India
Sanjeev Rana	Department of Computer Science & Engineering, Maharishi Markandeshwar Deemed University, Mullana, Ambala, Haryana, India
Sarbjeet Singh	University Institute of Engineering and Technology, Panjab University, Chandigarh, India
Sumindar Kaur Saini	University Institute of Engineering and Technology, Panjab University, Chandigarh, India
Sunita Dhingra	Department of Computer Science & Engineering, University Institute of Engineering & Technology, Maharshi Dayanand University, Rohtak Haryana, India

Stuti Mehla   Department of Computer Science & Engineering, Maharishi Markandeshwar Deemed University, Mullana, Ambala, Haryana, India

Taranjeet Singh   Mangalmay Institute of Engineering and Technology, Greater Noida, Uttar Pradesh, India
IFTM University, Moradabad, India

Tushar   Department of Computer Science & Engineering, Amity University, Noida, India

Vaishali Mehta   Panipat Institute of Engineering & Technology, Samalkha, Panipat, Haryana, India

Vaishali M. Wadhwa   Department of Information Technology, Panipat Institute of Engineering and Technology, Panipat, India

Vishal Dhull   University Institute of Engineering and Technology, Panjab University, Chandigarh, India

Yashpal Singh   Mangalmay Institute of Engineering and Technology, Greater Noida, Uttar Pradesh, India

CHAPTER 1

Challenges and Opportunities for Deep Learning Applications in Industry 4.0

Nipun R. Navadia[1,*], **Gurleen Kaur**[1], **Harshit Bhadwaj**[2], **Taranjeet Singh**[2], **Yashpal Singh**[2], **Indu Malik**[3], **Arpit Bhardwaj**[4] **and Aditi Sakalle**[5]

[1] *Dronacharya Group of Institutions, Greater Noida, Uttar Pradesh, India*

[2] *Mangalmay Institute of Engineering and Technology, Greater Noida, Uttar Pradesh, India*

[3] *Galgotias University, Greater Noida, Uttar Pradesh, India*

[4] *Bennett University, Greater Noida, Uttar Pradesh, India*

[5] *USICT, Gautam Buddha University, Greater Noida, Uttar Pradesh, India*

Abstract: Manufacturing plays a prominent role in the development and economic growth of countries. A dynamic shift from a manual mass production model to an integrated automated industry towards automation includes several stages. Along with the boost in the economy, manufacturers also face several challenges, including several aspects. Machine Learning can prove to be an essential tool and optimize the production process, respond quickly to the changes and market demand respectively, predict certain aspects of the particular industry to improve performance, maintain machine health and other aspects. Machine Learning technology can prove its effectiveness when applied to a specific issue in the sector— such as filtering out the primary use cases of Machine Learning manufacturing specifically, 'Predictive quality and yield' and 'Predictive maintenance.' Supervised Machine Learning and Unsupervised Machine Learning may provide the accuracy to predict the outputs and the underlying patterns.

Keywords: Artificial Intelligence, Instance-Based Learning, Intelligent Manufacturing System, Machine Learning, Manufacturing.

INTRODUCTION

Currently, the automotive sector is prone to massive shifts. This shift is triggered by various increasing global innovations, such as globalization, urbanization, individual autonomy, and demographic shifts. However, the coming years will significantly challenge the industrial manufacturing environment [1]. Increasing

* **Corresponding author Nipun R. Navadia:** Dronacharya Group of Institutions, Greater Noida, Uttar Pradesh, India; E-mail: nipunn2011@gmail.com

Vaishali Mehta, Dolly Sharma, Monika Mangla, Anita Gehlot, Rajesh Singh and Sergio Marquez Sanchez (Eds.)

globally connected business operations, on the one side, will increase the difficulty within production networks. On the other side of the table, the production and scheduling procedures will also be affected by market conditions and customized products.

These demanding specifications will force businesses to adapt their complete production approach, including structure, processes, and product lines.

It is possible to trace the origin of manufacturing back to 5500-3500 BC. The term manufacturing or manufacture did not even reveal before 1567, even though manufacturing got emerging in 1683, about 100 years later [2]. The Latin terms' manus' and 'facere' means 'hands' and 'to make' respectively were used to generate the word. Both were merged in Late Latin to create the term manufactus, implying 'made from hand' or saying 'hand-made' in short. Indeed, the terms' factory' and 'production' were introduced, taking 'manufactory' as the base word. Manufacturing is described in its broadest and most specific sense: "The translation of objects into stuff" [3].

In the Collins English Dictionary (1998), however, it is described in more succinct terms: transforming or manufacturing any final product using the raw materials, particularly in a large-scale production utilizing machines and technology.

This description can be extended in a new sense: The produce, according to a comprehensive schedule, of goods from raw materials using various methods, machinery, activities, and workforce. The raw materials undergo adjustments during manufacturing to become such a component of a commodity or product. It must have a demand in the market and future, or the product's value must be worth it after processing. Production is nothing but' adding value' to the raw form of material. To make the company profitable and smooth running, the value-added as worth to the product by manufacturing is always required to be strictly higher than the production cost or manufacturing of the products. It is then possible to describe the additional value as increased consumer value resulting from a shift in the shape, location, or supply of the goods, minus the expense of the products and services involved.

Eventually, an organization's income is most often alluded to the added value or gross revenue, measured by deducting the sales revenue's overall expenses. Companies focused on this concept of value-added throughout the past. Companies have used executive benefit or reward programs.

One of the most critical aspects of today's production is increasing sophistication, expressed in manufacturing systems and in the goods to be produced, processes, and business's architectures.

A preliminary prediction from another study [4] can be applied to the idea of Intelligent Production Processes (IMS). IMS is identified in another seminal paper by its next generation of manufacturing systems, all of which were created to solve, within some limits, unparalleled, unexpected problems based on even imperfect and inaccurate knowledge, using the outcomes of AI technologies.

The concept of learning, which is most commonly quoted, derives from [5]: "Learning signifies improvements in performance that are adaptive in the context that they make the system the next time to perform certain tasks or activities taken from the very same group more efficiently." As described [6], we need modern computer technology concerning advanced manufacturing automation that could produce, log and retrieve data, ingest and encode information into knowledge and better reflect this knowledge to help decision-making. It should be stressed that knowledge is closely associated with learning, and an essential characteristic of IMSs must be learning capacity.

HISTORY OF ML IN MANUFACTURING

In 1983, looking at the critical steps in the evolution of manufacturing systems (ONC, FMS, CIM), Intelligent Manufacturing Systems (lMSs) were identified as the next generation that, using the results of artificial intelligence (AI) study are supposed to solve unprecedented problems within certain limits, even based on incomplete and imprecise knowledge.

Hatvany pointed to the absence of such AI strategies in this essay, which seemed indispensable for designing individual systems. In specific, there was a shortage of successful situational rehabilitation and learning skills.

The concept of learning most commonly quoted comes from [7]: "Learning denotes improvements in the system that are adaptive in the sense that they make the system the next time to perform the same job or tasks taken from the same population more effectively." As regards to advanced automated engineering, as described in [8], "we need modern computing technologies that are not only capable of generating, recording and retrieving information, but also of digesting and synthesizing information into knowledge and properly representing that knowledge to help decision-making."

It is required to draw concern regarding that knowledge is closely associated with literacy, where an essential characteristic of lMSs must be learning ability.

The domains related to the architecture or the development and machine learning research have not been undertaken. The most remarkable advantage of all these research and innovation programs, with a few exceptions, was that, with a specific engineering problem, they implemented or integrated a specific ML solution or technique through a conventional modeling and decision-making system. Learning machines or data has become a plausible hypothesis, but ML must be discussed in the engineering workplace to grasp the details.

Learning was selected as the first subject as an essential function of any intelligent system. It turns out that the learning skills are rapidly at the forefront-primarily through the findings of an artificial neural network (ANN) study.

CHALLENGES IN THE REALM OF MANUFACTURING

Manufacturing is one of the most conventional sectors, but it might not be adequate for its worth. In recent decades, several developed economies have undergone a decline in manufacturing contribution to their GDP. However, numerous projects to revamp the industrial industry have been initiated in recent years. The challenges facing manufacturing today vary from the challenges of the past.

Several studies have been published which propose main production challenges on a global level. Most scholars agree on the main problems:

- Introduction of new development technology.
- Growing significance in the manufacture of Items of high added value.
- Green production and goods(processes).
- Agile and scalable capabilities and supply chains for businesses.
- Goods, programs, and process advancement.
- Near partnership for the implementation of emerging technology between industry and science.
- New paradigms in supply control.

These core problems illustrate the continued pattern of being more competitive and diverse in the manufacturing industry. The apparent difficulty is inherited not only in the production programs themselves but progressively in the product to be produced as well as in the organization and collaborative network (business) processes. The fact that today's manufacturing businesses' competitive market climate is influenced by volatility is an addition to the problem [9].

In particular, looking at fields that are more likely to be optimized, such as tracking and regulation, scheduling, and diagnostic testing, it becomes evident that increasing data access introduces another challenge: in addition to the vast volumes of available dates, the high dimensionality, and variation of data and in addition to whole NP nature.

INTRODUCTION TO TECHNOLOGIES

The concept of artificial intelligence has made tremendous strides in automating human thought over the past couple of decades. Symbolic approaches rely on the conceptual representation hypothesis — the idea that it is possible to model cognition and cognitive functions as obtaining, controlling, associating, and changing symbolic representations. The first and perhaps most known kind of intelligent and expert systems seeking to represent the "intelligence" of a human brain in a computer program are expert systems. In these structures, information processing continues in the context of output rules, frames, or highly optimized semantic networks.

Introduction to Artificial Intelligence and Machine Learning

The domain of AI and ML are closely interrelated. According to one of the industry leaders, AI is "the science and engineering of making smart machines, brilliant computer programs. It refers to the similar challenge of understanding human intelligence by using machines, but AI does not have to confine itself to scientifically detectable approaches" [10]. It is relatively generic and entails all sorts of activities, such as abstract thinking and generalizing about the universe, solving problems, preparing ways to accomplish goals, traveling across the universe, identifying things and sounds, communicating, interpreting, and managing robotics. And a machine's action is not only the algorithm's product. It is also shaped by its 'body' and the universe in which it is embedded biologically. However, while keeping it easy, if you can code an innovative program with some human-like actions, it may be called AI to keep it basic. "But because it is learned from data immediately, it is not ML: "ML is the science that is concerned with the issue of how to create computer programs that are concerned with computer programs Improve with practice automatically" [11]. So, both AI and ML create innovative computer programs, deep learning, being an example of machine learning, is no different. In many fields of object detection and recognition, speech detection and recognition, and control, deep learning that has made remarkable progress can be seen as a revolution in computer programs, including computing layers of abstraction using reusable constructs such as variational inference networks, pooling, convolution, Autoencoders, and soon a general overview of the correct algorithm. Data collection and collection in an in-depth neural network format. They are general feature approximators because of the inductive reasoning of neural networks. Training them usually needs broad labeled training sets. Although object recognition benchmark training sets sometimes store uncountable examples of every class name, generating classified data for training takes the most time and costly profound learning aspect for many AI applications.

On the other hand, creating an AI algorithm that covers any possible problem we want to solve-say, thinking about information and expertise to mark data automatically and, in turn, render, *e.g.*, deep learning less data-famished makes a lot of old-fashioned labor. Still, we know very well what is achieved by default in the algorithm. And can more readily research and appreciate the complexities of the problem it solves. This seems to be valuable, especially when a computer has to communicate with a person.

Supervised Machine Learning

Supervised ML methodologies are widely used in industrial applications because of enormous data and expertise-sparse problems and challenges. Furthermore, ML's supervised way may stand to gain from its information collection produced for qualitative simulation purposes in manufacturing, and the reality is that these kinds of data are classified [12]. Supervised ML is learning from an experienced external supervisor's classes. This might be partly because of the attainability of input from the expert and those instances which are labeled. Supervised ML is a prevalent one among them in numerous fields of development, tracking, and management. There are several phases in the overall supervised ML process to manage the data and set up the teacher's preparation and test data set, which is also supervised. The requisite data is defined and (if necessary) pre-processed based on a given problem.

- The training set concept is an essential factor since it affects the later classification outcomes to no small degree. Even if it always looks as if the algorithm's specification is only followed by the specification of the data set used for trying the model, it must also consider the algorithm collection criteria. Some of the algorithms are permitted to be tailored to the issue's particular nature by a 'kernel selection.' This seeks to pay attention to ML models' adaptability or algorithms' implementation and the number of concerns that might be resolved. The similarity criteria often refer to the recognition and pre-processing of data to some degree. Various algorithms have some strengths and disadvantages in dealing with specific data sets. The training dataset is used to train it after an algorithm is chosen. The qualified algorithm is then tested with a trial dataset to determine the willingness to perform the desired outcome's targeted processes. The dataset and parameter features can be modified to maximize the model results to assure that the results are promising. If the performance of the considered algorithm or model is not up to the mark or disappointing, the process, based on the actual performance, needs to be begun at an earlier point.

Unsupervised Machine Learning

A vast area of study is unsupervised machine learning. The distinguishing characteristic is that there is no input information provided externally inside unsupervised instruction. The algorithm itself is expected to describe clusters based on current data,*e.g.*, logical attribute cohesiveness. The aim here is to detect the hidden or unrevealed groups of objects by clustering the data, while classification (known labels) focuses on supervised learning. In essence, unsupervised ML identifies many ML approaches that attempt to learn in the absence of either an established performance or recommendations structure. Clustering, association rules, and self-organizing maps are three common manifestations of unsupervised learning [13]. Unsupervised approaches are becoming increasingly relevant, particularly in the sense of Big Data. However, as with the application of output, the primary assumption is that to identify the range of learning for the algorithm to be educated, experienced experts can drive states' classification. The priority would, therefore, is always placed over supervised processes. Any features in unsupervised instruction, however, could be helpful in the application in manufacturing after all. Second, there is the risk that no professional input will be available or, in the future, beneficial in certain circumstances.

Reinforcement Learning

Reinforcement Learning is re-defined by the supply of teaching information to the environment. A numerical feedback signal contains information about how well the device did in the initial round. Another distinguishing feature is that by attempting instead of being instructed, the learner has to dig up to see which actions produce the optimum of superior outcomes [14]. This differentiates RL from most of the other strategies of ML. RL is, however, seen as a special kind of guided learning' by some scholars. However, RL issues can also be identified by the lack of classified instances of different behaviors, unlike supervised learning issues. RL emulates the human learning process based on a sequential environmental reaction. Unlike supervised learning, RL is most fitting in situations where there is no competent supervisor. An agent is required in such uncharted terrain to benefit from contact and his own experience. Since Reinforcement Learning depends on action feedback, one fascinating and often daunting concern is that Not only can these acts have an immediate effect or not, but at a later moment and during a subsequent additional analysis, these effects may be observed. In a broad view, RL is characterized by characterizing a learning problem, not by characterizing learning methods. The tradeoff between discovery and extraction is a very particular problem for RL. To attain the goal, the agent should 'exploit' the practices he has to choose and identify others to 'explore' by actively following alternate approaches. RL is not commonly applied in development, and as of today, there are only a few examples of practical use. Expert guidance is available in the bulk of industrial applications today. Thus, RL is acceptable for industrial purposes.

INTRODUCTION OF SUPERVISED ML ALGORITHM IN THE REALM OF MANUFACTURING

It is a significant challenge to choose an appropriate method for specifications of the problems in manufacturing development. Initially, an ML algorithm or technique's practical feasibility with the parameters can be derived from comparisons [15]. However, ML algorithms' essential attributes and their modified 'siblings' represent most study problems because of human nature. It's not suitable to conclude solely on such a hypothetical and generalized selection for the ML algorithm. To be able to find an appropriate ML algorithm or technique.

The next requires a detailed analysis of ML algorithms' past execution on research studies with standard parameters for the problem-statement. It is not necessary to find the testing challenges in the same field. The main challenge in this selection is balancing the specified requirements. In this scenario, the capability to handle data sets makes several dimensions and multivariate and adapts to changing conditions.

Statistical Learning Theory (SLT) is an incredibly assuring and suitable supervised ML technique for industrial study. Under the principle of supervised learning, it means the computer's training to enable a function representing the relationship between inputs and output to be chosen (without being directly programmed) [16]. SLT concentrates on how well the selected function generalizes, or how well the performance for earlier unnoticed input is measured. There are some more practical algorithms based on SLT's theoretical context. NNs, SVMs, and Bayesian simulation. The diversity of potential application scenarios and potential design techniques significantly benefit SLT algorithms.

In some cases, SLT makes it possible to reduce the number of samples required. SLT is also able to help solve problems such as the variability of the observer than other approaches. SLT also requires a significant number of samples to work in several other instances. The possibility of over-fitting certain realizations is another problem for the SLT implementation. Steel found, however, the dimension is a strong indicator of the probability of using STL to over-fit. Besides, SLT does not eradicate computational complexity but rather prevents it by relaxing architecture problems.

Bayesian Networks (BNs) can be explained as a graphical model representing the statistical relationships among variables [17]. Among SLT's most well-known applications are BNs. A specific type of BNs is defined by Naïve Bayesian Networks, made up of directed acyclic graphs. Small storage needs, the ability to use it as an incremental learner, its robustness to missed values, and the simplicity to understand performance are among BN's benefits. Nevertheless, the resistance to redundant and interdependent characteristics is considered very small.

Instance-Based Learning (IBL) or Memory-Based Thinking (MBR) is primarily based on and applied to k-nearest neighbor (k-NN) classifiers, such as regression and classification [18]. While IBL/MBR techniques have proved in some cases to achieve high classification accuracy, reliability, and good efficiency and be applicable in several different domains, they do not seem to be the best fit when looking at the previously defined requirements. IBL/MBR's factors were exempted from any further research, include their difficulties in setting the feature weight matrix in new domains. The complex calculations required if massive amounts of training occurrences/test patterns and parameters are associated, less versatile learning processes, task-dependence.

The functionality of the brain inspires Artificial Neural Networks. The brain can perform excellent functions that can help implement engineering when converted to a machine/artificial device. By concurrent processing (in fact or simulated), NN simulates the decentralized 'computation' of the central nervous system and allows an automated system to conduct unmonitored, reinforcement, and supervised learning activities. Decentralization takes advantage of a vast set of simple, fully interconnected processing components or nodes. It incorporates the capacity to process data from all these nodes and their connexons to exogenous variables into a dynamic response [19]. In today's ML science, these NNs play a significant role. It is possible to see today's NN implementation as being at the level of representation and algorithm. NN is used in various industrial fields and numerous topics, highlighting their crucial advantage: their immense applicability.

There is an extensive range of various ML algorithms and techniques available, as outlined in the previous section. There are unique benefits and pitfalls to both. Selected implementations of a special supervised ML algorithm: SVMs, are outlined to summarize practical applications of ML in production systems.

Monitoring is a significant application field of SVM in manufacturing. SVM's consistently and smoothly applied areas are machine condition monitoring, tool wear, and fault detection. Quality tracking in development is also an environment where SVMs have been successfully introduced [27, 28].

Picture recognition is an application of the SVM algorithm with an intersection with the manufacturing application. It can be used in production to distinguish degraded goods. Such fields of use are, for example, recognition by handwriting. The forecasting of time sequence is also a field where SVM enhancement is sometimes introduced. As exemplified by the SVM algorithm, many popular ML applications are available in the manufacturing industry, and several of them are even infrequently used in industries worldwide.

APPLICATION OF ML TECHNIQUES IN MANUFACTURING

Machine-learning approaches may be valuable instruments for finding precious data patterns. Since there are no readily available alternatives, it is also essential to have a crystal clear perception of a specific problem's demands and select the algorithm and technique that perfectly suits those criteria. In a machine-learning device it should consist of the skills enlisted below to be helpful in a manufacturing application:

a. Concerned with numerous data types.
b. Processing inrun-time.
c. They are coping with massive data sets of very high-level.
d. The development of easy-to-understand results.
e. That they are easy to enforce.

Domain independent algorithms are machine-learning algorithms. They may, in theory, be a beneficial instrument for designing knowledge-based structures. A typical pattern is accompanied by attempts to implement machine-learning techniques. The process's significant phases are problem formatting, representation determination, training data selection, learning information evaluation, and knowledge base fielding [20].

There is a wide range of fields of growth upon which machine learning has also been applied effectively. An inductive-learning method was suggested and used to construct a qualitative knowledge base using a simulation experiment's findings. Inductive learning, given the class, was used to obtain a generalized definition of the control parameter values. The knowledge base produced could thus be used for deductive reasoning to guide the method.

To analyze process-planning decision-making challenges, we have been using inductive learning. To learn about manufacturing routes *via* a steel factory, they followed a mix of induction and interviews with experts [21]. While the experts were fairly descriptive, rule induction to support the experts in formalizing and structuring their expertise saved substantial time and effort. Inductive-learning approaches have allowed engineers to summarize vast quantities of knowledge to facilitate decision-making.

It is essential to build automatic scheduling systems to manage manufacturing processes as the production stages get more complicated. One of the functional approaches used to address this issue is scheduled based on learning, which requires the automated acquisition of dispatching rules. Various efforts have been made to use learning in planning problems. Flow-shop scheduling issues, job-shop scheduling issues, and adaptive production processes scheduling problems were added to proposed approaches for obtaining scheduling rules using inductive-Learning techniques. Experimental studies have demonstrated that efficient scheduling can be accomplished by applying the proposed techniques.

For just-in-time (JIT) output processes [22, 23], machine-learning algorithms and techniques have been put into practice. First, in an intricate JIT factory, neural networks and decision trees were being used to set the number of kanbans. For the successful operation of a JIT production system, the number of kanbans is essential. Results have shown that two functional methods with unique abilities to change the number of kanbans dynamically represent neural networks and decision trees. Second, to forecast JIT factory performance from past information that contains both good and lousy factory performance, a method focused on inductive learning was used. In particular, the CART decision-tree classifier was used to automatically produce rules in the JIT development environment. Based on shop variables, the rules obtained can reliably define and forecast factory output and recognize the significant relationships between shop variables that decide factory performance.

The application of machine-learning techniques to the metal etching problem was explored to evaluate, identify, and forecast metal etchings' consistency. They used three different techniques [24]. Neural networks, inductive learning, and case-based reasoning, a variant of example-based learning, adopted methods. The authors concluded that through their ability to simulate and simplify the processing of vast volumes of dynamic data in diverse production areas, machine-learning methods help minimize cycle time and scrap and increase energy usage. Modern sensor-equipped devices, such as airplanes produce extensive numerical and symbolic data to run and sustain. Few researchers developed an approach using these data to create models to predict when separate aircraft components can be replaced before they malfunction. Three distinct machine-learning methods were used to infer the desired models: inductive learning, instance-based learning, and Bayesian learning.

The manufacturing of semiconductors is a dynamic process requiring the control of a wide range of parameters from the early stages of production to the final product packaging. It takes a lot of data processing effort to increase the development process's efficiency and is only done by human engineers. In a standard wafer processing facility, the transaction rate is as many as one million wafers a day. The amount of knowledge involved makes the process of data processing incredibly time-consuming and demanding [25]. Several scholars recommended protocols for the use of semiconductor production of machine learning techniques. Studies have shown that in a large and dynamic process such as semiconductor manufacturing, machine-learning methods can be proper instruments for continuous quality management.

An intelligent data-mining method applied to the drop-test study of portable electronic goods has been developed to uncover valuable design information. The adopted rule-induction procedure is based on the algorithm C4.5. Studies of the proposed method have demonstrated that the methodology is scalable and can be extended to various design and development processes to minimize costs and increase efficiency and introduced an industrial visual inspection method that can be used to conduct bulk production quality controls. The method employs the inductive-learning algorithm RULES-3 [26].

To enhance the efficiency of development processes, a fuzzy inductive-learning-based intelligent-monitoring framework was developed. To ensure the consistency of goods, the procedure has been successfully applied to diagnose tapping operations conditions.

AREAS OF APPLICATION TO SUPERVISED MACHINE LEARNING IN MANUFACTURING AND ITS DEVELOPMENT

There is an extensive range of ML algorithms and techniques available, as outlined in the previous section. There are unique benefits and pitfalls to both. Selected implementations of a special supervised ML algorithm: SVMs, are outlined to summarize practical applications of ML in production systems. Monitoring is a significant application field of SVM in manufacturing. SVM's areas are consistently and smoothly applied are machine condition monitoring, tool wear, and fault detection. Quality tracking in development is also an environment where SVMs have been successfully introduced [27, 28].

Picture recognition is an application of the SVM algorithm with an intersection with the manufacturing application. It can be used in production to distinguish degraded goods. Such fields of use are, for example, recognition by handwriting. The forecasting of time sequence is also a field where SVM enhancement is sometimes introduced. As exemplified by the SVM algorithm, many popular ML applications are available in the manufacturing industry, and several of them are even infrequently used in industries worldwide.

MANAGEMENT OF METHOD/MACHINE LEVEL UNCERTAINTIES AND ADJUSTMENTS

Tool Condition Manufacturing

Through linear decision functions trained adaptively, computational PR (Pattern Recognition) techniques for control purposes began. The Fuzzy PR methods have proven to be practical methods to deal with cutting processes' unpredictable existence. Various multi-purpose monitoring systems have been developed based on PR, multi-sensor aggregation, and parallel processing by multiprocessor systems. For TCM (Tool Condition Monitoring) the author uses ANNs. It was shown that the ANNs for multisensory integration were applicable. The statistical analysis obtained by linear models and ANNs trained by the back propagation procedure (BP) demonstrated the more significant noise reduction and classification capabilities of the neural networks [29]. How to manage the changing operating conditions is one of the key-but frequently ignored concerns in controlling machining processes. Some proposals were shown in 1993 for integrating process attributes knowledge into the learning and classification phases. The best generalization capacity was obtained with the latter alternative by comparing the various methods, *i.e.*, the networks can search out the multiple method parameters' alarming results and generalize them. Due to TCM's numerical, run-time design, comparatively few studies have been reported on implementing symbolic learning methods in this area compared to generative approaches. The recognition of plunge grinding by decision tree generation using the grinding wheel's vibration signals was defined in [30]. A combined framework and feature learning technique was defined in four categories *via* a neuro-fuzzy (NF) method for categorizing fit states of tools used for milling. To evaluate the fuzzy rules and the membership parameters (MBF) functions, a four-step learning algorithm combining supervised BP learning, competitive learning, and self-organized clustering algorithms was applied.

Process Modelling

In various computer-integrated manufacturing disciplines, accurate predictive models are particularly significant, such as configuration, optimization techniques, control, and simulation of operations and equipment design. There are several challenges in modeling production processes: the vast range of additional machining operations, the multivariate, non-linear, probabilistic nature of machining, the partially understood parameter relationships, the absence of objective evidence, *etc* [31]. The need for sensor convergence, advanced models, multimodal systems, and learning capacity was highlighted in the CIRP Annals survey on advances and patterns in monitoring and controlling manufacturing parameters. The decision-making methodology involves many process models that relate process state variables such as friction coefficient or chip quality mark to process parameters such as feed rate, cutting speed, and angle of the instrument's rake. In 1993, inverse machining processes and techniques, *i.e.*, separate models, were often produced using other two processing parameters and force and vibration characteristics as network parameters for the three processing parameters (axial cutting depth, tooth feed, and cutting speed). Analytical models for forces or wear, resulting in profile grinding, are accessible and, through learning techniques, can be tailored to various amounts. Simulation methods, such as FEM(Finite Element Method) simulation, may incorporate these computational models to predict the workpiece's thermoelastic characteristics [32]. ANNs could also be efficiently used here because of their higher adaptivity and non-linearity. Adaptive quality management can lead to an application of multisensory integration, propound signal processing, dynamic systems, simulation techniques. A new method for creating multi-purpose models of conventional machining integrating machine learning and optimization algorithms is illustrated. Simulated annealing search is used in many applications, including all process chains' modeling work, to locate the multi-purpose model's unknown parameters.

Adaptive Control

Research studies to evaluate effective process models for manufacturing processes to realize robust advanced control schemes have been mentioned above. It is possible to define the task to be performed in a manner as there are some constraints on input variables like system limits. Certain output variables could be held close enough to the target values, and some may have higher limits. The suggested algorithm is dependent on an augmented Lagrangian approach to optimize a correctly chosen combined output index that takes the above criteria into account. Utilizing simulated data, their desirable algorithm, which involves forward and backward passes, has led to improved results. A so-called gradual approach was implemented to enhance further the whole "batch mode" strategy (where training and propagation are performed separately), where the training and propagation processes occur concurrently. However, just a portion of the potential input space, mainly the field close to the operating stage, is screened during this gradual process [33, 34]. The work showed harmful generalization properties when checked with values farther from this area. In 1987, among the most popular models for intelligent machine tools were introduced. Simultaneous calculation and processing of multiple signals) is the basis of the control technique. These signals are transformed into autonomous modeling techniques. The synthesis of the multiple sensor data is the central aspect of this structure. Two-hybrid AI systems were introduced in 1997 for manufacturing process monitoring and control on various hardware and software bases. Network outputs were transmitted to an expert framework in all these hybrid systems, which offers information about process management. Hybrid systems affect the impact of sub-symbolic stages based on cumulative information, produce optimum process parameters, and notify the user of the process's current state. The lower, sub-symbolic stage is created by an artificial neural network prototype named NEURECA in the HYBEXP method [35]. The higher symbolic standard is based on the widely available GoldWorksIII expert system shell.

The machine tool (the machine tool controller is integrated) is related to symbolic and neural subsystems. The symbolic component forwards information on the process parameters (feed rate, cutting depth, *etc.*) to the machining operation. The indirect signals produced are measured and transmitted to the hybrid system's sub-symbolic portion. SIMURECA calculates both the force and vibration signals' chosen features based on cumulative information and entire process parameters (cutting speed, feed rate, cutting depth). These features are transferred to the subsystem of NEURECA, which accomplishes the allocation of the estimate or classification [36]. As per previous studies, only if they manage method parameters will accurate ANN models be developed to sort cutting tools calculation by applying indirect signals. Consequently, the ANN models' inputs throughout HYBEXP often integrate cutting parameters with indirect signal characteristics. It is possible to use systems for both classification and evaluation.

Intelligent Approaches in System-Level Control of Difficulty, Modification, and Disruption

Difficulties emerge from unpredictable tasks and activities, non-linearities, and many encounters in today's production processes when trying to monitor diverse operations on complex shop floors. The efficacy of traditional management and (off-line, predictive) scheduling methods is severely constrained by difficulty and ambiguity [37]. Ultimately, the success manufacturing firms' relies on their capability to quickly adjust their manufacturing to new internal and external situations. Two primary methods are to increase the reactivity of historically organized structures by innovative modern controlling strategies and to develop autonomous, collaborative structures to deal with the enumerated issues. The creation of adaptive structures, which can benefit from recorded history, is another-often overlapping-method of coping with changes and disruptions.

Holonic Manufacturing Systems (HMSs)

A Holonic systems consist of independent, intelligent, scalable, dispersed, cooperative agents or holons as one of the new development paradigms. Three forms of fundamental holons are defined, namely order holons, substance holons, and resource holons, along with the key flows of data between all three. By using object-oriented principles such as grouping and specialism, these simple entities are organized. It is also foreseen that workers' holons can allow simple holons to do their jobs. The same paper presents a holonic production process reference architecture. Other scholars apply only to two categories of fundamental building blocks. A common characteristic of these methods is that in one basic form, the order and commodity holons' functions are in some way combined [38, 39]. The systems of hierarchical, heterarchical, and holonic regulation for something like an assembly cell are contrasted. Holonic systems have been shown to provide greater efficiency than their more-traditional counterparts in a broader range of scenarios. A transition between truly hierarchical and heterarchical structures is one of the most promising aspects of the holonic method. However, for reasons of industrial adoption of holonic, among many other reasons, the industrial recognition of holonic is comparatively limited [40].

a. The relative crudity of the concept of the agent and its implementations for output.
b. The more significant expenditure of the functioning of manufacturing systems in compliance with the values of agents.
c. The almost insurmountable obstacles in their incremental incorporation into current processes of development.

For solving the problems mentioned above, multiple methods are implemented and discussed. Here, methods where simulation is a core problem are considered.

Approaches to Improve the Efficiency of the Output System Dependent on Agents

Numerous researchers suggested a heterarchical solution to address the drawbacks of hierarchical power. Heterarchical control is a highly hierarchical mode of control, enforced without unified or precise direct control by a system of autonomous agents. Control decisions are made by mutual consent, and information between the involved agents is freely shared. Thus, heterarchical control architectures deliver comparable prospects of decreased sophistication, high resilience, and high robustness against output disruptions. As such, transparent reactive scheduling is not necessary [41]. Experiments and analytical implications have partly proven these expectations. Interestingly, it turns out that the heterarchical control does not guarantee optimal efficiency, preventing all types of hierarchy. It may be much more critical that a system's actions under the heterarchical influence can be unpredictable.

ADVANTAGES AND CHALLENGES IN THE USE OF MACHINE LEARNING IN THE DEVELOPMENT OF MANUFACTURING

Advantages

ML's available benefits have been described in previous sections, specifying that Ml algorithms can deal with complete NP problems that frequently arise when it approaches optimization problems in innovative and intelligent manufacturing systems [42]. Here, the focus is on ML techniques' capability to handle data with high dimensions and multivariate and large data sets to derive implicit relationships in a dynamic, varied, sometimes even chaotic universe. 'Because most engineering and manufacturing topics are rich in data yet knowledge - sparse,' ML offers a tool for enhancing domain comprehension. The benefits are presented in this segment to generalize the entire type of ML. Nonetheless, it must be understood that the benefits' specificity can vary based on all the ML techniques or algorithms selected [43].

The ability to manage high-dimensional topics and information is an advantage of ML algorithms. In the future, this is likely to become even more critical, specifically concerning the rising accessibility of massive information with little clarification in manufacturing. However, this could not be applied, as it is valid for ML techniques and algorithms' other benefits and drawbacks. Specific algorithms can accommodate high dimensionality better than some others [44 - 46]. As mentioned earlier, ML algorithms can manage high-dimensional data that are mainly applicable to manufacturing. An advantage of ML in production is often known to be the capacity to function with high dimensionality.

The improved accessibility of algorithms attributable to rapid miner programs is another benefit of the ML technique. In certain instances, this makes (relatively) simple deployment and, also, comfortable modification of all the parameters to improve the utility of classification [47].

As stated before, finding previously hidden (implicit) information and defining implicit associations in data sets is a significant benefit of ML algorithms. The ML algorithm's comprehensive ability is to produce outcomes in a development environment; however, it has been successfully demonstrated.

Because of the unique existence of complex, unpredictable, and complex development processes, ML algorithms do have the potential to learn first from complex structures here and modify to the uncertain dynamic environment automatically to such a degree [48 - 50]. Depending on the ML algorithm, the adaptation is relatively simple and quicker than conventional approaches in nearly all situations. Implementing ML in development can contribute to deriving trends from extent sets of data that may provide a foundation for approximating the possible behavior method. In decision-making processes, this new experience (knowledge) can support process owners and be used directly to automatically refine the system. Ultimately, some ML methods' goal is to identify specific relationship-characterizing trends or regularities [43, 51].

Challenges

The collection of appropriate data is a popular problem for ML applications in the industry. This is also a constraint since the availability, accuracy, and structure of the manufacturing information at hand have a significant impact on the success of machine learning algorithms. For example, high-dimensional data can represent a significant amount of unnecessary and redundant details for certain ml algorithms, which can negatively impact the output of learning algorithms.

The majority of machine learning algorithms today only work for data that has continuous and nominal values. The degree to which the effect is important is determined by a number of variables, including the algorithm and parameter settings. Due to security issues or a simple lack of data capture during the operation can be considered a general obstacle for most industrial analysis, not just ML applications, to obtain some data. Even though machine learning allows for the extraction of information and produces stronger outcomes than other conventional approaches with less criteria for accessible data in most situations, certain types of available data must be considered to ensure a good implementation. This, along with the next issue, emphasises the growing need to recognise data in order to implement machine learning. In contrast to conventional approaches, where a lot of time is spent extracting information, ML spends a lot of time preparing the details.

The topic of which machine learning methodology and algorithm to use is becoming increasingly important (selection of ML algorithm). While efforts to define "common machine learning methods," the variety of problems and their specifications emphasise the need for advanced algorithms with specific strengths and weaknesses. A large number of different ML algorithms, or at least derivatives of ML algorithms, are usable, owing to the increased interest of scholars and practitioners in the field of ML in manufacturing. Combinations of various algorithms, so-called "hybrid methods," are becoming more and more popular, offering better outcomes than "individual" single algorithm implementation, adding to the already established difficulty. Many experiments exist that demonstrate the efficient implementation of machine learning methods to particular problems. Simultaneously, in certain ways, test evidence is not publicly accessible. As a consequence, a neutral and impartial evaluation of the outcomes, as well as a final comparison, is difficult. As of today, the widely agreed method for selecting a fitting machine learning algorithm for a given problem is as follows:

To select between a controlled, unsupervised, or RL method, one must first examine the available data and how it is represented (labelled, unlabeled, available expert information, *etc.*).

Second, the general applicability of usable algorithms to the study issue criteria (*e.g.*, being able to accommodate high dimensionality) must be assessed. The structure, data formats, and total volume of usable data that can be used for testing and assessment must all be given special attention.

Third, in order to find a fitting algorithm, prior implementations of the algorithms on related problems must be investigated. In this context, the word "related" refers to study problems with similar criteria, such as those found in other disciplines or domains.

The analysis of the data is often a problem. It is important to remember that not only the output format or diagram is important for interpretation, but also the algorithm parameters, parameter settings, the "planned result," and the data, including its pre-processing. Certain more distinct constraints (again, based on the selected algorithm) may have a significant effect on the understanding of the data. Resistant to over-fitting, prejudice, and variation (and hence the bias-variance trade-off) are only a few of them.

CONCLUDING REMARKS

In today's era, manufacturing can be very complex to understand and implement for those who do not have the right technology and tools to build quality goods. Artificial Intelligence (AI) and Machine Learning (ML) algorithms can be a perfect option to enhance the entire process of manufacturing in terms of improving quality and certain other essential aspects, respectively, since Artificial

Intelligence (AI) and Machine Learning (ML) are interrelated somehow. They individually play an essential role, as well. Supervised Machine Learning is used in industrial applications and stands to gain from its qualitative manufacturing simulation information collection. Unsupervised learning proves to be beneficial in the respective sector in specific ways, particularly in the sense of Big Data. Statistical Learning Theory (SLT) proves to be a perfect Supervised Machine Learning algorithm for industrial study. To have a good view of manufacturing requirements, a clear vision must know which technology suits you here. Some of the manufacturing skills required in manufacturing are:

1. The Development of easy-to-understand results.
2. Numerous data types (numerical, nominal, text, and images)
3. Outliners, Fuzzy data handling
4. Processing in real-time. Since Holonic Manufacturing Systems (HMS) consists of intelligent, independent, and scalable agents as one of the new development paradigms, it proves to be an excellent fit for industrial adoption reasons.

CONSENT OF PUBLICATION

Not applicable.

CONFLICT OF INTEREST

The author declares no conflict of interest, financial or otherwise.

ACKNOWLEDGEMENTS

Declared none.

REFERENCES

[1]   C.J. Bartodziej, *The concept industry 4.0: An Empirical Analysis of Technologies and Applications in Production Logistics.* Springer Gabler: Wiesbaden, 2017, pp. 27-50.
        [http://dx.doi.org/10.1007/978-3-658-16502-4_3]

[2]   S. Kalpakjian, "Competitive Aspects of Manufacturing", In: *Manufacturing Engineering and Technology* 3rd edition. Addison Wesley Publishing Company, 1995, pp. 1216-1243.

[3]   J.T. Black, and R.A. Kohser, *DeGarmo's materials and processes in manufacturing.* 13th ed. John Wiley & Sons, 2020.

[4]   J. Hatvany, and L. Nemes, "Intelligent manufacturing systems—a tentative forecast", *IFAC Proceedings Volumes,* vol. 11, no. 8, pp. 895-899, 1978.

[5]   H.A. Simon, Why should machines learn?*Machine learning.* MorganKaufmann: USA, 1983, pp. 25-37.

[6]   S.C.Y. Lu, "Machine learning approaches to knowledge synthesis and integration tasks for advanced engineering automation", *Comput. Ind.,* vol. 15, no. 1-2, pp. 105-120, 1990.
        [http://dx.doi.org/10.1016/0166-3615(90)90088-7]

[7]   D. Partridge, and K. Paap, "An introduction to learning", *Artif. Intell. Rev.,* vol. 2, no. 2, pp. 79-101, 1988.
[http://dx.doi.org/10.1007/BF00140398]

[8]   H.K. Tönshoff, and A. Walter, "Self-tuning fuzzy-controller for process control in internal grinding", *Fuzzy Sets Syst.,* vol. 63, no. 3, pp. 359-373, 1994.
[http://dx.doi.org/10.1016/0165-0114(94)90222-4]

[9]   L. Monostori, "AI and machine learning techniques for managing complexity, changes and uncertainties in manufacturing", *IFAC Proceedings Volumes,* vol. 35, no. 1, pp. 119-130, 2002.

[10]   D. Acharya, S. Goel, H. Bhardwaj, A. Sakalle, and A. Bhardwaj, "A long short term memory deep learning network for the classification of negative emotions using EEG signals", In: *2020 International Joint Conference on Neural Networks (IJCNN)* IEEE., 2020, pp. 1-8.
[http://dx.doi.org/10.1109/IJCNN48605.2020.9207280]

[11]   T.M. Mitchell, "Machine Learning", In: *MacGraw-Hill Companies. Inc Boston,* 1997.

[12]   J.A. Harding, and M. Shahbaz, "Data mining in manufacturing: a review", *Transactions of the ASME, Journal of Manufacturing Science and Engineering,* vol. vol. 128, pp. 1-9, 2006.
[http://dx.doi.org/10.1115/1.2194554]

[13]   Y. Zhao, and G. Karypis, "Evaluation of hierarchical clustering algorithms for document datasets", *Proceedings of the eleventh international conference on Information and knowledge management,* pp. 515-524, 2002.
[http://dx.doi.org/10.21236/ADA439551]

[14]   A. Bhardwaj, A. Tiwari, M.V. Varma, and M.R. Krishna, "An analysis of integration of hill climbing in crossover and mutation operation for EEG signal classification", *Proceedings of the 2015 Annual Conference on Genetic and Evolutionary Computation,* pp. 209-216, 2015.
[http://dx.doi.org/10.1145/2739480.2754710]

[15]   S. B. Kotsiantis, I. Zaharakis, and P. Pintelas, "Supervised machine learning: A review of classification techniques", *Emerging artificial intelligence applications in computer engineering,* vol. 160, no. 1, pp. 3-24, 2007.

[16]   T. Evgeniou, T. Poggio, M. Pontil, and A. Verri, "Regularization and statistical learning theory for data analysis", *Comput. Stat. Data Anal.,* vol. 38, no. 4, pp. 421-432, 2002.
[http://dx.doi.org/10.1016/S0167-9473(01)00069-X]

[17]   R. Battiti, M. Brunato, and A. Villani, *Statistical learning theory for location fingerprinting in wireless LANs. Technical Report.* University of Trento, 2002, pp. DIT-02-DIT-0086.

[18]   P. Kang, and S. Cho, "Locally linear reconstruction for instance-based learning", *Pattern Recognit.,* vol. 41, no. 11, pp. 3507-3518, 2008.
[http://dx.doi.org/10.1016/j.patcog.2008.04.009]

[19]   W.S. Lim, and C.S. Tang, "Optimal product rollover strategies", *Eur. J. Oper. Res.,* vol. 174, no. 2, pp. 905-922, 2006.
[http://dx.doi.org/10.1016/j.ejor.2005.04.031]

[20]   N. Lavrač, H. Motoda, T. Fawcett, R. Holte, P. Langley, and P. Adriaans, "Introduction: Lessons learned from data mining applications and collaborative problem solving", *Mach. Learn.,* vol. 57, no. 1/2, pp. 13-34, 2004. [Kluwer Academic Publishers. Manufactured in The Netherlands].
[http://dx.doi.org/10.1023/B:MACH.0000035516.74817.51]

[21]   S.C-Y. Lu, D.K. Tcheng, and S. Yerramareddy, "Integration of simulation, learning and optimization to support engineering design", *CIRP Ann.,* vol. 40, no. 1, pp. 143-146, 1991.
[http://dx.doi.org/10.1016/S0007-8506(07)61954-4]

[22]   T.R. Rakes, L.P. Rees, F.C. Siochi, and B.A. Wray, "Estimating the number of kanbans using neural networks", *Advances in Artificial Intelligence in Economics, Finance, and Management,* vol. 1, pp.

125-139, 1994.

[23] I.S. Markham, R.G. Mathieu, and B.A. Wray, "Kanban setting through artificial intelligence: a comparative study of artificial neural networks and decision trees", *Integrated Manuf. Syst.*, vol. 11, no. 4, pp. 239-246, 2000.
[http://dx.doi.org/10.1108/09576060010326230]

[24] H. Bhardwaj, A. Sakalle, A. Bhardwaj, and A. Tiwari, "Classification of electroencephalogram signal for the detection of epilepsy using Innovative Genetic Programming", *Expert Syst.*, vol. 36, no. 1, 2019.e12338
[http://dx.doi.org/10.1111/exsy.12338]

[25] S. Létourneau, F. Famili, and S. Matwin, "Data mining to predict aircraft component replacement", *IEEE Intell. Syst. Their Appl.*, vol. 14, no. 6, pp. 59-66, 1999.
[http://dx.doi.org/10.1109/5254.809569]

[26] D. Devarriya, C. Gulati, V. Mansharamani, A. Sakalle, and A. Bhardwaj, "Unbalanced breast cancer data classification using novel fitness functions in genetic programming", *Expert Syst. Appl.*, vol. 140, 2020.112866
[http://dx.doi.org/10.1016/j.eswa.2019.112866]

[27] U. Çaydaş, and S. Ekici, "Support vector machines models for surface roughness prediction in CNC turning of AISI 304 austenitic stainless steel", *J. Intell. Manuf.*, vol. 23, no. 3, pp. 639-650, 2012.
[http://dx.doi.org/10.1007/s10845-010-0415-2]

[28] K. Salahshoor, M. Kordestani, and M.S. Khoshro, "Fault detection and diagnosis of an industrial steam turbine using fusion of SVM (support vector machine) and ANFIS (adaptive neuro-fuzzy inference system) classifiers", *Energy*, vol. 35, no. 12, pp. 5472-5482, 2010.
[http://dx.doi.org/10.1016/j.energy.2010.06.001]

[29] L. Monostori, "Learning procedures in machine tool monitoring", *Comput. Ind.*, vol. 7, no. 1, pp. 53-64, 1986.
[http://dx.doi.org/10.1016/0166-3615(86)90009-6]

[30] M. Junkar, B. Filipič, and I. Bratko, "Identifying the grinding process by means of inductive machine learning", *Comput. Ind.*, vol. 17, no. 2-3, pp. 147-153, 1991.
[http://dx.doi.org/10.1016/0166-3615(91)90027-7]

[31] H.K. Tönshoff, J.P. Wulfsberg, H.J.J. Kals, W. König, and C.A. van Luttervelt, "Developments and trends in monitoring and control of machining processes", *CIRP Ann.*, vol. 37, no. 2, pp. 611-622, 1988.
[http://dx.doi.org/10.1016/S0007-8506(07)60758-6]

[32] L. Monostori, and Z.J. Viharos, "Multipurpose modelling and optimisation of production processes and process chains by combining machine learning and search techniques", *Proc. of The 32nd CIRP Int. Seminar on Manufacturing Systems*, pp. 399-408, 1999.

[33] S. S. Rangwala, and D. A. Dornfeld, "Learning and optimization of machining operations using computing abilities of neural networks", *IEEE Transactions on Systems, Man, and Cybernetics*, vol. 19, no. 2, pp. 99-314, 1989.

[34] D. Barschdorff, L. Monostori, G.W. Wöstenkühler, C. Egresits, and B. Kádár, "Approaches to coupling connectionist and expert systems in intelligent manufacturing", *Comput. Ind.*, vol. 33, no. 1, pp. 5-15, 1997.
[http://dx.doi.org/10.1016/S0166-3615(97)00007-9]

[35] L. Monostori, *Hybrid AI approaches for supervision and control of manufacturing processes.*, 1995, pp. 37-40.

[36] L. Monostori, and J. Prohaszka, "A step towards intelligent manufacturing: Modelling and monitoring of manufacturing processes through artificial neural networks", *CIRP Ann.*, vol. 42, no. 1, pp. 485-488, 1993.

[http://dx.doi.org/10.1016/S0007-8506(07)62491-3]

[37]   E. Szelke, and L. Monostori, Reactive scheduling in real time production control.*Modeling manufacturing systems.* Springer: Berlin, Heidelberg, 1999, pp. 65-113.
[http://dx.doi.org/10.1007/978-3-662-03853-6_5]

[38]   P. Valckenaers, F. Bonneville, H. Van Brussel, L. Bongaerts, and J. Wyns, "Results of the holonic control system benchmark at KU Leuven", In: *Proceedings of the Fourth International Conference on Computer Integrated Manufacturing and Automation Technology* IEEE., 1994, pp. 128-133.
[http://dx.doi.org/10.1109/CIMAT.1994.389083]

[39]   L. Bongaerts, L. Monostori, D. McFarlane, and B. Kádár, "Hierarchy in distributed shop floor control", *Comput. Ind.,* vol. 43, no. 2, pp. 123-137, 2000.
[http://dx.doi.org/10.1016/S0166-3615(00)00062-2]

[40]   B. Kádár, and L. Monostori, Agent-Based control of novel and traditional production systems. pp. 33-38. 1998.

[41]   T. Vamos, "Cooperative systems based on non-cooperative people", *IEEE Contr. Syst. Mag.,* vol. 3, no. 3, pp. 9-14, 1983.
[http://dx.doi.org/10.1109/MCS.1983.1104762]

[42]   G. Köksal, İ. Batmaz, and M.C. Testik, "A review of data mining applications for quality improvement in manufacturing industry", *Expert Syst. Appl.,* vol. 38, no. 10, pp. 13448-13467, 2011.
[http://dx.doi.org/10.1016/j.eswa.2011.04.063]

[43]   A. Bhardwaj, and A. Tiwari, "A novel genetic programming based classifier design using a new constructive crossover operator with a local search technique", In: *International Conference on Intelligent Computing* Springer: Berlin, Heidelberg, 2013, pp. 86-95.
[http://dx.doi.org/10.1007/978-3-642-39479-9_11]

[44]   A. Bar-Or, A. Schuster, R. Wolff, and D. Keren, "Decision tree induction in high dimensional, hierarchically distributed databases", In: *Proceedings of the 2005 SIAM International Conference on Data Mining* Society for Industrial and Applied Mathematics., 2005, pp. 466-470.
[http://dx.doi.org/10.1137/1.9781611972757.42]

[45]   T.N. Do, P. Lenca, S. Lallich, and N.K. Pham, Classifying very-high- dimensional data with random forests of oblique decision trees.*Advances in knowledge discovery and management.* Springer: Berlin, Heidelberg, 2010, pp. 39-55.
[http://dx.doi.org/10.1007/978-3-642-00580-0_3]

[46]   B. Filipič, and M. Junkar, "Using inductive machine learning to support decision making in machining processes", *Comput. Ind.,* vol. 43, no. 1, pp. 31-41, 2000.
[http://dx.doi.org/10.1016/S0166-3615(00)00056-7]

[47]   X. Guo, L. Sun, G. Li, and S. Wang, "A hybrid wavelet analysis and support vector machines in forecasting development of manufacturing", *Expert Syst. Appl.,* vol. 35, no. 1-2, pp. 415-422, 2008.
[http://dx.doi.org/10.1016/j.eswa.2007.07.052]

[48]   K.J. Wang, J.C. Chen, and Y.S. Lin, "A hybrid knowledge discovery model using decision tree and neural network for selecting dispatching rules of a semiconductor final testing factory", *Prod. Plann. Contr.,* vol. 16, no. 7, pp. 665-680, 2005.
[http://dx.doi.org/10.1080/09537280500213757]

[49]   E. Alpaydin, and J.P. Gee, *Introduction to Machine Learning The MIT Press.* 2nd ed. Cambridge, MA, USA, 2010.

[50] T. Wuest, D. Weimer, C. Irgens, and K.D. Thoben, "Machine learning in manufacturing: advantages, challenges, and applications", *Prod. Manuf. Res.,* vol. 4, no. 1, pp. 23-45, 2016.
[http://dx.doi.org/10.1080/21693277.2016.1192517]

[51] S. Tiwari, S. Goel, and A. Bhardwaj, "Machine Learning approach for the classification of EEG signals of multiple imagery tasks", In: *11th International Conference on Computing, Communication and Networking Technologies (ICCCNT)* IEEE., 2020, pp. 1-7.
[http://dx.doi.org/10.1109/ICCCNT49239.2020.9225291]

CHAPTER 2

Application of IoT–A Survey

Richa Mishra[1,*] and **Tushar**[1]

[1] *Department of Computer Science & Engineering Amity University, Noida, India*

Abstract: Internet of Things (IoT) is surely a term that gives us the thought that everything is related to the internet. IoT is an assembly of machines that can share and transfer data. In this way, IoT can make our lives more convenient and easy because no physical interaction is required between machines and humans. As there are so many benefits of this technology there arise some challenges too. In today's scenario, humans rely very much on the smart applications of the IoT, which will affect our lives to the core. IoT is widely used to exchange information either remotely or locally with the help of sensors. These IoT devices can then process the information according to their needs and can take necessary steps as well. For example, IoT devices can sense the temperature and if the temperature rises above a certain level, they can act as actuators. This chapter provides us with an overview of the recent technologies in the field of IoT and to learn more about some of its very relevant applications. However, this document provides an opportunity for young researchers to gather more and more information about the Internet of things.

Keywords: Artificial Intelligence, Deep Learning, Internet of Things, Wireless Sensor Networks.

INTRODUCTION

Internet of Things (IoT) is an advanced technology that connects various computing devices or mechanical machines without any physical interaction among them by using wireless sensor networks. Internet of Things is a catchphrase in the world of computing. IoT can affix acumen in heartfelt global matters and connect it with another. Technologies such as Wi-Fi (Wireless Fidelity), Bluetooth, Wireless Sensor Networks, RFID (Radio Frequency Identification), *etc.*, have a significant impact on IoT services in making them reliable, accurate, and time-saving. IoT has observed significant employment in the world of healthcare. IoT also lends itself to smart monitoring and tracking system for patient's health, treatment history, diet plan, *etc.* [1]. Wearable fitness

[*] **Corresponding author Richa Mishra:** Department of Computer Science and Engineering, ASET, Amity University, Noida, India; E-mail: richas.phoenix@gmail.com

Vaishali Mehta, Dolly Sharma, Monika Mangla, Anita Gehlot, Rajesh Singh and Sergio Marquez Sanchez (Eds.)

bands enable personalized attention, including calorie count, variations in blood pressure and heart rates, *etc.* In a comprehensive view of all these, this chapter reviews the latest IoT based applications in the domain of the healthcare sector. Massive studies have been done for the exploration of different technologies such as Information Technologies (IT) in complementing and amplifying offered healthcare services in the present generation. In particular, the IoT has been extensively functional to interlock these checkup possessions and endow the more reliable, helpful, and smart healthcare assistance to the elderly and patients with a habitual illnesses [2]. Continuous evolution in the healthcare sector has led the way to the invention of wireless devices. Nowadays, a wide-ranging view of the patient's whole health preserve can be obtained through the prototypes of the next generation monitoring that has not only a look at the patient's health but also provides the prevention measures, diet plan for the patient, recovery state of patient's health, *etc.* IoT technology facilitates intercommunication that can alert the hospital personnel based on the patient's vitals in case of any emergency. It transforms the healthcare sector to be more efficient and economically feasible, and thus enhances the quality of service. Currently, the modern advancements in the healthcare field have resulted in a towering range of data which further needs more technologies to organize and use it in the best way possible [3].

Healthcare organizations take the services of technical persons and engineers to create a luring future in healthcare by inventing advanced equipment and thus, making this sector a more accurate and effective one. They are also very well allied with gigantic Internet-connected things/devices that engender vast amounts of data that can be used in different ways. An upper-level healthcare system outcome is the leading objective joint by hospitals, clinics, and health organizations across the world. Healthcare vitals collected through IoT drives the innovation of medicinal assistances in addition to cost reduction, precision improvement, and providing this ample butter of the healthcare advancements to more and more population.

Despite all these advancements in the healthcare sector, several problems have been unleashed during the current pandemic Covid-19. The best solution for this today is social distancing. This paper gives an innovative and needy solution promoting the idea of social distancing to prevent the spread of the pandemic. Here, a brief description of the methodology and working of this system is also given. We have also given some ideas for its applications keeping in mind today's requirements due to this outbreak.

IoT IN MANUFACTURING

Internet of Things (IoT) is a way to digital transformation in manufacturing. IoT employs a number of sensors to collect the data and uses cloud software to turn this data into valuable information. The main adoption drivers for the IoT include:

- **Cost reduction**. Due to optimized asset and inventory management, companies *reduce operational costs and create new sources of revenue.*
- **Shorter time-to-market**. Efficient manufacturing and supply chain operations allow reducing product cycle time.
- **Mass customization**. Tracking the inventory and the manufacturing operations is difficult and sometimes, it is not feasible. IoT is used to track a source of real-time data required for *shop floor scheduling and routing.*
- **Improved safety**. IoT addresses safety issues in potentially hazardous environments. It can be used in health care sectors, for instance.

IoT technologies are changing the way production systems are constructed and run, driving degradation in three ways: They are; visibility into shop floor and field operations, visibility into the manufacturing supply chain and visibility into remote and outsourced operations.

LITERATURE SURVEY

The internet of things helps the world to live their lives more comfortably and work smartly in both their personal and professional lives. With the revolution of technology in the past few years, IoT has completely changed the lives of humans, if it is getting the groceries sitting on your couch or ordering food from the restaurants while watching the T.V., or switching on our air conditioners before arriving at the houses or commanding 'Alexa' to inform us about the happening around the globe. OT has completely changed the way of our living and has made our lives so easy and comfortable that now we can't even imagine our life without it.

IoT [4 - 8] has been very useful for the business and corporate world as it provides companies to look more efficiently in the company's work chain and process of working. It helped a lot to take the work to a more automatic level rather than working manually, which significantly lowers the labor cost and wastage and thus provides efficient working in the manufacturing unit. IoT also provides better transparency to the customers as everything is working automatically, so there are always fewer chances of error and there is a proper record of every single product in the database [9, 10]. IoT has changed the market to a whole another level. In today's scenario, it is very difficult to survive if companies do not adopt technological advancements. As such, there are infinite areas in which IoT is playing its role very accurately. And we will cover many of them in the next coming pages. But as much we have learned so far it can easily be deduced that IoT has been playing an important and huge role in our lives for the past few years. As a result, the role of IoT in our life cannot be neglected even for once.

Business Organization: IoT provides several benefits to Business organizations [10 - 15]. Some of the common benefits which IOT introduce businesses to are as follows:

1. IoT provides total monitoring over their complete business process.

2. IoT provides a better experience to the customers.

3. IoT reduces the labor cost of the company and also limits the work hours to very low.

4. IoT helps to increase the productivity rate.

5. IoT connects the enterprises to multinational companies and makes their interaction easy which produces much more business outcomes and better business relations.

IoT encourages the companies to review their way of approach towards the business and try them to think for new ideas for better business outcomes which lead to the better growth of the company. IoT also provides every possible piece of equipment to improve the business ideas of the company. Generally, IoT is most used in manufacturing units, delivery of the product, monitoring of the data, business process, *etc.* It makes the transaction process much easier, which also boosts up the business in terms of growth.

Health Care: IoT has played a role of a revolutionary in the field of health and medicine [16 - 20]. It has taken the medical sciences to a whole different level and saved lives when there is no hope. IoT changed the way how we look after ourselves and made us more aware of our health and encourage us for living a healthy and safe life for our betterment.

Nowadays, humans are living restless lives; they have no time to give about their health and their body conditions. In this busy schedule of life, they keep on ignoring their health conditions and end up lying on a hospital bed. But if they properly know about their body conditions, their body vitals like pulses, heart rate, blood sugar level [21 - 30], their working hours, then they have better chances to live a better life. This is where IoT comes into the limelight. There are so many gadgets nowadays that can keep a check on our vitals at every moment and alerts us immediately when there is a need to see a doctor need to take a tablet. These small things like gadgets and apps turned out to be lifesaving as well as changing, especially for the people who work like horses. Gadgets like smartwatches, when tied to the wrist, keep a proper count on our vital and also suggests the actions in accordance. These apps and gadgets suggest that we eat chocolate when our sugar level goes low and take a deep breath when our blood pressure is high and calm down and do breathing exercises when we have a panic attack or something just like that; it also helps us in other ways. So we can feel the difference, like if we do not switch to wearing these smart gadgets, then there will be consequences. And also every time we cannot go to see a doctor and have to take care of ourselves on our own, this concept of IoT [31 - 35] came in and suggested to us the ways to operate immediately in the condition of emergency. So there are so many other ways in which IOT helps us to live a healthy and comfortable life for ourselves as well for our future generations. For instance, it warns us immediately not to take an infant to a place where the pollution level is above the safety level . People don't see the change easily, but there is a very big change, and IOT has become an essential tool to live a healthy and safe life. By the interference of IoT in the health care department it has also taken a huge space of the market for the same. Now there are so many companies in the market which are selling products and devices for our health care. Even some of the biggest technology companies like Apple and Samsung are also launching their products like smartwatches and safety bands in the market with better technology. So IOT has opened a very big market [35 - 42] for the investors and firms and also for the startups. People are launching mobile applications on which they provide fitness programs and nutrition advice. Also, there are several apps on which we can have the guidance of the doctor [43] while sitting in our drawing-room. Hence, we can realize that IoT can serve as a boon for a healthy life style.

IoT in Cars: IoT in cars is a venture which is still developing because in introducing a car which is connected to the internet and also works as per the need of the environment still needs some time. But even now, many big automobile companies have launched their internet-connected cars. IoT not only enhances the comfort level of the owner but it also changes the whole driving experience for the owner. IoT makes the car safer to drive. And it gives full backup at the time of emergency. When we talk about driving our car fast on the road, then the first thing came to our mind is our safety. What if we are not able to control the car, then we may crash it on the roadside. But by the equipment of the smart technology of the internet and equipping the car with smart sensors, a car can easily handle itself like if the car feels it may crash, then it will automatically apply the emergency brake and protect the driver from getting injured and still, we have a bit of bad luck and we had an accident. Then here comes the involvement of IoT as soon as cars airbags break out to protect the driver that very moment with the help of smart sensors the smart software will know that there has been an accident and the passenger may need medical care. So with the help of IoT, the car will automatically call the ambulance and will tell them about the exact location of the happening. This turns out to be life-saving for the driver. And when we talk about the security of the drive, then here also the IoT does its work. Whenever the sensors find someone much closer to the car, it starts beeping and if some thief tries to steal the car, it automatically goes on the lock mode and now the engine will not start and it will give a direct message to the owner that the car is not safe. There is more technology which the automobile companies should work on. But by, introducing some of the IoT technologies like GPS, antitheft alarm, Bluetooth, *etc.*, has already made our drive more convenient and secure.

IoT in WSN: IoT is widely used in WSN [44 - 46]. It is used to measure temperature or process information of any kind and send the data to the rest of the world.

Every invention is made for the benefit of society to make their work easier, safer, and more accurate. This proposed idea of COVID-19 would also have a wide range of applications in society as more than 185 countries are being affected by the COVID-19. Here are some of the areas where it could be extremely beneficial:

a. Police for Clearing Masses During the Pandemic Spread - Since most security forces have been working during this pandemic spread, their personal lives are also at risk. They have been working hand-to-hand with the hospital staff to tackle this deadly situation. They have been provided with all the safety requirements to ensure their full safety during working hours. But this smart COVID-19 prevention kit could be extremely beneficial for these forces in ensuring their safety while doing jobs which includes clearing masses in this pandemic spread.
b. Hospital Staff -The hospital employees who are given tasks at the isolation centers, taking the suspiciously infected person from their places or testing them for COVID-19 have more chances of being infected by the COVID-19. This proposed smart prevention kit can ensure them full guidance, hygiene, and, most importantly, safety.
c. Personal Uses of the public for going into several public spaces - General public also needs to go out of their homes for various important purposes during this time when social distancing is advised. They can also use this prevention kit easily to ensure their safety from the coronavirus spread in public places.

d. Traffic Police -The job of traffic police services is mainly at the various public spaces, so this smart prevention kit becomes extremely useful in their case. The coat can be made of the same shade fabric as their uniforms are off so that it could be easily worn over their specific uniforms.

e. Workers in Industries - As most of the pharmaceutical product- based companies have been working during this outbreak also, so it's important to provide a safe, secure and hygienic workplace to the labor and other employees. This kit could be used by all the workers as a dress from their specific companies to minimize the risks of this pandemic spread.

ROLE OF IOT IN PANDEMIC COVID-19

Nowadays the world is going through very hard times. This fight against the novel COVID-19is the fight for the existence of the human race. There are more than 2 lakh deaths all over the world. And more than 2 million cases of COVID-19. This a very alerting condition for the whole world. As we have been seeing that the whole world is in an emergency now and some nations have been locked down completely. So COVID-19is affecting our lives to the cores.. And as there is no antidote has been found for this virus so this very important for us to be safe and try not to be in contact with an infected person. So we must be thinking about how IoT can help to stop this chain of COVID-19. But it is helping the world very crucially and making more chances to win this fight with this virus. Like police have been putting motion sensors in parks and gathering places if there is a gathering, it immediately alerts the police authorities to take action and stop the gathering. Our security forces are also getting the live coverage with the help of the drones to find out if there is any gathering of the people happening. And this time of lockdown, people can order the food that is just because of IoT. The biggest example of the contribution of IoT in stopping this chain of the virus is AROGYA SETU APP, "Covid India Seva" platform, and e-Sanjeevani OPD.

ArogyaSetu App: AROGYA SETU APP is developed by the government of India to make people aware of the nearby cases of the virus. This also tells us about the place where there is an outbreak of the COVID-19 and is not safe to go there. It is a Bluetooth working COVID-19 tracing app. The other motives of this app are to be aware of the risks, best practices, and how to prevent themselves by coming in contact with an infected person.

It is a Bluetooth-based technology app that keeps track of the COVID-19 patients. So now, let's focus on how it works. When you install this app on your phone, it asks you to switch on your GPS setting, and now it can trace your location. Now, suppose you go somewhere In a place where there are some people around you. In that case, the app will automatically match with the person who has the same app and then when you were lying safe in your home and the person you were in contact with the app match happened is found to be positive with the virus then the AROGYA SETU app will notify you and tell you that the person you met in founding infected and it will also tell you the places where you should avoid to go. This is how this app functions.

Benefits of AROGYA SETU App

1. As it works on Bluetooth so it identifies the danger on the user on his location.

2. It has the complete data of that particular location, so it gives proper info for the user about the places which has been quarantined.

3. It informed the user if he/she has crossed someone who later found positive of the virus even if he was 6 feet away at the time of crossing.

4. It recommends the user about the safety measure, self-assessment test, and symptoms of the virus.

5. It also suggests the users how to be safe and how we should follow the social distancing at the time of this pandemic

6. The app also suggests to the user to go for a test if he/she might be infected or in serious danger of catching the virus.

7. This app comes with a Chabot who answer all the quires related to COVID-19.

These are the benefits of this app which functions under the IoT. So we have seen how magically this app works and how it is saving our families and us from this global COVID-19 And this app also helping or fighters who are risking their lives so that our families could be safe. In this way, no one can neglect the benefits of IoT, IoT has become a boon for us in these hard times, whether it is AROGYA SETU app or it is online money transactions or is online food ordering or anything. It would not have been a close fight without the introduction of IoT. We could have won this fight without IoT, but there was a very big chance that we could have born an immense loss in our lives like so many countries are still paying to their fate but if they would have switched to this technology life would not be that hard in this time of the global pandemic.

Covid India SevaPlateform: Covid India Seva is a digital initiative to bring transparency to the Government of India's e-governance initiative, especially in this crisis of the Covid-19 pandemic. Covid India Seva was launched by the Central government on 21st Apr 2020; this new digital platform provides an interactive platform to establish a direct channel of communication with millions of Indian people. This initiative tries to bring transparency in the e-governance system, which includes delivery of necessary services in real-time and answering citizens' queries swiftly, at a large scale, especially in crises like the ongoing global Covid-19 pandemic.

People can post their queries to the @COVID INDIA SEVA Twitter handle to get swift replies from the team of trained and expert medical staff across the country. This platform helps trained experts to share authoritative public health information smoothly at a large scale, helping to build a large channel for communication with citizens. The responses by the trained and experts will be available for everyone and users will not require to share any personal details/health records on this account.

e-Sanjeevani OPD: The e-Sanjeevani is a telemedicine service that is implemented under Ayushman Bharat Yojna, an initiative of the Ministry of Health & Family Welfare, Government of India. The aim of this is to connect the entire 1.5 lakh health and wellness center established under Ayushman Bharat Yojna. It is the second teleconsultation service that helps patient-to-doctor interaction, ensuring the physical distancing amid this Covid-19 pandemic. The OPD has provided essential healthcare at a critical time when conventional medicine is perceived to be risky because of the nature of the pandemic. The App was launched on 13th April 2020 this year in the aftermath Covid-19 pandemic. This has turned to be a boon by containing the spread of Covid-19 besides providing essential healthcare for Non-Covid patients. e-Sanjeevaniis a management information system (MIS) based application, designed for users to choose as per their need. It provides specialties including telecardiology and tell-Opthalmology. The striking features of the app include Comprehensive Electronic Medical Record (CEMR), video conferencing, and teleconsultation. eSanjeevaniOPD- stay home has been developed by the Centre for Development of Advanced Computing (C-DAC) in Mohali. Salient features of this citizen-friendly web-bases National Teleconsultation Services include Patient Registration, Token generation, Queue Management, Audio-Video Consultation with a Doctor, e-Prescription, SMS/Email Notifications, Serviced by State's Doctors, Free Service *etc.*

Advantages of IoT

The Internet of Things has a lot to offer in almost every domain we can link to, starting with data. IoT generates a large amount of data. The more information is analyzed, the easier it gets to make the right decisions. With cognitive data insights, we can predict consumer patterns, which strongly impact current and future marketing strategies and customer experience. And since IoT seeks to heighten accuracy, it is set to eliminate errors while monitoring and tracking things in real-time. This high-level of precision will facilitate the automation process of routine and repetitive tasks, which would otherwise be very time-consuming. And as time is money, you will also feel it in your pocket.

INFORMATION

IoT provides a whole lot of information about things as the internet got access to all the information of the world. And if we got the right and instant knowledge about things, then it is very easy for us to take the right step in a particular situation. And also, sharing of information among the devices through IoT makes our daily chores much easier and more convenient for us; not only does it saves our energy and time but it also saves money too. IoT means a network of devices and objects that are connected to the internet. Being connected to the Internet means that it can collect data or send it through Internet, receive information from the Internet, or do both things; wired and wireless connectivity between the devices and processors is essential and is always through the Internet. The amount of data collected by IoT is humongous.

Tracking

Computers and other IoT devices keep a proper track record of the things and food items present in our kitchen, and by this, they can easily suggest us to buy what we need at the time and what is the item which is running out or about to expire, this helps a lot. Not only on the things but also with the help of IoT devices, we can track the locations of our family members and vehicles for safety purposes and also we can contact them at the time of need. IoT provides the great capacity to generate important amounts of data from the physical world. Which once analyzed by computer tools, can be used to improve decision making as well as the performance of daily activities, thus facilitating the lifestyle of people, with the advent of IoT technology and location-based sensors (such as GPS). We now have the ability for a personal security solution to include a location tracking capability. Rapid assistance from danger or threat can now be a button push away.

Time

This is the biggest advantage of the IoT. If we talk about this generation, the basic thing which we need the most is "TIME" because one can buy anything but not time. If we spent much time doing other things then we won't be able to save time for ourselves and this is the main problem with this generation, 'we all are fighting with time'. But IoT has given a lead to us in this fight with time. By switching to the IoT smart appliances and digital devices, the time saved has a tremendous value. Now a day, we even can't imagine doing those works without the introduction to the IoT. And this is the biggest boon that comes along with the IoT in that it 'saves time for our lives'.

Money

The financial aspect is the biggest advantage of the IoT. It is very much convenient for our pocket. As we get every information of our smartphones. So we don't have to waste extra money on things. Also if we switch to online money transactions and online bill payments, then we are experiencing there countless offers given by these apps, which not only saves our money but also saves a whole lot of time and energy for ourselves.

Better Quality Of Life

This is the basic need of this generation; everyone wants the best of the comfort and facilities in their lives and IOT is doing that for them. By upgrading smart homes and wearables, it gives us the power of doing so many things without even moving our legs; it is never less than a superpower and this is all done under the action of IoT.

Energy

We know that for MSMEs, the cost of energy is a significant proportion of their operational expenses; hence any product or service that can help reduce their energy cost will be valued. Organizations can lower their energy needs by switching off lights or adjusting heating and ventilation systems. By lowering their energy use at peak hours, entities like supermarkets, hotels, offices, campuses, hospitals, and factories can help the National Grid manage peak loads, and receive dividends for doing so. Regulatory norms need to be eased up a bit so that the smart grid market can progress upward.

The key to the efficiency-enhancing power of IoT lies in peak usage periods. Electricity is much more expensive in the hours when everyone is using a lot of it. For example, if it's 3 pm on a hot day, the cost of electricity can be 3 times what it is at 2 pm on another day, but in India, the dynamic pricing model is seldom practiced. Homes and offices still get charged solely on how much power they consume every month.

Disadvantages of IoT

There are countless advantages of IoT as we have been discussing in the above paper and also how it is our life magically. But everything comes at a cost and every idea has its consequences so as the IoT. The main problems and disadvantages IOT is struggling with are privacy and security issues, too much reliance on technology, a distraction from the real world, slothfulness, unemployment, and lack of craftsmanship. Working within a network means you are vulnerable to virtual attacks that can comprise your information and threaten your private data. Now let's have a look at what the real problem is with these issues.

Privacy and Security

This is the main issue with which we are dealing with. We are unaware of this that how much easy this is for any anonymous person to steal our privacy and our personal information. As everything is available on the internet, you can have access to it. We never know that the tiny apps present in our phones are a major threat to our privacy and security. They got the exact location of us and know more about us than any of our family members do. And this should not be the way this is. IoT must be secured and should be under proper security of the cyber theft.

Too Much Reliance On The Technology

This is also the issue we should all be worried about because relying too much on these gadgets will make us more used to it there will be no way we can cut from them even if we want to so as there is a quote " too much of everything is bad " this same goes with IoT. If we keep on using the technology the same way, then surely this will kill us someday because not doing any of our basic stuff makes us lazy and this will put many health issues in our body, which will later cause a big problem for us. So if we want to live a healthy and long life then we need to use technology smartly and in a very limited manner.

Distraction From The Real World

THIS is the main issue with which the present generation is dealing. If we see the kids today they don't want to play outside in the field but on their phones and play stations. There is very limited social interaction that has left today and all the credit goes to IoT. We are getting more virtual than social. Not only socially this distracts from our studies too, and kids are switching more to online-based study than working manually on the books and making self-notes this surely affects their studies in some way or the other.

Unemployment and Lack Of Craftsmanship

This is one of the major issues from which the present world is suffering from by switching to digital machines and self-commanding devices, we are snatching the work from the labor class workers and the people who are experts in working with their hands not only it is creating the unemployment, but also it is killing the real art which was the true heritage of our nation.

CONCLUSION

Right now, each day, the enormous universe of the web has 2.9 quintillion bytes of information all the time as per the measurements of the level of information that has been started in the most recent two years. The Internet of Things (IoT) vows to have a major impact by including another measurement in the manner individuals will collaborate with the encompassing things. As we all know that there is an abundant amount of data that has been traveled at every corner of the world, which results in a high tendency of data hacking and misuse of our private information. Through this technology, there will be an increment in productivity which will improve the economy of the country. The main IoT playing in our life is, it is improving the quality of life and now IOT is enhancing its range to the most fundamental sectors of our lives like education, health care, transportation, security, agriculture, *etc.* and there is a huge competition in the market by the introduction of the IoT in this field. In the future, IoT is going to touch almost every aspect of the lives of people within the next few years. IoT stages can assist associations with diminishing expense through improved process effectiveness, resource usage, and profitability. To improve a following of gadgets and articles utilizing sensors and availability, they can have an advantage from constant experiences and examination, which would enable them, to settle on more intelligent choices. In this paper, we review best-in-class techniques, design of IoT, characterization, biological system, a reference model of the Internet of Things (IoT), and applications in this new rising region, which additionally features probably the most significant innovations. This current paper motivates us to endure a considerable outline and enormous picture of peruses of this developing zone.

CONSENT OF PUBLICATION

Not applicable.

CONFLICT OF INTEREST

The author declares no conflict of interest, financial or otherwise.

ACKNOWLEDGEMENTS

Declared none.

REFERENCES

[1]   B. Singh, S. Bhattacharya, C.L. Chowdhary, and D.S. Jat, "A review on internet of things and its applications in healthcare", In: *Journal of Chemical and Pharmaceutical Sciences* vol. 10. , 2017, no. 1, pp. 447-452.

[2]   Y. Yuehong, Y. Zeng, X. Chen, and Y. Fan, "The internet of things in healthcare: An overview", *J. Ind. Inf. Integr.,* vol. 1, pp. 3-13, 2016.

[3]   Bhatt Chintan, Dey Nilanjan, and S Ashour Amira, "Internet of things and big data technologies for next-generation healthcare", In: *Springer International Publishing*, 2017, pp. 978-3.

[4]   K. Ashton, "That 'internet of things' thing", *RFID journal,* vol. 22, no. 7, pp. 97-114, 2009. http://www.rfidjournal.com/articles/view?4986

[5]   D.L. Brock, "The Electronic Product Code (EPC) a naming scheme for physical objects", *Auto-ID Centre, White Paper,* 2001.https://citeseerx.ist.psu.edu/viewdoc/download?doi=10.1.1.61.6514&rep=rep1&type=pdf

[6]   International Telecommunication Union., "ITU internet report 2005: the internet of things", https://www.itu.int/net/wsis/tunis/newsroom/stats/The-Internet-of-Things-2005.pdf

[7]   M.A. Albreem, A.A. El-Saleh, M. Isa, W. Salah, M. Jusoh, M.M. Azizan, and A. Ali, "Green internet of things (IoT): An overview", *2017 IEEE 4th International Conference on Smart Instrumentation, Measurement and Application (ICSIMA),* pp. 1-6, 2017.

[8]   Q. Meng, and J. Jin, "The Terminal Design of the Energy Self-sufficiency Internet of Thing", *2011 International Conference on Control, Automation and Systems Engineering (CASE),* pp. 1-5, 2011. [http://dx.doi.org/10.1109/ICCASE.2011.5997619]

[9]   G. Verma, and D. Sharma, "Seeing through the walls with wireless technology: A Review", *International Journal of Sensors, Wireless Communications and Control, Bentham Science,* vol. 12, 2022no. 9, .https://www.eurekaselect.com/article/121888

[10] S. Tozlu, M. Senel, Wei Mao, and A. Keshavarzian, "Wi-Fi enabled sensors for internet of things: A practical approach", *IEEE Commun. Mag.,* vol. 50, no. 6, pp. 134-143, 2012. [http://dx.doi.org/10.1109/MCOM.2012.6211498]

[11] F.K. Shaikh, S. Zeadally, and E. Exposito, "Enabling Technologies for Green Internet of Things", *IEEE Syst. J.,* vol. 11, no. 2, pp. 983-994, 2017. [http://dx.doi.org/10.1109/JSYST.2015.2415194]

[12] V. Ovidiu, and F. Peter, *Internet of Things: Converging Technologies for Smart Environments and Integrated Ecosystems.* River Publishers: Aalborg, Denmark, 2013. http://www.internet-of-things-research.eu/pdf/Converging_Technologies_for_Smart_Environments_and_Integrated_Ecosystems_IERC_Book_Open_Access_2013.pdf

[13] G. Santucci, *The internet of things: Between the revolution of the internet and the metamorphosis of objects.,* 2010. https://docplayer.net/37795045-The-internet-of-things-between-the-revolution-of-the-internet-and-the-metamorphosis-of-objects.html

[14] F. Mattern, and C. Flörkemeier, "Vom Internet der Computer zum Internet der Dinge", *Informatik-Spektrum,* vol. 33, no. 2, pp. 107-121, 2010. [http://dx.doi.org/10.1007/s00287-010-0417-7]

[15] T. Lindner, "The supply chain: changing at the speed of technology", *Connected World,* 2015.

[16] Y. Erlich, "A vision for ubiquitous sequencing", *Genome Res.,* vol. 25, no. 10, pp. 1411-1416, 2015. [http://dx.doi.org/10.1101/gr.191692.115] [PMID: 26430149]

[17] H. Garg, and M. Dave, "Securing IoT Devices and Securely Connecting the Dots Using REST API and Middleware", In: *4th International Conference on Internet of Things: Smart Innovation and Usages (IoT-SIU)* Ghaziabad, India, 2019. [http://dx.doi.org/10.1109/IoT-SIU.2019.8777334]

[18]   G. Noto La Diega, and I. Walden, *Contracting for the 'Internet of Things': Looking into the Nest.* vol. Vol. 7. Queen Mary School of Law Legal Studies Research Paper, 2016, pp. 1-38.https://papers.ssrn.com/sol3/papers.cfm?abstract_id=2725913

[19]   O.B. Sezer, E. Dogdu, and A.M. Ozbayoglu, "Context-Aware Computing, Learning, and Big Data in Internet of Things: A Survey", *IEEE Internet Things J.,* vol. 5, no. 1, pp. 1-27, 2018.
[http://dx.doi.org/10.1109/JIOT.2017.2773600]

[20]   W. Na, J. Park, C. Lee, K. Park, J. Kim, and S. Cho, "Energy-Efficient Mobile Charging for Wireless Power Transfer in Internet of Things Networks", *IEEE Internet Things J.,* vol. 5, no. 1, pp. 79-92, 2018.
[http://dx.doi.org/10.1109/JIOT.2017.2772318]

[21]   J. Jin, J. Gubbi, S. Marusic, and M. Palaniswami, "An Information Framework for Creating a Smart City Through Internet of Things", *IEEE Internet Things J.,* vol. 1, no. 2, pp. 112-121, 2014.
[http://dx.doi.org/10.1109/JIOT.2013.2296516]

[22]   Q. Wu, G. Ding, Y. Xu, S. Feng, Z. Du, J. Wang, and K. Long, "Cognitive Internet of Things: A New Paradigm Beyond Connection", *IEEE Internet Things J.,* vol. 1, no. 2, pp. 129-143, 2014.
[http://dx.doi.org/10.1109/JIOT.2014.2311513]

[23]   S. Xia, H. Wu, and M. Jin, "GPS-Free Greedy Routing With Delivery Guarantee and Low Stretch Factor on 2-D and 3-D Surfaces", *IEEE Internet Things J.,* vol. 1, no. 3, pp. 233-242, 2014.
[http://dx.doi.org/10.1109/JIOT.2014.2320260]

[24]   Z. Ren, X. Qi, G. Zhou, and H. Wang, "Exploiting the Data Sensitivity of Neurometric Fidelity for Optimizing EEG Sensing, IEEE Internet of Things Journal, June 2014, Vol. 1, pp. 243-254. L. Yu, T. Jiang, Y. Cao, Q. Qi, "Carbon-Aware Energy Cost Minimization for Distributed Internet Data Centers in Smart Microgrids", *IEEE Internet Things J.,* vol. 1, pp. 255-275, 2014.

[25]   J. Kharbanda, R. Madan, V. Passi, and D. Sharma, "Mobile Application Deployment on Cloud", *IEEE Internet of Things Journal,* 2022.

[26]   M.S. Khan, M.S. Islam, and H. Deng, "Design of a Reconfigurable RFID Sensing Tag as a Generic Sensing Platform Toward the Future Internet of Things", *IEEE Internet Things J.,* vol. 1, no. 4, pp. 300-310, 2014.
[http://dx.doi.org/10.1109/JIOT.2014.2329189]

[27]   Y. Zhang, L. Sun, H. Song, and X. Cao, "Ubiquitous WSN for Healthcare: Recent Advances and Future Prospects", *IEEE Internet Things J.,* vol. 1, no. 4, pp. 311-318, 2014.
[http://dx.doi.org/10.1109/JIOT.2014.2329462]

[28]   K. Framling, S. Kubler, and A. Buda, "Universal Messaging Standards for the IoT From a Lifecycle Management Perspective", *IEEE Internet Things J.,* vol. 1, no. 4, pp. 319-327, 2014.
[http://dx.doi.org/10.1109/JIOT.2014.2332005]

[29]   Xiang Sheng, Jian Tang, Xuejie Xiao, and Guoliang Xue, "Leveraging GPS-Less Sensing Scheduling for Green Mobile Crowd Sensing", *IEEE Internet Things J.,* vol. 1, no. 4, pp. 328-336, 2014.
[http://dx.doi.org/10.1109/JIOT.2014.2334271]

[30]   Pin-Yu Chen, Shin-Ming Cheng, and Kwang-Cheng Chen, "Information Fusion to Defend Intentional Attack in Internet of Things", *IEEE Internet Things J.,* vol. 1, no. 4, pp. 337-348, 2014.
[http://dx.doi.org/10.1109/JIOT.2014.2337018]

[31]   B. Kantarci, and H.T. Mouftah, "Trustworthy Sensing for Public Safety in Cloud-Centric Internet of Things", *IEEE Internet Things J.,* vol. 1, no. 4, pp. 360-368, 2014.
[http://dx.doi.org/10.1109/JIOT.2014.2337886]

[32]   S.C. Lin, C.Y. Wen, and W.A. Sethares, "Two-tier device-based authentication protocol against PUEA attacks for IoT applications", *IEEE Trans. Signal Inf. Process. Netw.,* vol. 4, no. 1, pp. 33-47, 2018.
[http://dx.doi.org/10.1109/TSIPN.2017.2723761]

[33]   A.J Shreedhar, K. Srijay, R.Y Rahul, and S.S Singh, "IoT based smart energy meter", *Bonfring International Journal of Research in Communication Engineering,* pp. 89-91, 2016.

[34]   S. Gopinath, N. Gunasundari, and P. Gowthami, *Internet of Things (IoT) Based Energy Meter, International Research Journal of Engineering and Technology.* vol. Vol. 3. IRJET, 2016, p. 4.

[35]   O. Vermesan, P. Friess, and P. Guillemin, "Internet of things strategic research roadmap, Internet of Things", *Global Technological and Societal Trends,* vol. 1, pp. 9-52, 2011.

[36]   I. Mashal, O. Alsaryrah, T.Y. Chung, C.Z. Yang, W.H. Kuo, and D.P. Agrawal, "Choices for interaction with things on Internet and underlying issues", *Ad Hoc Netw.,* vol. 28, pp. 68-90, 2015.
[http://dx.doi.org/10.1016/j.adhoc.2014.12.006]

[37]   O. Said, and M. Masud, "Towards internet of things: survey and future vision", *International Journal of Computer Networks,* vol. 5, no. 1, pp. 1-17, 2013.

[38]   H. Ning, and H. Liu, "Cyber-physical-social based security architecture for future internet of things", *Advances in Internet of Things,* vol. 2, no. 1, pp. 1-7, 2012.
[http://dx.doi.org/10.4236/ait.2012.21001]

[39]   R.A. Kjellby, L.R. Cenkeramaddi, A. Frøytlog, B.B. Lozano, J. Soumya, and M. Bhange, "Long-range & Self-powered IoT Devices for Agriculture & Aquaponics Based on Multi-hop Topology", In: *IEEE 5th World Forum on Internet of Things (WF-IoT)* Limerick, Ireland, 2019.
[http://dx.doi.org/10.1109/WF-IoT.2019.8767196]

[40]   A.R. Deshmukh, S.A. Dhawale, and S.S. Dorle, "Analysis of Cluster-Based Routing Protocol (CBRP) for Vehicular Adhoc Network (VANet) in Real Geographic Scenario", In: *2020 IEEE International Conference on Electronics, Computing and Communication Technologies (CONNECT)*, 2020, pp. 1-5.Bangalore, India
[http://dx.doi.org/10.1109/CONECCT50063.2020.9198669]

[41]   S.N. Swamy, and S.R. Kota, "An Empirical Study on System Level Aspects of Internet of Things (IoT)", *IEEE Access,* vol. 8, pp. 188082-188134, 2020.
[http://dx.doi.org/10.1109/ACCESS.2020.3029847]

[42]   E.P. Yadav, E.A. Mittal, and H. Yadav, "IoT: Challenges and Issues in Indian Perspective", *3rd International Conference On Internet of Things: Smart Innovation and Usages (IoT-SIU), Bhimtal,* pp. 1-5, 2018.
[http://dx.doi.org/10.1109/IoT-SIU.2018.8519869]

[43]   R. Mishra, "MRI Based Brain Tumor Detection Using Wavelet Packet Feature and Artificial Neural Network", *International Conference and Workshop on Emerging Trends in Technology (ICWET 2010),* pp. 26-27, 2010.

[44]   R. Mishra, R. K. Tripathi, and A. K. Sharma, "Corona based Node Distribution Scheme Targeting Energy Balancing in Wireless Sensor Networks for the Sensors Having Limited Sensing Range", *Wireless Networks.*

[45]   R. Mishra, V. Jha, R.K. Tripathi, and A.K. Sharma, "Energy-efficient approach in wireless sensor networks using game-theoretic approach and ant colony optimization", *Wirel. Pers. Commun.,* vol. 95, no. 3, pp. 3333-3355, 2017.
[http://dx.doi.org/10.1007/s11277-017-4000-2]

[46]   R. Mishra, V. Jha, R.K. Tripathi, and A.K. Sharma, "Design of probability density function targeting energy-efficient network for coalition-based WSNs", *Wirel. Pers. Commun.,* vol. 99, no. 2, pp. 651-680, 2018.
[http://dx.doi.org/10.1007/s11277-017-5134-y]

CHAPTER 3

Cloud Industry Application 4.0: Challenges and Benefits

Abhikriti Narwal[1,*] and **Sunita Dhingra**[1]

¹ Department of Computer Science & Engineering, University Institute of Engineering & Technology, Maharshi Dayanand University, Rohtak Haryana, India

Abstract: The latest advancements in the manufacturing industry due to ICT (Information and Communication Technologies) has promoted the wave of Industry 4.0 in today's world. This has transformed the traditional mass-production model into the mass customization model. The vision of Industry 4.0 is to make machines that have the capability of self-learning and self-awareness for improving the planning, performance, operations, and maintenance of manufacturing units. This paper analyses the fundamental technologies behind the success of I4.0, namely Cloud computing and big data analysis, in great detail. The Cloud is the heart of Industry 4.0. It is the primary enabler of innovative, more efficient, and practical strategies in business processes by using artificial intelligence, intelligent sensors, and robotics. It has additionally examined numerous applications where this concept is being used along with various issues and challenges.

Keywords: Big Data Analyses, Cloud Computing, Cloud Manufacturing, Cyber-Physical Systems, Digital Shadow of Production, Healthcare, Industry 4.0, Nine Pillars.

INTRODUCTION

An industrial revolution of the 18th century known as the 1st revolution marked the beginning of the steam engine. The 2nd revolution gave rise to the mass production epoch with industrial electrification. Information Technology (IT) with computers and embedded hardware resulted in the 3rd revolution in the 20th century. Now, the 4th revolution, which is marked by Industry 4.0, gives a novel organization hierarchy and control over the industrial value chain. It is embarked by using the potential of IT (Information technology) in various production processes to make everything digital. Since the 1st revolution, it is evident how technology has evo-

* **Corresponding author Abhikriti Narwal:** Department of Computer Science & Engineering, University Institute of
Engineering & Technology, Maharshi Dayanand University, Rohtak Haryana, India;
E-mail: richas.phoenix@gmail.com

Vaishali Mehta, Dolly Sharma, Monika Mangla, Anita Gehlot, Rajesh Singh and Sergio Marquez Sanchez (Eds.)

lved to make the manufacturing procedure more automated and sustainable for its easy and effective use [1].

With the worldwide integration of the industries and digital transformation, there is a paradigm shift from mass production to mass customization (MC). MC's production approach provides personalized products and services designed explicitly by modularized and flexible methods with the integration of supply chain members [2]. This focuses more on value creation than merely reducing the production costs by fulfilling the client's needs and increasing responsiveness. The fast evolution of IT, cloud computing, and the Internet of Things (IoT) have embarked on Industry 4.0 and Cloud Manufacturing, where the things (or machines) are interconnected but can communicate and analyze the data to make intelligent decisions.

The vision of Industry 4.0 is to make machines that have the capability of self-learning and self-awareness for improving the planning, performance, operations, and maintenance of manufacturing units [3]. Furthermore, it aims at developing intelligent manufacturing units for client-specific applications [4]. Data monitoring and tracking the status and locations of products in real-time are the basic needs of this industry [5]. CM is the latest service-oriented paradigm that works along the same lines as that of cloud computing. However, both of them represent different business theories but work for the same purpose. These new unfolding philosophies are connected, where Industry 4.0 takes up the concept of manufacturing as a service from CM, and CM borrows the idea of an intelligent factory from Industry 4.0.

Intelligence and digital transformation of manufacturing units is a new wave that has revolutionized the entire business. So, if you will not dive into it, you will be left behind. Therefore, for all industries, it is imperative to consider the new technologies and adapt their policies to comply with the expectations of the modern world. Ever since the evolution of the latest technology in the business world, businesses have never been more fickle. Digitization is all around us, whether the automobile industry is moving towards driverless cars or the consumer industry unfolding the various technologies in the form of smart homes. According to [6], approximately nearly 7 billion things were connected to the internet in 2014, and this number is expected to reach nearly 25 billion in 2020. Cloud computing is a pivot in all contemporary business companies and institutes. It means to get the computing services like storage, databases, networking, analytic, servers, and access to data all over the Internet rather than on your system. Furthermore, it provides the flexibility to offer a "pay–as–you–use" feature that allows the industries to pay for only those services that they have used. This helps them reduce their operational costs, run their infrastructure more efficiently, and scale the business as per the requirement.

In India, cloud-based services have become omnipresent. This is so much that it is challenging for some businesses to manage their work without cloud computing. It is essential for small industries as it decreases operational costs and improves speed and accuracy. It helps the industry hold its position on a worldwide platform by providing them with software solutions, scaling, flexibility, big data analytics, and collaboration. Top Biggies also boast this concept, wherein they are using the culture of work from home that is only possible due to cloud computing. They also rely on cloud computing to store their crucial and critical data as it provides very high security.

Many industries have reached new heights by adopting cloud computing in their business processes. Many new technologies have evolved, but nothing could take away the strategic significance of cloud computing. It is the pivot of all technologies as it gives location and device independence, network virtualization, scalability, reliability, faster recovery, reducing ownership costs, offline accessibility, and many more. It has its footprints in all industries, whether entertainment, banking, or the marketing sector, by providing innovative and better services to the targeted clients. The cloud market is expanding very quickly and, as per NASSCOM reports, will reach $ 7.1 billion in 2022 [7]. On the other hand, we could see little advancement like wafting away modular and social software with low-cost hardware soon. According to many industrial reports around the world, it is believed that cloud technology is one of many technologies that are driving the fourth industrial revolution by providing innovative business ideas.

FUNDAMENTAL CONCEPTS

Industry 4.0 (I4.0)

Smart Factory, Factories of the Future, Intelligent Factories, or Industrial value chain Initiative are interchangeably for Industry 4.0. It is the digitization of production or manufacturing units with control over the value chain in the industry. It is marked by more automation, a digital and physical world collaboration by cyber-physical systems, customization of services or products, and a tremendous shift from traditional industrial systems to modern control systems. To fully understand this concept, one must know the entire value chain from the origin of raw material to supplier and things required for intelligent manufacturing and the ultimate destination of production units. In a nutshell, it led to the substitution of autonomous systems with cyber-physical systems either entirely or partially by incorporating the information systems. As described in Fig. (**1**), intelligent factories have become the centre for analysis and promote digitization in manufacturing units. It further introduces a new level of organization and control all over the system by sharing the complete product life cycle with the clients to fulfill their needs.

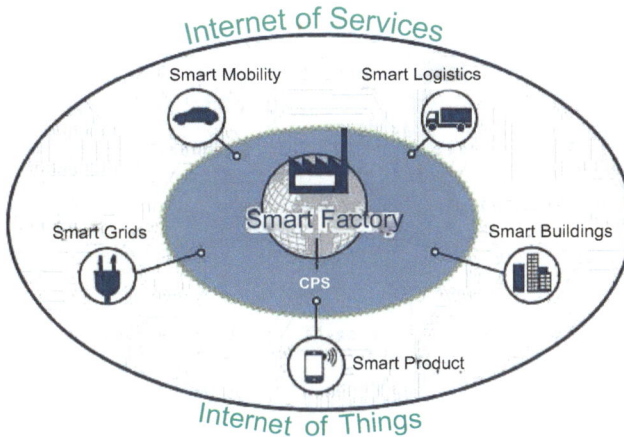

Fig. (1). Smart Factories as Industry 4.0 [8].

It is vital to amalgamate the physical and digital systems for the realization of I4.0. This introduces the cyber-physical systems in the manufacturing domains. Its scope is not just limited to connecting the physical objects like sensors or machines with the cyber functionality but also to adding the applications as services to provide the additional functionality to the clients. Fig. (**2**) describes the concept of Industry 4.0 with all its objectives and characteristics.

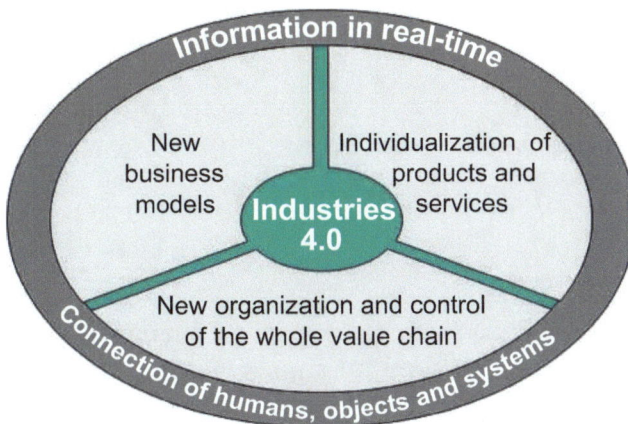

Fig. (2). Industry 4.0 along with its features.

I4.0 uses Information and Communication Technologies (ICT) for producing customized goods and services to make clients happy. This approach has changed the old automation model to a new interconnected, networked model by collaborating IT and operational technology. This created an environment that entertains more flexible production processes by sharing the data and establishing new connections.

This way of communication between machine to machine or machine to humans usage of clients data for customization of products have made the life of people very easy. One could trace the entire production process effectively. The revolution of this century has made it possible for the production machines to be operated efficiently and autonomously. With such innovation, all game players of the supply chain are its suppliers, producers, or consumers cone on the same line and access and analyze the entire data of their production processes.

Cyber-physical systems and mechanical devices are different in their way of functionality. Therefore, it is appropriately described in Fig. (3), which introduces the 4 different layers in the entire process. The first one is the socio-technical value-added systems, the second device or components like sensors, humans, actuators, the third being the platform for smooth communication and connection, and the last is the application layer that provides the extra functionality to the physical domain.

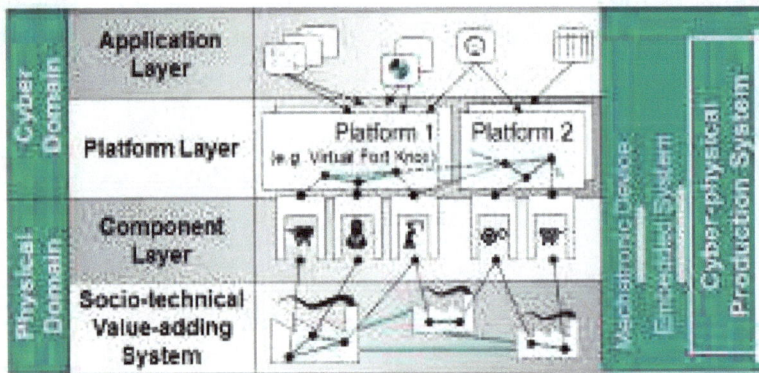

Fig. (3). Cyber-Physical System.

Keeping in mind the widespread usage of ICT empowered manufacturing methods in industries, there is a need for some reference architecture that would further lead to their continuous adoption and evolution [9]. Reference Architectural Management Industrial 4.0 (RAMI 4.0) of Germany aimed at implementing and developing I4.0 according to the strategies issued by the

German Federal Government. Due to its widespread acceptance, RAMI 4.0 has now matured into the German standard DIN SPEC 91345 [10]. Similar initiatives have also been started in various countries like China, the U.S.A., France,`123- and many more. USA has taken the help of giant IT industries like Intel, At&T, Cisco, IBM, and General Electric to start up an Industrial Internet Consortium (IIC) to build Industrial Internet, and they named it as Industrial Internet Reference Architecture(IIRA) [10].

The fundamental goal of RAMI 4.0 and IIRA is to promote digitization in business processes and to enable them with intelligent technology. Overall, the objective is to make significant changes in the present production models, optimize various methods of manufacturing processes, build customized products and services, reduce the cost, and finally, strengthen the industries ultimately. This will improve economic growth more employment and create an environment where the suppliers and consumers are closely coupled [11].

I4.0 allows real-time access to the entire product life cycle by integrating horizontal and vertical software applications. It promotes quick decision-making policies by providing autonomous information without the help of humans, encourages the transparent traceability of the entire production process, helps in detecting the errors of manufacturing procedures and rectifying them immediately. It also includes preventive maintenance planning remotely monitoring of the manufacturing plants to minimize the cuts in production due to failure in the equipment, leading to many manufacturing plants at a different geographical location. In addition, it promotes transparent communication between different suppliers across the entire production process, lowering the response time to delivery, and gaining new information on the life of the product for the future use of new business models.

The interconnection between the fundamental business components of I4.0 generates Big Data. This data generated from different sources in real-time is available in many formats and needs to be stored and processed for analysis with advanced technologies and algorithms. It is due to this reason that cloud computing and big data are to be applied to I4.0. They are the connective issue of this industry. These two fundamental approaches provide all the necessary and relevant components required for this novel industrial paradigm. Fig. (**4**) represents the relationship between these two technologies and I4.0.

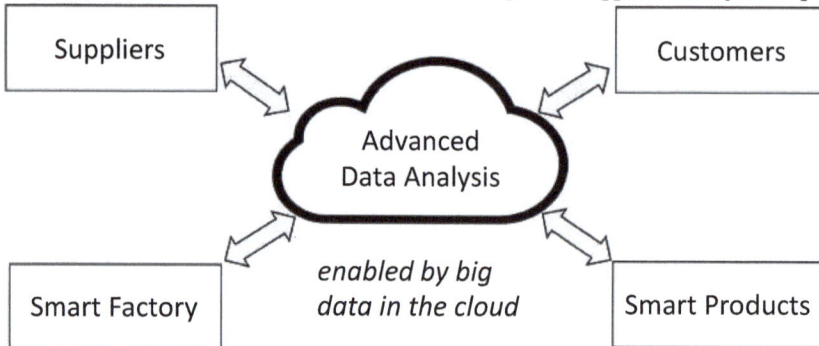

Fig. (4). Relationship between I4.0 and Cloud and big data.

NINE PILLARS OF INDUSTRY 4.0

Industry 4.0 is emerged as the winning technology in many logistics and manufacturing systems by incorporating the cyber-physical systems globally. It extensively uses the globally available information and communication network for the required business processes. The technology enabler of I4.0 is intelligent manufacturing, IoT, Industrial IoT, and cloud-based manufacturing, which makes it easy to build digital and intelligent business processes [12, 13]. The nine digital industrial technologies, also known as the nine pillars, will change the optimized and isolated production units to fully automated, integrated, and customized flow of production processes to improve the efficiency of the systems. Fig. (5) portraits the 9 pillars of I4.0 along with their functionality. These are as follows:

Fig. (5). Nine pillars of I4.0.

Advanced Robotics

With advancements in technology, robots are becoming more flexible, autonomous, and cooperative, helping them interact with other machines or humans more quickly and efficiently. They are also becoming intelligent to take up their own decisions and learn from their own mistakes. In industries, they perform the production activities more precisely and where humans could not go. As a result, they complete their work accurately, more precisely, and intelligently in less time without not compromising the versatility, safety, flexibility, and collaboratively of their work. Table **1** represents some of the robots used in industry [14].

Table 1. List of robots used in industry.

Sr. No.	Name of Robot	Functionality	Company
1.	*Roberta*	It is an industrial robot with 6 axes that are used for efficient and flexible automation of the different process	*Gomtec*
2.	*Baxter*	It is an interactive robot that is used in packaging activities	*Rethink Robotics*
3.	*BioRob Arm*	It lives near the humans and assists them in their tasks	*Bionic robotics*
4.	*Kuka L.B.R. iiwa*	It is light in weight and used for sensitive industrial tasks	*Kuka*

Additive Manufacturing

Additive manufacturing methods are widely used in Industry 4.0 to provide highly customized products in decentralized systems. It includes 3-D printing for prototypes and spare parts. The highly decentralized system using additive manufacturing reduces transport distances and inventory [15]. The production becomes less costly and faster using various additive manufacturing technologies like selective laser melting, fused deposition method, *etc.* [16]. For example, we could see many variations in the engine, interiors, bodywork, and equipment in the cars of the same model to fulfil the needs of highly demanding clients.

Augmented Reality

Industries with augmented reality provide many services such as communicating real-time information like repair instruction or selecting different parts in the warehouse to workers on their smartphones. This helps in improving the decision making policies and their working procedures [15]. For example, if a chopper is struck in some remote area and needs maintenance. This will take around much time. The mechanic will need to go on another flight and check for the faults. In turn, if the chopper's driver is acquired with augmented glasses connected with the central computer, the full details of the chopper will be known, and the repair action will be performed in less time.

Simulation

Simulations are used mainly in those industries that use real-time data to pretend the physical world into virtual reality. For example, simulations in the manufacturing procedures reduce the downtime and the risk of production failures in the start-up phase [17]. It also enhances the decision making quality.

Horizontal/Vertical Integration

Industry 4.0 is catered by three types of integration: the first is a horizontal integration that requires integration across the entire value creation network, the second is vertical integration, and the third is the end-to-end integration of the entire life cycle of products [18]. Self-optimization and integration techniques are the two methods that are used in industries these days.

Industrial Internet and Internet of Things

IoT has its roots in Information and Communication Technology (ICT) that uses the internet infrastructure. It comprises the intelligent object interconnection of the various sensory devices and systems. The critical point is to interconnect everything, be it resources, objects, machines, information, or humans, with the internet to create the Internet of Things and services.

IoT means the worldwide interconnection of objects, each with a unique identification address, complying with all standard protocols [18]. The other interchangeable terms for IoT are Internet of Services, Internet of Everything, Internet of Manufacturing Services, Internet of People, or Integration of Information and Communication Technology (IICT) [19].

The key characteristics of IoT are context-driven, omnipresent, and optimization, where context-driven means the object interaction and understanding of the real environment. Its ability to respond quickly if something changes, omnipresent means to get the information of location and its surrounding atmospheric conditions and optimization emphasizes that objects are more than just physical interconnection to a network of human operators at the machine-human interface [20].

Industrial internet refers to the value chain that intelligently interconnects the human factors, physical objects, smart sensors, intelligent machines, and production lines in the organization. Data and software are the prime components of intelligent planning and control over the industries of the future. For example, intelligent pallets and intelligent shelving will take place in modern inventory management in warehouse storage. In the carriage industry, tracking and tracing of goods become more safe, precise, and faster [21].

Cloud

Cloud serves as the backbone for communication and connection in Industry4.0. The industries require more data sharing among many companies and sites and look for faster response times. "Digital production", a new term that recently emerged, requires connecting the various devices to the same Cloud for sharing information [22]. This is possible only with the help of cloud computing.

With this technology, I4.0 can store large chunks of data generated from various production processes that are interconnected with each other. Machines and sensors always generate more data when compared to humans. It provides agility, flexibility, and adaptability by allowing the processing capacity and storage space to be contracted on demand. It promotes a scalable structure where the users could consume the resources as per needs. It cuts the operation cost to a large margin as the clients don't need to empty their pockets to purchase licenses, servers, or any professional personnel for maintenance. This also saves energy to a large extent. Adding more in the cloud perspective also led you to access the storage anytime, irrespective of the devices used and the platform.

All of this promotes the healthy and friendly collaboration between the suppliers and consumers in the manufacturing ecosystems. In short, the consumer can participate in all the steps of the production procedure, which in turn improves their satisfaction. Sometimes, as a result of a large volume of data, a latency time is observed that could affect the performance of the production process. To overcome this issue, a new concept could be used, which is "Fog Computing". It processes the large volume of data coming from IoT things for proper analysis and control functions. It improves the latency time as the node that processes the data is located in the same network as the IoT devices. These nodes are capable of storage and computing processes. Compared with cloud computing, fog computing improves the stability and quality of services and reduces congestion [23]. Further, to improve security and data privacy, it is advisable to use private clouds for confidential functionality.

Cyber Security and Cyber-physical Systems

Industry 4.0 results in the widespread use of connectivity and various standard communication protocols, thus increasing cybersecurity threats drastically. Due to this reliable and secure communication and secured access to the management of machines is the need of the hour. The powerful bond between the digital and physical world helps improvise the quality of information needed in manufacturing systems for their planning, optimization, and cost operations [16]. The cyber-physical systems (CPS) involve the close integration of cyberspace systems like communication, computation, and control systems with physical systems like natural or hand-made [24]. The main characteristics of CPS are automation and decentralized production processes. It has become easy to find out the faults in machines and automatically repair them with the help of proper sensors in CPS. The Cloud plays a significant role in CPS. It helps communicate with the machine by using the 5C structure, whether the communication is from machine to human or machine to machine [21]. For example, the smart vehicle uses the CPS to predict the routes.

The CPS and IoT are the backbones of I4.0. It is pretty evident from Fig. **(6)**, which represents the relationship of CPS and IoT with I4.0. It incorporates ubiquitous computing in which users can access the required information anywhere and anytime [25]. For example, an exciting application of CPS could be seen at the floor tools and equipment of the shops where they have enabled the machine to machine communication [26]. It also allows the interaction between real and virtual systems or *vice versa*. With the help of virtual systems, it is easy to design, model, and simulate the products to be delivered to the real world. Also, the physical processes in the manufacturing industries would be easily viewed by virtual environments like augmented reality or 3-D.

Both IoT and CPS deploy the Internet of Services over cloud infrastructure where they store, share, exchange, and analyze the data from all manufacturing processes. To add more, all the supply chain players could share and deploy the manufacturing processes as services. These resources could be used in an integrated and collaborative platform to design and model the new services and products through a virtual environment for a more dynamic, sophisticated, and demanding market.

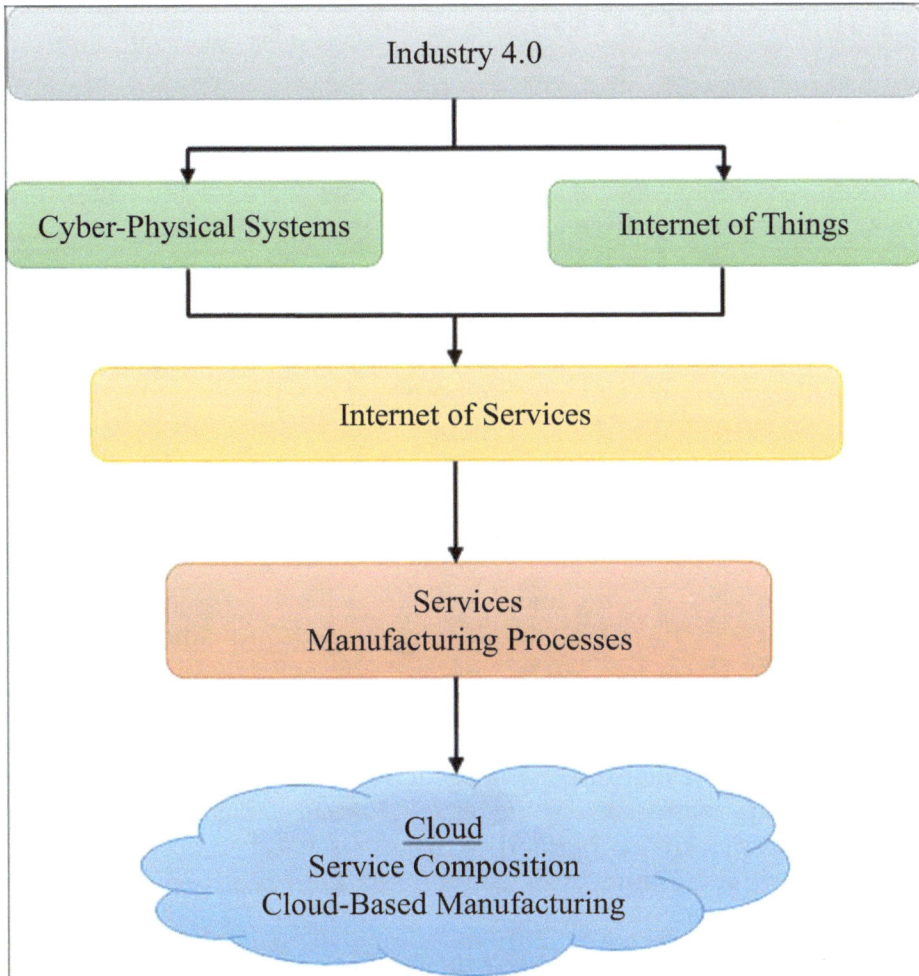

Fig. (6). I4.0 with CPS and IoT in a cloud-based manufacturing.

Big Data Analytics

With the digitization of many industries, there is enormous data that is flowing in. Therefore for collecting and analyzing it, we require specific tools that support the real-time decision-making policies. Big data constitutes four V's: volume, velocity, variety, and value of data. The evaluation of the earlier recorded data could be used to find out the threats that occurred in various production processes and to foretell any new problems and the new solutions to prevent them from occurring again and again in the industry [24].

THE CLOUD AND INDUSTRY4.0

The partnership between Industry 4.0 and Cloud is a winning combination. Companies' main agenda nowadays is to integrate the IoT into their processes, thus developing entire automated management and the extensive use of digital technologies. In short, the main driving force behind the intelligence in technologies that is pervasive and ubiquitous is the Cloud.

With this advancement, monitoring and control operations steps are doubled, but the industries could now comply with the quality control measures more efficiently and with less cost and time. In addition, the plethora of advanced sensor technology, augmented reality, artificial intelligence, 3D printing, and strong collaboration of supply chain members in smart factories have increased customer satisfaction.

The Cloud is the heart of Industry 4.0. It is the primary enabler of innovative, more efficient, and practical strategies in business processes by clouting artificial intelligence, intelligent sensors, and robotics. As per the research, six out of ten industries feel like going for cloud infrastructure for their manufacturing operations. It is thereby a real catalyst of digital transformation in manufacturing companies. It helps industries reach new heights by giving them the required computing power and analyzing the information from the wide range of data captured. Although artificial intelligence, robotics, extensive data analysis are the prime assets of digitization in the industrial process, we can't ignore the Cloud. Due to the Cloud that gives the facility of pay as you use and various onboard services, the small or big industries could enjoy the benefits of the technologies mentioned above.

The Cloud is being known for its various key features.

Pay as You Use

The clients are required to pay for only those resources they have used and that for the duration they have used.

Agility and Flexibility

You could scale your business, storage, and network as per your need quickly. It ensures the elasticity in infrastructure that makes the company reliable enough to withstand the sudden changes in the market like seasonal changes, attacking market campaigns, or digitization in production-sensitive solutions.

Zero Deployment Time

It helped in enhancing operational efficiency by reducing the operational activities and maintenance of infrastructure significantly.

Cost Reduction

It helps in decreasing the cost related to infrastructure and eases up the maintenance.

Shorter Innovation Cycles

It led to the ongoing improvement of the involved services with simplicity.

The presence of the Cloud in many industrial sectors has introduced the eight leading indicators that would help understand the present and future needs of various businesses, thus enabling them to explore the true potentials of the Cloud more accurately. These are the eight indicators:

Increase in the Speed and Rate of Innovation

The Cloud offers low cost in adopting any new service or maintaining the older one compared to the on-premise situation. Moreover, it provides additional privileges like effort and time reduction in many decision-making activities and their transition into new offers and products.

Total Cost of Ownership Optimization

The clients have the opportunity to use and configure the infrastructure as per the needs and requirements of their business processes.

Rapid Provisioning of Resources

Consumers get access to their required resources very efficiently and promptly. Earlier the traditional systems used to take many weeks, which is now reduced to a few hours. The economic benefits of decreasing the cost of cloud services have increased due to the severe competition of the key vendors.

Increased Control over Costs and Savings

When you get the service on the Cloud, you save a considerable chunk of money which could further be invested in developing new products and services.

Dynamic use of Resources

The services provided by the Cloud are highly granular, such that they could quickly fulfill all the requirements of end-users.

Sustainability and Privacy

The Cloud comply with all security and data protection standards to ensure the entire safety of the client's crucial data

Optimization in IT Functionality

It makes the optimal usage of IT infrastructure without causing any redundancies.

Skills

It helps improve the skills by making full use of innovative and specific IT solutions on the Cloud.

APPLICATIONS

Cloud Manufacturing (CM)

At present, many manufacturing industries are turning to the latest digitization paradigms by enhancing the alliance of all players on the supply chain. With this, they are making themselves capable of standing and shining on the global front. It is a consolidated business model that uses cloud computing to provide virtual production resources to industries quickly. It reduces operational costs and increases the productive capacity with great flexibility for each player on the supply chain. CM combines many innovative technologies like CPS, Industrial IoT, Data Management manufacturing, and a significant player, the Cloud, to start a new type of service called Manufacturing-as-a-Service (MaaS). It has become a new frontier for cloud computing in I4.0 that provides instant access to large manufacturing units at a reasonable cost [27].

Keeping in mind the manufacturing aspect, all the resources and their states, objects, features, information, and operational mode are all considered services in cloud manufacturing. All these services are well published, described, located, and invoked on the internet to perform tasks as requests between providers and clients [28]. This service could be deployed on either a large or single server using cloud-based technology. However, the stand-alone services require more time to complete and sometimes even face difficulty accomplishing the per user demands. Therefore, to solve this problem, a new concept of service composition is coined to combine various enterprises' existing and available services to perform either complex or simple tasks [29]. The novel method for implementing CM architecture is discussed in [30]. They used a reusable platform to map the CM providers and users so that each client could get the service of their own choice at a reasonable cost and time. Their method uses the ASDI platform that uses two parameters, namely the study of the system and the domain.

I4.0 takes all the hardware, software, and cyber-physical systems as services. All of them form an integrated service that strives to solve the problems of common interests when published in a collaborative environment. For example, Fig. (7) represents a single condition where partners or stakeholders publish or deploy the services on a cloud platform to develop a virtual environment to meet customer needs satisfiability. Here in the client ask for a service, the back end systems will check for its availability and work hard to meet their requirement in the best possible way.

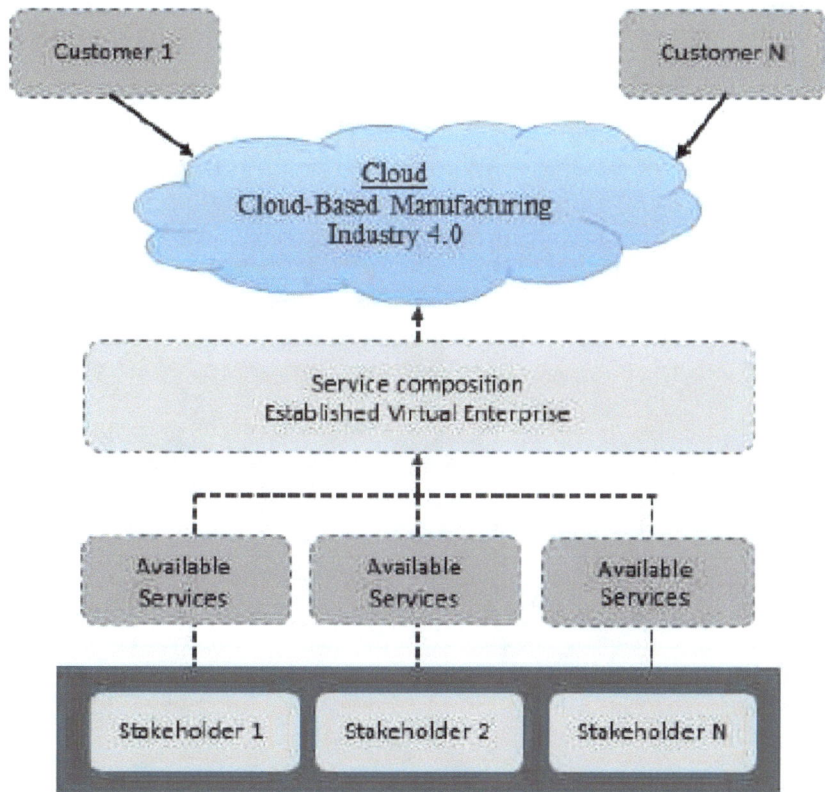

Fig. (7). Stakeholders providing services in a virtual environment to meet the client's need.

Digital Shadow of Production

The Digital Shadow of Production is considered the theoretical backbone of the Application Center. Fig. (**8**) represents the holistic digital image and Digital Factory (DF) and its fundamental understanding of the missing link between the two. DF uses historical knowledge, data, and experiences [31]. For the industrial control of production with permanently altering products, there is a need for a near real-time production image.

This novel concept of the digital shadow of production improves the digital image of the enterprises by providing them with the real-time information and data of the present value-added system. This is further accomplished by using the information technologies on a large scale by exploring the data from various sources like humans, sensors, orders, controls, or possibly the delivered products. I4.0 is highly atomized and generates a massive amount of data. This big data usually is not structured and heterogeneous, making it difficult to analyze it for better decisions. Digital shadow elevates this problem by linking all the required data with the help of a data lake. It combines up all the data which is specific to the given problem [32].

Accepting the digital shadow of production on a broad scale is a challenging task for the coming years. Thereby, an advanced and intelligent platform is needed for its production. Virtual Fort Knox has taken the initial step towards this direction [33]. The basic architecture of the same is illustrated in Fig. (**8**).

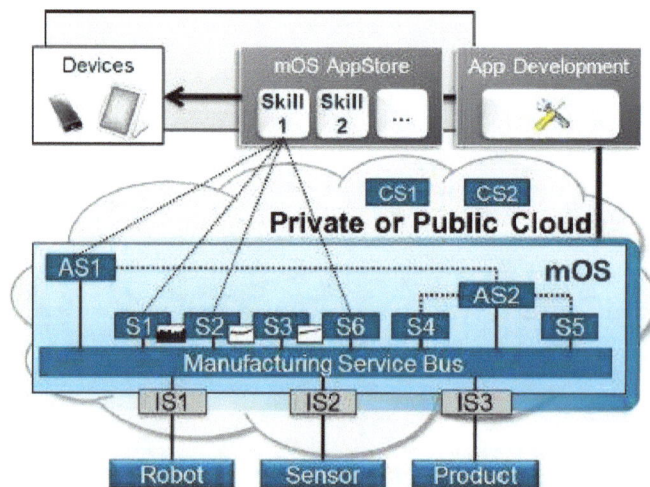

Fig. (8). The Virtual Fort Knox [36].

This cloud-enabled IT platform served as the strong backbone for the communication and connection of many objects in application-oriented I4.0. With the help of this, we could even control the machines remotely, give instructions to the robots, or even manipulate the settings of various decoupled sensors like temperature probes or cameras. The orchestration of highly dynamic sources is done by the manufacturing service bus. This architecture allows accessing the multiple industrial resources in a cloud system in a standardized manner by using various industrial standards like ReST, OPC, ROS, or UA. Further from the user's perspective, all the services provided by the manufacturing service bus could collaborate into superior apps for the help of planners and workers. It is even visible in the creation and intelligent use of various big data concepts in the I4.0. Manufacturing service buses serve as an excellent platform for integrating different data sources in a large number to look for new and creative information in the non-structured production data.

Healthcare

With the rapidly evolving technology and the increasing governmental efforts, the healthcare sector is not left behind from the influence of I4.0. They are now moving from eHealth to healthcare 4.0 also referred to as HC 4.0. Smart health is a widely adopted technology that incorporates ICT into health care solutions. It is worth noting that smart health is different from HC4.0, as HC4.0 has its peculiarities. It is indeed represented by three main technologies: Cloud Computing, Big Data, and the Internet of Things. All paradigms above continuously revolve around eHealth and its surrounding environment [35, 36].

Cloud computing makes use of Utility Computing, where you lend or lease your computing resources like computing power, network resources, and storage in real-time with very little interaction with the provider. By doing this, it simplifies the operations by making the use of pay as you go billing feature. It does not require the careful prediction of the needed resources hence it can utilize the Cloud on a short-term basis without the direct commitment from the user. Apart from this, a client who uses the Cloud enjoys the benefits of a wide range of on-demand resources and can either lease or deliver everything as a service. The most frequently used services are Infrastructure-as-a-Service, Platform-as-a-Service, and Software-as-a-Service [37]. The latest variations include Function-as-a-Service, also known as "Serverless Computing". The Cloud is a must to satisfy the needs of IoT; in fact, on some IoT systems, it is a part of IoT top layers. The extended functionality in the embedded field devices that make them more intelligent and flexible triggers their move to adopt the Cloud with high scalability and responsiveness [38].

Apart from the benefits above, Cloud observed a few shortcomings over the last few years. Most of them are related to the communication between the datacentre hosting the cloud services and the end device, such as latency, cost, bandwidth, and connection availability. Furthermore, the widespread use of mobile devices further makes the situation even worse for the cloud paradigm. In fact, in many cases, the Cloud fails in meeting all the requirements of many applications, particularly in the healthcare domain. As a result, many concepts and technologies have been proposed; Fog computing is one among them. Fog computing takes up the cloud computing services to the nodes in the same network as end devices, thus distributing the load between the base data centre, edge nodes, and end device [39]. This results in low latency rates, fast response, long-term security, and improved scalability. It also improves the on-time service delivery rates and reduces the number of problems related to cloud computing like delay, cost overheads, and jitter while transferring the information to the Cloud.

It likewise underpins client portability, asset, and interface heterogeneity; what's more, circulated information examination to address the necessities of conveyed applications requiring low dormancy. Also, it improves the administration and programming of processing, stockpiling, and systems administration administrations between datacenters furthermore end gadgets. Along these lines, Fog processing is an integral asset to help the decentralized and shrewd handling of extraordinary information volumes produced by IoT sensors sent to incorporate physical and digital conditions, helping the IoT arrive at its vast potential.

When clients are mobile nodes and their computing capacities are moved to the radio access network, this idea coins a new terminology called mobile edge processing. The mobile Cloud unfold so many concepts, which are as follows: (i) mobile devices act like thin clients with most of the application being run on remote server (ii) cell phones are utilized as asset suppliers for the Cloud in a versatile distributed network; (iii) mobile phones offload their entire workload to an edge cloud. In this setting, Carnegie Mellon University created the possibility of cloudlet, making a middle tier between the cell phone and the conventional Cloud. The cloudlet is a self-guided and self-managed data center in a container, a mini cloud with assets adequate to have tremendous burdens for a small bunch of (portable) clients simultaneously. Cloud computing is inferred in different mainstays of HC4.0, particularly Big Data and IoT, yet additionally for Visual/Virtual Computing and other medical care applications.

The trademark advantages of Cloud Computing in containing integration costs and optimized resources are explicitly noted worthy in the medical services situation. Cloud computing meets the IT needs of the medical care area to improve health processes [40 - 42], encourage the adoption of best medical services, and encourage and inspire more developments. The application of Cloud innovations regarding medical care has been named Healthcare as a Service (HaaS) [43]. Contrasted with the primary drivers with the appropriation of Cloud advancements in more broad applications and the IoT worldview with big data [44], HaaS applications share advantages from versatile, on-request, and practically endless calculation capacity. Systems administration assets; not with standing these, other perspectives have been discovered to be significant, for example, simplicity of information sharing, simplicity of information assortment and coordination, and now and again improved execution, accessibility, unwavering quality furthermore, security. Besides, the portable and individual gadgets benefit from Cloud and Fog Computing for dealing with the advanced information and any place and whenever there is a demand for clinical administrations. With many devices and objects becoming more and more part of the regular lives of doctors, patients, and nurses, availability and computation latency becomes a critical issue that needs to be resolved. This adversary affects the forecasting and decision-making procedures, which impacts the delivery of health care services. Mobile Cloud mitigates or unravels these issues and gives frameworks with logical data, considering all the more user-friendly, customized services and adaptive quality of service management. To summarize, Cloud, Fog, and Mobile Edge Computing comprise a significant piece of HC4.0, with positive impacts on medical care examination and improvement of services such as improving quality, making them affordable for a more significant chunk of individuals than presently possible, and improving the results for patients.

According to the latest scientific literature review and market trends, healthcare witnesses a considerable role in driving the I4.0 visions. IoT is very important among the various pillars of I4.0 for remotely monitoring all the resources and allowing healthcare implementation in different settings, from home monitoring and elderly care to specific healthcare rehabilitation. These IoT-enabled settings produce a large amount of data, for which new big data technologies are required to make intelligent interpretation from the raw data. This further makes the healthcare industry rely on the Cloud for storing and processing the data to make further predictions and enhance the reliability and security of data. The latest application of Industry 4.0 could be witnessed during the COVID 19 pandemic, which has created a massive demand for medicines and healthcare equipment. I4.0 has catered to customized needs with the help of cloud technology, big data analytics, IoT, and many intelligent brains [44].

Cloud-based architecture is widely adopted in various cases to simplify and strengthen the development, design, and deployment of information systems. They simplify the procedures of gathering, processing, and sharing healthcare information like medical images, hospital administrative data, or the patient's clinical records. Cloud systems help enhance the data collection process by providing mobile user interfaces to all the entities of cloud services to obtain and process healthcare information. Further, sharing of relevant data among the different medical structures or across patients and hospitals has also gained importance. Security and privacy aspects are also taken care of properly.

BENEFITS OF CLOUD IN INDUSTRY 4.0

The use of CPS and IoT in the end-to-end engineering of I4.0 and the horizontal and vertical integration has extensively increased. Even more, it is predicted that we could observe an exponential growth in the number of projects and services that rely on cloud infrastructure. In this way, the cloud-based designing frameworks can profit the developing Industry 4.0 to offer platform, software, and infrastructure among the partners. And it is also leading to the designing of intelligent manufacturing environments.

With the help of the Cloud, resources, services, and data become accessible to anyone regardless of the operating system or platform. It offers a decentralized technology that benefits the various project members to share and deploy their products and services anywhere. At the worldwide level, where the stakeholders are required to deliver their products or services quickly, it is mandatory to improve the ICT to handle the upcoming demands rapidly. This could only be possible with the help of cloud-based infrastructure as this structure is highly dynamic, scalable, faster, and reliable. Apart from this, they should reinforce the service composition based on service-oriented architecture to form the virtual environment, where an intelligent manufacturing environment should be adopted to develop the new services and products faster. They also handle the rapid market fluctuation efficiently and effectively. The virtual environment in I4.0 requires a more scalable and flexible environment and autonomous system reconfiguration to handle the market concerns. At last, cloud-based manufacturing systems must deploy the task as consumer-centric, demand-driven, and service-oriented to support the industrial flexibility, control systems, and control systems.

CHALLENGES AND ISSUES

The innovation of the latest technology has made the drastic shift in the industrial development systems, from mechanical systems to highly automated and intelligent systems, to become more responsive and capable of handling the current dynamic demands and requirements. This has catered to many issues and challenges such as flexibility, embedment, predictability, and reliability. However, I4.0 faces a few fundamental issues in the present manufacturing industries such as:

Intelligent Negotiation Mechanism and Decision Making

The smart industries require more social capability and autonomy as fundamental steps in self-organized systems. But, the present industries use the 3C's functionality; they lack autonomy in their systems, whereas today's system has 3C Capabilities, *i.e.*, lack of autonomy in the systems.

Industrial Wireless Network (IWN.) Protocols with High Speed

Although the IWN network is better than the weird network of old manufacturing industries, it fails to provide appropriate bandwidth to transport a high volume of data and heavy communication these days.

Manufacturing Specific Big Data and Analytics

It is challenging to ensure the good quality and moral integrity of data coming from various manufacturing units. The data annotations are very diverse, and it is becoming challenging to process and do advanced data analysis with different semantics.

System Analysis and Modelling

System modelling in complex cases is still an undiscovered search area. System modelling is done to minimize the dynamical equations and deploy an appropriate control model in the self-organized manufacturing system.

Cyber Security

There is an urgent need to protect the highly confidential and critical data generated from smart industries. With the increase in the interconnectivity of entities and standard communications, cybersecurity threats have increased drastically.

Flexible and Modularized Physical Artifacts

The processing and deployment of any product in distributed cloud environment require grouped machinery and testing strategies. So, there is the requirement to create a modularized and smart conveying unit that could drastically change the production methods.

Investment Issues

This is the most common issue faced by almost all new technologies in manufacturing. The nine pillars of I4.0 require a large amount of investment.

CONCLUSION

Industry 4.0 introduces the concept of digitization in the market where all the objects are interconnected. A huge amount of data is being generated from various organizations, which must be stored, processed, and analyzed to create valuable information to satisfy a highly competitive global market. The fundamental technologies behind the success of I4.0 are CloudComputing and Big data. Both technologies are independent of the industrial size and the

reference architecture model used. The use of big data and cloud computing for I4 opens up a wide range of opportunities for future research. Similarly, communication from Cloud to company and from Cloud to Cloud is still an undiscovered area.

In the future, it will be mandatory to develop training programs to facilitate human to explore the undiscovered areas in big data and cloud computing. Furthermore, the term Industry 5.0 has also been introduced in the research areas considered the next industrial revolution. It is expected that this revolution will highly impact the society and government structure apart from only manufacturing ramifications.

CONSENT OF PUBLICATION

Not applicable.

CONFLICT OF INTEREST

The author declares no conflict of interest, financial or otherwise.

ACKNOWLEDGEMENTS

Declared none.

REFERENCES

[1]   F. Almada-Lobo, "The Industry 4.0 revolution and the future of Manufacturing Execution Systems (MES)", *Journal of Innovation Management,* vol. 3, no. 4, pp. 16-21, 2016.
        [http://dx.doi.org/10.24840/2183-0606_003.004_0003]

[2]   F.S. Fogliatto, G.J.C. da Silveira, and D. Borenstein, "The mass customization decade: An updated review of the literature", *Int. J. Prod. Econ.,* vol. 138, no. 1, pp. 14-25, 2012.
        [http://dx.doi.org/10.1016/j.ijpe.2012.03.002]

[3]   J. Lee, H.A. Kao, and S. Yang, "Service innovation and smart analytics for industry 4.0 and Big Data Environment", *Procedia CIRP,* vol. 16, pp. 3-8, 2014.
        [http://dx.doi.org/10.1016/j.procir.2014.02.001]

[4]   J. Qin, Y. Liu, and R. Grosvenor, "A categorical framework of manufacturing for Industry 4.0 and Beyond", *Procedia CIRP,* vol. 52, pp. 173-178, 2016.

[http://dx.doi.org/10.1016/j.procir.2016.08.005]

[5]   M.A. Kamarul Bahrin, M.F. Othman, N.H. Nor Azli, and M.F. Talib, "Industry 4.0: A review on Industrial Automation and robotic", In: *Jurnal Teknologi* vol. 78. , 2016, pp. 6-13.

[6]   R. van Delden, "Towards a socially adaptive digital playground", *Proceedings of the 11th International Conference on Interaction Design and Children - IDC '12,* 2012. [http://dx.doi.org/10.1145/2307096.2307166]

[7]   *Gartner says 6.4 billion connected 'things' will be in use in 2016, up 30 percent from 2015.* Available: https://www.gartner.com/en/newsroom/press-releases/2015-11-10-gartner-says-6-billion-connected-things-will-be-in-use-in-2016-up-30-percent-from-2015 [Accessed: 30-Jul-2022].

[8]   R. Neugebauer, S. Hippmann, M. Leis, and M. Landherr, "Industrie 4.0 - From the Perspective of Applied Research", *Procedia CIRP,* vol. 57, pp. 2-7, 2016. [http://dx.doi.org/10.1016/j.procir.2016.11.002]

[9]   V.P. Kupriyanovsky, D.E. Namiot, and O.N. Pokusaev, "Physical internet and logistics transportation systems of the Digital Economy", *World of Transport and Transportation,* vol. 19, no. 1, pp. 92-109, 2021. [http://dx.doi.org/10.30932/1992-3252-2021-19-1-92-109]

[10]   P. Radanliev, D. De Roure, J. R. C. Nurse, R. Mantilla Montalvo, and P. Burnap, *Supply chain design for the Industrial Internet of things and the industry 4.0,* 2019, pp. 1-10. [http://dx.doi.org/10.2139/ssrn.3346528]

[11]   S. Erol, A. Jäger, P. Hold, K. Ott, and W. Sihn, "Tangible industry 4.0: A scenario-based approach to learning for the future of production", *Procedia CIRP,* vol. 54, pp. 13-18, 2016. [http://dx.doi.org/10.1016/j.procir.2016.03.162]

[12]   F. Almada-Lobo, "The Industry 4.0 revolution and the future of Manufacturing Execution Systems (MES)", *Journal of Innovation Management,* vol. 3, no. 4, pp. 16-21, 2016. [http://dx.doi.org/10.24840/2183-0606_003.004_0003]

[13]   *Productivity growth in a liberalizing economy: Evidence from Indian Manufacturing Industry.* Productivity in Indian Manufacturing, 2014, pp. 187-211.

[14]   S. Simons, P. Abé, and S. Neser, "Learning in the AutFab – The Fully Automated Industrie 4.0 Learning Factory of the University of Applied Sciences Darmstadt", *Procedia Manuf.,* vol. 9, pp. 81-88, 2017. [http://dx.doi.org/10.1016/j.promfg.2017.04.023]

[15]   T. Stock, and G. Seliger, "Opportunities of sustainable manufacturing in industry 4.0", *Procedia CIRP,* vol. 40, pp. 536-541, 2016. [http://dx.doi.org/10.1016/j.procir.2016.01.129]

[16]   J. Lee, and V. Quan, *Smart Manufacturing in China's fashion industry.* Bloomsbury Fashion Business Cases, 2019.

[17]   K. Witkowski, "Internet of things, Big Data, industry 4.0 – innovative solutions in logistics and supply chains management", *Procedia Eng.,* vol. 182, pp. 763-769, 2017. [http://dx.doi.org/10.1016/j.proeng.2017.03.197]

[18]   D. de S. Dutra, and J.R. Silva, "Product-service architecture (PSA): Toward a service engineering perspective in industry 4.0", *IFAC-PapersOnLine,* vol. 49, no. 31, pp. 91-96, 2016. [http://dx.doi.org/10.1016/j.ifacol.2016.12.167]

[19]   E. Marilungo, A. Papetti, M. Germani, and M. Peruzzini, "From PSS to CPS design: A real industrial use case toward Industry 4.0", *Procedia CIRP,* vol. 64, pp. 357-362, 2017. [http://dx.doi.org/10.1016/j.procir.2017.03.007]

[20]   S. Misra, C. Roy, and A. Mukherjee, "Overview of Industry 4.0 and Industrial Internet of Things", *Introduction to Industrial Internet of Things and Industry,* vol. 4, no. 0, pp. 27-50, 2021.

[http://dx.doi.org/10.1201/9781003020905-2]

[21]   B. Bagheri, S. Yang, H.A. Kao, and J. Lee, "Cyber-physical systems architecture for self-aware machines in Industry 4.0 environment", *IFAC-PapersOnLine,* vol. 48, no. 3, pp. 1622-1627, 2015. [http://dx.doi.org/10.1016/j.ifacol.2015.06.318]

[22]   Y. Wang, G. Wang, and R. Anderl, "A holistic approach for introducing the strategic initiative Industrie 4.0", *Iaeng transactions on engineering sciences: special issue for the international association of engineers conferences,* pp. 263-274, 2018. [http://dx.doi.org/10.1142/9789813230774_0019]

[23]   N. Jazdi, "Cyber physical systems in the context of Industry 4.0", In: *In 2014 IEEE international conference on automation, quality and testing, robotics.* IEEE, 2014, pp. 1-4. [http://dx.doi.org/10.1109/AQTR.2014.6857843]

[24]   S. Dustdar, Y. Guo, B. Satzger, and H.L. Truong, "Principles of Elastic Processes", *IEEE Internet Comput.,* vol. 15, no. 5, pp. 66-71, 2011. [http://dx.doi.org/10.1109/MIC.2011.121]

[25]   W. Liu, and J. Su, "A solution of dynamic manufacturing resource aggregation in CPS", *2011 6th IEEE joint international information technology and artificial intelligence conference,* vol. 2, pp. 65-71, 2011. [http://dx.doi.org/10.1109/ITAIC.2011.6030279]

[26]   E. Hoos, "Design method for developing a Mobile Engineering-Application Middleware (MEAM)", *2014 IEEE International Conference on Pervasive Computing and Communication Workshops (PERCOM WORKSHOPS),* pp. 176-177, 2014. [http://dx.doi.org/10.1109/PerComW.2014.6815193]

[27]   M. Hasan, and B. Starly, "Decentralized cloud manufacturing-as-a-service (CMaaS) platform architecture with configurable digital assets", *J. Manuf. Syst.,* vol. 56, pp. 157-174, 2020. [http://dx.doi.org/10.1016/j.jmsy.2020.05.017]

[28]   D. Stock, M. Stöhr, U. Rauschecker, and T. Bauernhansl, "Cloud-based platform to facilitate access to manufacturing it", *Procedia CIRP,* vol. 25, pp. 320-328, 2014. [http://dx.doi.org/10.1016/j.procir.2014.10.045]

[29]   I. Parmentola, "Tutore, and M. Costagliola Di Fiore, "Environmental side of Fourth Industrial Revolution: The positive and negative effects of i4.0 technologies," Handbook of Smart Materials, Technologies, and Devices, pp. 1–31, 2021. A. Talhi, V. Fortineau, J.-C. Huet, and S. Lamouri, "Ontology for cloud manufacturing based product lifecycle management,"", *J. Intell. Manuf.,* vol. 30, no. 5, pp. 2171-2192, 2017.

[30]   P.D. Kaur, and I. Chana, "Cloud based intelligent system for delivering health care as a service", *Comput. Methods Programs Biomed.,* vol. 113, no. 1, pp. 346-359, 2014. [http://dx.doi.org/10.1016/j.cmpb.2013.09.013] [PMID: 24139021]

[31]   G. Schuh, A. Gützlaff, F. Sauermann, and J. Maibaum, "Digital Shadows as an enabler for the internet of production", *IFIP Adv. Inf. Commun. Technol.,* vol. 591, pp. 179-186, 2020. [http://dx.doi.org/10.1007/978-3-030-57993-7_21]

[32]   J. Schlechtendahl, M. Keinert, F. Kretschmer, A. Lechler, and A. Verl, "Making existing production systems Industry 4.0-ready", *Prod. Eng.,* vol. 9, no. 1, pp. 143-148, 2015. [http://dx.doi.org/10.1007/s11740-014-0586-3]

[33]   L.M. Vaquero, and L. Rodero-Merino, "Finding your way in the fog", *Comput. Commun. Rev.,* vol. 44, no. 5, pp. 27-32, 2014. [http://dx.doi.org/10.1145/2677046.2677052]

[34]   G.L. Tortorella, F.S. Fogliatto, A. Mac Cawley Vergara, R. Vassolo, and R. Sawhney, "Healthcare 4.0: trends, challenges and research directions", *Prod. Plann. Contr.,* vol. 31, no. 15, pp. 1245-1260, 2020. [http://dx.doi.org/10.1080/09537287.2019.1702226]

[35]   J. Al-Jaroodi, N. Mohamed, and E. Abukhousa, "Health 4.0: On the way to realizing the healthcare of the future", *IEEE Access,* vol. 8, pp. 211189-211210, 2020.
[http://dx.doi.org/10.1109/ACCESS.2020.3038858] [PMID: 34976565]

[36]   N. Hanner, T. Ermakova, J. Repschlaeger, and R. Zarnekow, *Designing a business model for a cloud marketplace for Healthcare.* Trusted Cloud Computing, 2014, pp. 285-294.
[http://dx.doi.org/10.1007/978-3-319-12718-7_17]

[37]   S.P. Ahuja, S. Mani, and J. Zambrano, "A Survey of the State of Cloud Computing in Healthcare", *Network and Communication Technologies,* vol. 1, no. 2, pp. 12-19, 2012.
[http://dx.doi.org/10.5539/nct.v1n2p12]

[38]   F. Sadoughi, R.F. El-Gazzar, L. Erfannia, and A. Sheikhtaheri, "How the Health Information Systems can overcome the challenges of migrating to the cloud? A framework based on a mix method approach", *Frontiers in Health Informatics,* vol. 11, no. 1, p. 107, 2022.
[http://dx.doi.org/10.30699/fhi.v11i1.342]

[39]   N. John, and S. Shenoy, "Health cloud-Healthcare as a service (HaaS)", In: *2014 International Conference on Advances in Computing, Communications and Informatics (ICACCI)* IEEE, 2014, pp. 1963-1966.
[http://dx.doi.org/10.1109/ICACCI.2014.6968627]

[40]   A. Botta, W. de Donato, V. Persico, and A. Pescapé, "de Donato, V. Persico, and A. Pescapé, "Integration of cloud computing and internet of things: A survey,"", *Future Gener. Comput. Syst.,* vol. 56, pp. 684-700, 2016.
[http://dx.doi.org/10.1016/j.future.2015.09.021]

[41]   M. Chen, "NDNC-BAN: Supporting rich media healthcare services via named data networking in cloud-assisted wireless body area networks", *Inf. Sci.,* vol. 284, pp. 142-156, 2014.
[http://dx.doi.org/10.1016/j.ins.2014.06.023]

[42]   A.M.H. Kuo, "Opportunities and challenges of cloud computing to improve health care services", *J. Med. Internet Res.,* vol. 13, no. 3, p. e67, 2011.
[http://dx.doi.org/10.2196/jmir.1867] [PMID: 21937354]

[43]   F.F. Costa, "Big data in biomedicine", *Drug Discov. Today,* vol. 19, no. 4, pp. 433-440, 2014.
[http://dx.doi.org/10.1016/j.drudis.2013.10.012] [PMID: 24183925]

[44]   M. Javaid, A. Haleem, R. Vaishya, S. Bahl, R. Suman, and A. Vaish, "Industry 4.0 technologies and their applications in fighting COVID-19 pandemic", *Diabetes Metab. Syndr.,* vol. 14, no. 4, pp. 419-422, 2020.
[http://dx.doi.org/10.1016/j.dsx.2020.04.032] [PMID: 32344370]

CHAPTER 4

Uses And Challenges of Deep Learning Models for Covid-19 Diagnosis and Prediction

Vaishali M. Wadhwa[1,*], Monika Mangla[2], Rattandeep Aneja[1], Mukesh Chawla[1] and Achyuth Sarkar[3]

[1] *Department of Information Technology, Panipat Institute of Engineering and Technology, Panipat, India*

[2] *Department of Information Technology, Dwarkadas J Sanghvi College of Engineering, Mumbai, India*

[3] *Department of Computer Engineering, National Institute of Technology, Arunachal Pradesh, India*

Abstract: Recent advancements in artificial intelligence and machine learning, specifically in the domain of natural language and computer vision, involve deep neural networks. Deep learning technology is evolving rapidly to enhance the advanced computing power across the globe in every industry. The uses of deep learning technology are becoming more apparent as the amount of available data is increasing enormously. It is being used to solve numerous complicated applications in real life with surprising levels of accuracy. Besides all the benefits, the large-scale deployment of artificial intelligence and deep learning-based models has several associated challenges due to the huge and rapidly changing data and its accessibility to common people. In this study, the authors provide a review of existing deep learning models to study the impact of artificial intelligence on the development of intelligent models in the healthcare sector, specifically in dealing with the SARS-CoV-2 coronavirus. In addition to reviewing the significant developments, the authors also highlight major challenges and open issues.

Keywords: Artificial Intelligence, Covid 19, Deep Learning.

INTRODUCTION

Artificial Intelligence is gaining popularity in every domain. AI is becoming an essential part of our daily life with the emergence in the field of microprocessors that are available with high computational power and large memory. People are now able to perform complex tasks with personal computers, which were only

* **Corresponding author Vaishali M. Wadhwa:** Department of Information Technology, Panipat Institute of Engineering and Technology, Panipat, India; E-mail: drvaishali.it@piet.co.in

Vaishali Mehta, Dolly Sharma, Monika Mangla, Anita Gehlot, Rajesh Singh and Sergio Marquez Sanchez (Eds.)

possible with supercomputers in the earlier decade. General-purpose GPUs (Graphics Processing Units) are the core of such complex systems with which authors can perform parallel processing in a combination of CPUs [1]. GPUs are capable of faster graphical data processing and are also used in scientific computing. Starting from very simple applications to very complex computing systems or decision-making devices, authors can see the usage of AI everywhere. A lot of toys are also designed and developed with AI technologies nowadays. Before detailing Deep Learning (DL), one must be aware of Machine Learning (ML). Machine Learning is a branch of Artificial Intelligence in which machines (or computers) are trained by providing a defined set of features extracted from given data or images. At the time of feature extraction, one needs to be extra cautious for selecting the features by which authors can train the machines and later on can be used for predicting the test data. However, Machine Learning works faster than Deep Learning, but there is a limitation that authors have to extract the features for ML and then only it will be working fine. On the other hand, Deep Learning accepts the images directly and produces results after making complex computations over the input. Deep Learning is a specialized branch of Machine Learning (ML) that requires fast computational machines and a large set of images for processing or making decisions. Not only for computer vision, deep learning algorithms are gaining popularity in Natural Language Processing, specifically speech recognition. Some of the powerful applications of deep learning technology include Automatic Text Classification, Automatic Translation of Text and Automatics Image Caption Generation. It works on the general data and is not dependent on any task-specific algorithm. Data itself makes the ways to provide the solutions to any problem. A high level of accuracy can be achieved with Deep Learning at the cost of specialized hardware consisting of high memory and computation speed [2].

Due to the continuous advancements in the field of artificial intelligence and machine learning, authors can see a significant improvement in the medical sector as well. There is a revolution in diagnosing, screening, prediction, medication, and treating several severe diseases. Covid19 is one such harmful disease that has been threatening the world since its origin. The researchers in artificial intelligence and data analytics are working day and night to fight this and develop a vaccine for its cure. Several models have been developed to reduce human intervention in the entire process, starting from disease diagnosis to final treatment. However, maximum models are not completely deployed to show their actual operation in real problems, but to tackle the SARS-Covid19 epidemic, they are still beneficial for healthcare professionals. But on the other hand, deep learning and machine learning algorithms for disease diagnosis and prediction are still vulnerable to various types of security attacks.

In this chapter, the authors present a study on different deep learning and AI-based models developed to fight the covid19 pandemic. Section 2 discusses the working of deep neural networks and the privacy issues involved in employing such models. In section 3, authors present a survey on the recent research in deep learning models for covid19 and other severe diseases. Finally, in section 4, authors discuss the challenges and issues involved in deploying such models and possible ways to minimize them.

WORKING OF DEEP NEURAL NETWORK

One can consider Deep Learning as Artificial Neural Networks (ANNs) that are designed by taking into consideration the natural human neurons. Artificial neurons are just like natural neurons that pass the signal to the next neuron in the body and, in turn, are used for making any decision or performing any action. Deep Learning is used in many application areas such as Image processing, categorization of images or patterns, speech recognition, predictions, decision-making, modeling, natural language processing, computer vision, and big data analysis [3]. Nodes in the network are connected in such a way that input layer nodes are connected with the first hidden layer nodes, the first hidden layer nodes are connected to the second hidden layer nodes, and so on until authors reach the final output layer nodes. Each connecting edge has some weight that is used to multiply with the input and summed at the node of the next layer. Then the summed value is passed to the Mathematical activation function so that error can be calculated easily at each node and then this error is minimized by changing the values of weights. In most cases, tan-hyperbolic or sigmoid activation functions are used. Each layer creates a mesh with the adjacent/next layer so that each input node will contribute to the generation of intermediate/final output from the nodes. Tan hyperbolic and sigmoid activation functions also play an important role in converting the range of inputs into a narrow range *i.e.,* -1 to +1 OR 0 to 1, respectively [4]. The output of the final layer is considered as the solution to the problem. A structure diagram of Deep Neural Network [5] is shown in Fig. (1) below:

Deep Neural Networks in Fig. (1) shows 8 inputs, 3 hidden layers of 9 nodes each, and 4 outputs. For Deep learning, the number of hidden layers may be greater than 150 and in some cases, it may be few thousand depending on the computation complexity of the network.

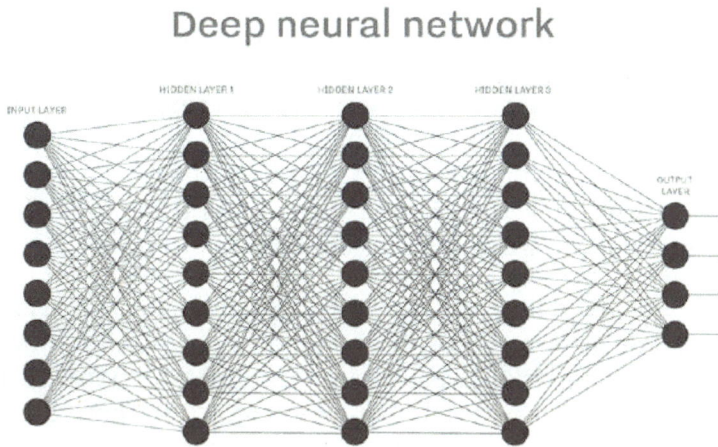

Fig. (1). ANNs consisting of the Input layer, Hidden layers, Output layer.

Designing a deep learning network is not a tedious task, but the training of the model includes the high cost in terms of space and time complexity as authors need a lot many iterations for a model to be trained and predict the results with the least error and high accuracy. A large set of parameters is considered for the inference that takes many computations to consider each aspect of the input data or images. That is the reason for requirements for high-end computational machines and high resource consumption.

A feed-forward ANN used particularly for processing/recognition of images is known as Convolutional Neural Networks (CNN). It is a deep neural network with many layers for extracting different attributes/features of the images. The architecture of a typical CNN [5] is shown in Fig. (2).

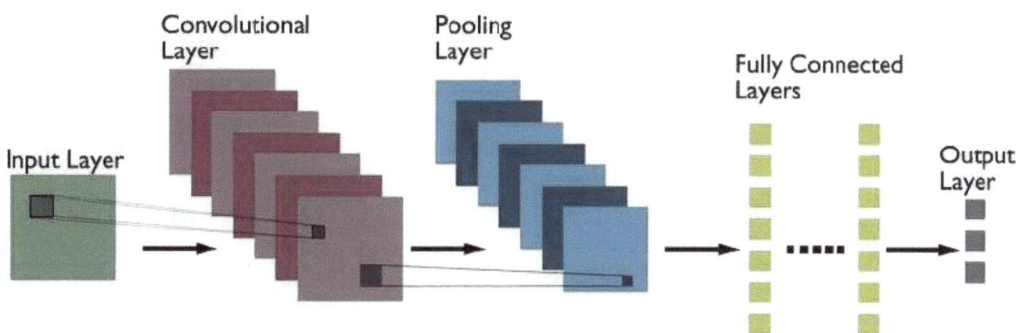

Fig. (2). A typical CNN Architecture

CNN and Long Short Term Memory (LSTM) are combined to take advantage of unsupervised learning that is the basis of any DL. Now, the authors will discuss some of the application areas of DL [1]:

Healthcare: Radiological diagnosis, Robot aided surgery, drug delivery, drug discovery are some of the application areas in Healthcare where DL is becoming popular. Deep Learning is applied to Digital imaging and Medical imaging to recognize the problematic areas and provide possible solutions for the same.

Driverless Cars: DL is being used in driverless cars that make use of sensors and cameras for sensing and imaging of the surrounding environment for making decisions that include varying speed, turning left/right, blowing the horn, *etc.* GPS is used for navigation purposes in such cars that are supported by a high-speed internet connection. Very high accuracy is provided to the driverless cars with the help of DL technology along with other electronic components like Ultrasound technology, Radar system, laser light beams, *etc.*

Weather forecast: DL can be useful for predicting weather conditions based on the images captured from the environment and matching the patterns with already stored images in the system. This helps forecast the sudden weather changes and save human lives by issuing any warnings for the weather. This may be useful in situations where people rely on solar energy, and early forecasting will help those people to make alternating arrangements.

Agriculture: Visiting the agricultural sites and doing surveys for crops is one of the tedious tasks that require human involvement and consumes a lot of time. By making use of DL technology, one can take images of the sites and analyze the crops by sitting in an office that saves time.

Manufacturing: Whether it is related to quality assurance of the product or packaging of the final product, there is always the need for a monitoring system that can ensure the right product is delivered at the consumer's end. DL technology can be applied in the area of manufacturing and can give tremendous results with the quality maintained and delivered to consumers resulting in the company's goodwill.

VULNERABILITIES IN DEEP LEARNING ALGORITHMS

Advancement in Machine learning and artificial intelligence has brought disruptive advancements in technologies. A lot of services depend on AI and data-driven approaches that control the massive amount of information available from dissimilar sources like people, computing devices, and sensor nodes.

Deep learning has a vast range of applications domain, including computer and information security. Thus deep learning is at the heart of most non-signatur--based intruder detection systems, like spam, malware, network intrusions, or fraudulent activities. Deep learning has capabilities f generalization, *i.e.*, learning algorithms which can produce predictions for data.

THE SECURITY OF DEEP LEARNING SYSTEMS

Although deep learning has many benefits, learning algorithms can be attacked by cybercriminals for malicious activities. Deep learning algorithms are vulnerable to several attacks [5, 6]. Deep learning acts as the weakest link in the security chain and by exploiting it, the whole system can be compromised.

An intruder can inject false data at the test time to poison the learning process to manipulate data. A number of these types of attacks are reported by anti-virus engines, spam filters, or fake profile and fake news detection systems [7]. These attacks have fostered the investigation of the security properties of deep learning. There is a strong requirement of the research area, a combination of deep learning and cybersecurity. This area will explore various vulnerabilities in deep learning and help in developing more secure learning algorithms [8].

SECURITY ATTACKS ON DEEP LEARNING MODELS

Attacks in Deep learning may be classified into two broad categories, namely poising attack and evasion attack. It depends on the various phases of deep learning algorithms. These two attacks are namely, the poisoning attack and evasion attack. In a poisoning attack, the attacker compromises the training phase and destroys the model while training. Another type of attack occurs in the interference phase and generally misclassifies the input. This type of attack is called an evasion attack. Both types of attacks are further classified as white box and black box attack

Various classifications, definitions, models, and categories of security threats on deep learning (DL) systems exist. Various parameters for classification are based on the adversarial capabilities, knowledge, goals, resources, and target criteria [6, 9]. Adversarial security attacks of DL systems can be explained along with the following schemes:

Influence

Causative attack: This type of attack targets the training process and alteration of training data is done. The output of this attack is manipulated data. This type of attack is also called the poisoning attack.

Exploratory attack: This type of attack targets the training process. However, it does not alter the training process. In this, attackers can exploit misclassification and probe the learning process for useful information.

Evasion attack: This attack also targets the training process. It alters the input data of the learning process which results in incorrect predictions.

Specificity

Targeted attacks: This type of attack targets specific points. The attacker exploits the continuous stream.

Indiscriminate. This type of attack targets the general class of points, instances of the learning process. The attacker exploits randomly with no specific target.

Security Violation

Integrity attack. Integrity preservation means there is no modification in data. This attack is performed with the help of false negatives, which will be considered normal traffic.

Availability attack. Availability means the system is available for legitimate users all the time. In this type of attack, the attacker makes the system busy with classification errors, denial of service, false negatives and positives, *etc.*

Privacy violation attack. Privacy preservation means the data is revealed only to the sender and receivers. In this attack, the attacker reveals sensitive and confidential data. It is also known as model extraction, inversion, or hill-climbing attack.

Authentication attack: Authentication means there is a guarantee of the origin of the information. In this type of attack, the attacker can spoof the address of a legitimate user to mislead other users in the process.

Table 1. Classification of various attacks on deep learning algorithms.

Influence	Specificity	Security Violation
Causative attack	*Targeted attacks*	*Integrity attack*
Exploratory attack	*Indiscriminate*	*Availability attack*
Evasion attack		*Privacy violation attack*

Deep Learning for COVID 19 Diagnosis and Prediction

The outbreak of COVID-19 Coronavirus, also known as SARS-CoV-2, has created a devastating situation worldwide. The aggregate rate of COVID-19 cases is rapidly increasing every day.

Since world war two, the biggest health challenge faced by the world is the coronavirus. No continent is left untouched with its serious impact all around the world. The world has now reached the terrible situation of over one million deaths, and every common man is under an unbearable burden of loss. However, the pandemic is not only a health crisis but also a major socio-economic crisis. The pandemic has left devastating social, economic, and political effects that will affect human life for ages. A lot of people have lost jobs and income. About 400 million jobs will be lost, as estimated by the International Labor Organization [10]. Not only this, even the basic needs will not be fulfilled by the majority of people.

To fight this global pandemic, the World Health Organization (WHO), scientists, and researchers are looking for new technologies to identify victims of the disease at various stages and are trying hard to control the spread of this virus further by tracing the contacts of victims. Scientists and medicines are putting all their efforts into developing a vaccine for the treatment of affected people. The latest research depicts that the next-generation technologies, including machine learning and artificial intelligence techniques, can be incorporated to meet the above objectives as they are proven to provide accurate results in a very less amount of time. They are much more reliable and even outperform humans sometimes [11]. Therefore, many medical industries have employed these techniques to tackle the Covid-19 pandemic.

The novel coronavirus disease has threatened the globe since its origin. The major cause of anxiety among people is its spreading rate is exponential. WHO has provided clear guidelines and measures to be followed for human health and to reduce the risk of infection. In such a scenario, prediction methods can be helpful to present an estimated number of confirmed or new cases, hospitalized cases, death cases, *etc*. Such prediction methods can help clinicians in several ways. For example, the number of approximate hospitalized cases depending upon their level of seriousness can help identify the required number of medical facilities, including beds, ventilators, and other equipment. In other words, prediction methods are a very useful tool for a reliable estimation of the spread of infection and necessary measures that can be taken beforehand. The Centers for Disease Control and Prevention (CDC) has analyzed that the prediction models not only help in the forecasting of mortality and hospitalization but a systematic plan can be prepared as per present scenarios to prevent future loss [12].

Because of their accurate and reliable prediction methods, Machine Learning (ML) and deep learning techniques have been effectively deployed to track the virus, predict the growth of its spread, and design protocols to manage its spread. For this purpose, faster analysis of radiography images is required. Therefore, a lot of artificial intelligence and deep learning-based systems [12, 13] have been proposed recently. These models have proven to be quite accurate for the detection of covid19 infected patients *via* radiography CT imaging techniques [14 - 18]. However, even after many efforts being made on developing the deep learning models for covid19 detection, most of these models are not accessible to the general public and hence they are of no practical use. Although, a lot of efforts have been made to provide AI-based models that have open access for COVID-19 disease detection using radiography images [16]. In this direction, Cohen *et al.*16 built a dataset for SARS and COVID-19 cases with a proper description of CT scans and CXR images. This was very helpful for the researchers, clinicians as well as common people so that they can build intelligent systems for COVID-19 diagnosis by exploring this dataset. Similarly, a lot of work has been done in the field of COVID-19 diagnosis using X-ray images [19 - 21], most of which are based on different variants of the COVIDx dataset or COVID-Net, which help conduct such studies [12, 14, 16, 22]. The generic structure to detect COVID-19 using deep learning uses following steps as shown in Fig. (**3**).

I. Collection of X-ray images of COVID-19 patients and healthy persons for creating dataset.
II. Generation of a huge number of x-ray images using data augmentation.
III. Representation of image in feature space so as to apply DL.
IV. Splitting of data into training, testing, and validation set.
V. Performance evaluation of the model using validation dataset.

For instance, as per the model proposed in [15], X-ray images are given to the proposed model, which resizes them to 224 by 224 pixels to maintain compatibility with the proposed CNN model.

Authors in [17] suggested design of a human- machine collaborative design that detects COVID-19 cases through CXR images. In this work, the authors have also created an open-access dataset COVIDx that can be used to train and evaluate the performance of COVID-Net. The proposed dataset consists of 13,975 CXR images across 13,870 patient cases, the largest open access available in COVID-19 positive patients. Here, authors design a prototype that makes various predictions such as no infection, non-covid infections and finally covid infection.

This predictive model can prove to be a helping hand to health professionals in order to prioritize the patients. Additionally, it may also suggest the treatment strategy, as infections of covid-19 and other diseases require different treatment. Authors in [22] also presented a model that extracts features from chest CT images. Similarly, authors in [23] also employed CNN to classify covid-19 infected and non-infected patients using the softmax activation function. Authors in [31] address the small dataset issue by using transfer learning to train deep CNN as state-of-the-art CNNs necessitate large-scale datasets to perform efficient classification and extraction. The proposed model is compared with state-of-t-e-art models in terms of various error metrics that establish the efficacy of the proposed model.

For disease prediction and identification, researchers have primarily focused on exploring deep learning methods, specifically deep CNNs, that achieved success in several computer-based imaging and visualization activities [13, 21, 23, 24]. Due to the rapid increase in covid19 patients on a daily basis, the covid-net and covidx datasets keep changing regularly. And on regular basis, this information is made available to the public.

Jain *et al.* in their work presented a CNN-based deep learning model for covid19 prediction. A two-stage approach was proposed to identify covid19 victims. In the first stage, they proposed a differentiation mechanism of normal/healthy people and pneumonia induced by bacterial or viral infection. The second stage models how to detect the presence of COVID-19. The proposed model is quite accurate, fast, and reliable and requires fewer computational requirements, making it useful to provide timely and appropriate treatment to patients infected from covid19 from viral-induced pneumonia [19].

In [22], a Capsule Network-based model was proposed to diagnose covid-19 patients using X-ray images. In their work, the focus is given to the class imbalance problem, and to overcome it authors designed a model that uses different convolution layers and capsules. The results show that with 90% sensitivity and 95.80% specificity, the suggested model presents an accuracy of 95.7%. In [14], a chest CT scan of 21 covid-19 victims was conducted in Wuhan, China. The major focus of the authors was to demonstrate the effect of covid19 disease on the lungs of the human body. Further in [19], the authors proposed a CNN-based COVID-RENet model that deals with the boundary and region-based constraints. The authors in their research extracted these features by using CNN classification and then to further improve the performance, they implemented the SVM on obtained classifications. In [25], using machine learning and deep learning algorithms, the authors proposed an artificial intelligence-based hybrid model. The proposed uses chest X-ray scan data for identifying Covid-19 infected patients. Similarly, in [19] the authors presented an analysis of the treatment of covid-19 patients. This model was also applied to the dataset of chest X-ray and CT scan images. In [26], the authors discussed the protocols to be followed by clinical staff and the necessary precautions to be taken to reduce the risk for uninfected or healthy patients. In [20], to diagnose pneumothorax, the authors used the SVM model. A Local Binary Pattern (LBP) was used to extract the properties of lung images. In this model, for the elimination of the impurities of chest images of abnormal lungs, the authors suggested a multi-scale texture segmentation approach. After this, the obtained information was applied to find out multiple overlapping blocks due to change of texture. Finally, to find out the whole region of disease with the abnormal organ, the authors used the rid boundary technique. Also, in [18], the authors proposed a deep learning-based model to detect the severity of covid 19 patients who were suffering from pneumonia and lung disease. They also used the collected data set of chest scan images.

Further, in [19], the authors presented a report on the impact of covid-19 on kidney and acute renal dysfunctioning. In [25], the authors presented a report of the total number of Covid-19 victims and fatal cases throughout the world. In [14], the authors suggested a deep learning-based approach (with vector gadget classifier) for the diagnosis of Covid-19 infected patients using chest X-ray scan images. It was very useful for medical professionals for the early detection of covid-19 cases. Their model was found to be 97.48% accurate for lung classification using different parameters. Further, in [27], various methodologies were discussed for covid-19 detection and prediction and the challenges faced under different scenarios. Then, after analyzing some X-ray images to identify pneumonia and lung infection, they concluded that it is hard to predict that any other symptoms related to flu or pneumonia can cause Covid-19. In [28], the authors presented a deep anomaly detection method for reliable screening of Covid-19 patients. In [11], the authors presented a study about the role AI tools play in the healthcare sector and the challenges they face while working on a small dataset of X-ray images. In [17], the authors proposed an automatic detection model for the identification of Covid-19 patients with the help of X-ray scan images. The proposed model is based on two different classification models - binary class and multi-class to give an accurate diagnosis. Authors in [19], presented a study of covid-19 coronavirus to some isolated persons who have been admitted to a hospital ward at Rawalpindi. By using chest X-ray data images, they proposed a CNN-based algorithm for analyzing pneumonia and applied SVM for better results. After studying and analyzing the research done on covid19 and analyzing the views of various researchers, authors can conclude that covid19 is a viral infection that is harmful not only for an individual as a human being but also for the country as a whole.

Due to the rapid rise in covid19 cases all around the globe, scientists and researchers are trying to have expertise in the area to minimize the risk of the spread of the virus. Due to limited resources and manpower, this has led to the development of smart detection systems based on emerging techniques. To provide immediate assistance to the victims, such fast and accurate models can be very helpful. These AI-based models have been proven extremely useful in handling insufficient resources such as RT-PCR test kits, hospital staff, and other medical facilities to diagnose and treat the disease. To diagnose covid-19 using X-ray images, Hemdan *et al.* [29] proposed a deep-learning based COVIDX-Net model made up of seven CNN layers. Wang and Wong [16] also proposed a deep learning model for COVID19 identification (COVID-Net), with 92.4% accuracy. Further, Ioannis *et al.* [30] proposed the deep learning model using 224 confirmed COVID-19 cases. Their model was proved to be 98.75% accurate. Narin *et al.* [31] also achieved a 98% accuracy for COVID-19 detection using X-ray images.

Similarly, there are several recent experiments and research on COVID-19 prediction and identification that used various artificial intelligence and deep learning models with CT scans and X-ray images [11, 32, 36].

However, such models are not recommended where the amount of available data is very little or not possible to collect. In particular, these models require data visualization tools to elaborate and visualize predictive analytics, such as in the case of the Covid 19 outbreak. However, data visualization tools are themselves not used as prediction models, but they can help estimate the trend. It has been researched and experimented that the AI tools play a vital role in perceiving data using multiple techniques [12]. As discussed above, these tools require an ample amount of data for a reliable and accurate prediction. The predictive results may be deviated and convey a different meaning even if one or two features are not present in the gathered data.

Big data, the fast-growing advancements in the emerging areas of AI, ML, and DL provide the ability to process massive amounts of diverse unstructured data and possess powerful computing capabilities. These techniques have been used effectively to extract valuable actionable information from a large amount of unstructured data [37].

Deep Learning makes use of crowdsourcing as a prediction method. Crowdsourcing is a technique where a task or a job is transmitted to the general public like an open call. This technique has been successfully employed to collect data and information from various sources such as blogs, messages in the form of text and images, news updates, posts on social media, *etc.* For mapping tragic locations, the collected data and information are then analyzed and harmonized to further facilitate the initiation of trace and search procedures. This technique was proven to be very helpful during the 2010 Haiti earthquake [37].

In healthcare systems, emerging technologies and big data analytics are bringing a gigantic transformation in the way the usual medical analysis and treatment process is followed. It's a revolution in medical science that integrates data collected from various resources such as patient's medical records, real-time wearable sensors, *etc.* to analyze and diagnose the victim's present health status and provide alarming signs if observed considering patient's current health track. This proves to be helpful to tackle such harmful diseases in the early stages and in taking appropriate prevention measures. To continue further, a comparative analysis report was presented by Pervaiz *et al.* where the performance of various machine learning algorithms was illustrated that are deployed on Google Flu Trends [38] to detect alarming signs of a probable pandemic breakout.

However, none of the revolutions comes without challenges. The use of emerging technologies for the prediction and analysis of coronavirus disease also presents some challenges for both the researchers and the general people, which are used as a resource for gathering massive data.

Challenges Involved

The COVID-19 pandemic has led scientists and researchers around the world to develop and employ new techniques and big data tools to observe the spread of coronavirus.

No doubt, data science, machine learning, and deep learning technologies can be promising tools to deal with such life-threatening diseases [37]. As an example, to determine and understand the movement patterns of people, the location data collected from telecom industries can be very helpful which gives an insight into the spread of the virus. Developers of private industries are in the process of developing apps that help volunteers to share their social contacts and location. Set up of virtual classrooms has proven to be helpful for teachers to interact with students during the lockdown period. Moreover, the teachers themselves are getting exposure to upcoming technologies and exploring pathways of digital classrooms with innovative interaction methods [40]. Also moving this further, the government of China has co-developed a mobile app that informs its users whether they have been in the vicinity of a COVID-19 victim. Its prediction results are based on the analysis of collected location data obtained from telecom service providers, the internet, satellites, and other monitoring systems that produce data that tells about the location of people in groups or alone.

However, such large-scale intrusion into public data leads to serious consequences concerning privacy and data protection. To deal with the crisis, the use of public data obtained from telecom companies was a feasible choice. Still, all legal regulations and instructions provided by the government and technology companies do not help protect people's privacy against misuse. Nonetheless, the established privacy rules and most human rights agreements are prepared considering the data protection and privacy norms in case of emergency. But, this does not ensure the privacy of individuals and groups. Nevertheless, the use of such technologies can be a promising tool for such critical situations, but it is equally important to observe that their use has severe consequences in terms of privacy and data protection worldwide [40]. The fact that every individual has a personal life's own secrets can not be overlooked just because it might be an emergency.

Even though disasters like the coronavirus epidemic require immediate and effective actions to be incorporated, authors should not ignore the fact that every individual's data is sensitive and contextual. It means that the same dataset might be meaningless in some contexts while it can be sensitive in some other context. The use of deep learning techniques to analyze location data to control the deadly disease can be useful to fight the crisis more quickly. But, the use of such abundant data and information brings a lot of challenges and the biggest challenge today is interference in individual and/or collective freedom and independence. Therefore, the appropriate framework has to be designed by the government to ensure that this data is being collected, monitored, placed, and shared authentically and responsibly.

The use of big data analytics and prediction models to deal with the pandemic provides both an opportunity as well as a challenge to scientists and developers.

CONCLUSION

The continuous development in emerging technologies has greatly improved the prediction, contact tracing, treatment, screening, medication, and vaccine development procedure for the coronavirus epidemic. Also, the use of AI, ML, and deep learning techniques has reduced human intervention in such practices.

Deep Learning has several advantages such as rapid response even for complex problems, reducing human efforts by providing huge automation, the ability to work on unstructured data, providing reliable and accurate results, and no requirement of data labeling. But, it also has some limitations as well like opaqueness, needs a huge amount of data for the problem at hand, and using very complex algorithms. Moreover, sometimes Deep Learning models may create difficulty in real-life if they produce misprediction due to internal and/or external malicious effects. Furthermore, training models based on deep learning technology generally use sensitive information of their users. Therefore, it is highly demanded that these models should not be susceptible to security and privacy. The deep learning users and industries must be aware of security threats and related countermeasures techniques for avoiding its counter effects.

CONSENT OF PUBLICATION

Not applicable.

CONFLICT OF INTEREST

The author declares no conflict of interest, financial or otherwise.

ACKNOWLEDGEMENTS

Declared none.

REFERENCES

[1]   S. Dutta, "An overview on the evolution and adoption of deep learning applications used in the industry", *Wiley Interdiscip. Rev. Data Min. Knowl. Discov.,* vol. 8, no. 4, 2018.
        [http://dx.doi.org/10.1002/widm.1257]

[2]   J. Chen, and X. Ran, "Deep Learning With Edge Computing: A Review", *Proc. IEEE,* vol. 8, pp. 1655-1674, 2019.
        [http://dx.doi.org/10.1109/JPROC.2019.2921977]

[3]   A. Shrestha, and A. Mahmood, "Review of Deep Learning Algorithms and Architectures", *IEEE Access,* vol. 7, pp. 53040-53065, 2019.
        [http://dx.doi.org/10.1109/ACCESS.2019.2912200]

[4]   S. Shi, Q. Wang, P. Xu, and X. Chu, "Benchmarking state-of-the-art deep learning software tools", *Proc. - 2016 7th Int. Conf. Cloud Comput. Big Data, CCBD,* pp. 99-104, 2017.
        [http://dx.doi.org/10.1109/CCBD.2016.029]

[5]   W.D. Jang, Y.J. Yoon, M.S. Cho, J.H. Jung, S.H. Lee, J. Jang, J.H. Bae, and I.M. Kang, "Design and Optimization of Germanium-Based Gate-Metal-Core Vertical Nanowire Tunnel FET", *Micromachines (Basel),* vol. 10, no. 11, p. 749, 2019.
        [http://dx.doi.org/10.3390/mi10110749] [PMID: 31683726]

[6]   B. Darvish Rouani, M. Samragh, T. Javidi, and F. Koushanfar, "Safe Machine Learning and Defeating Adversarial Attacks", *IEEE Secur. Priv.,* vol. 17, no. 2, pp. 31-38, 2019.
        [http://dx.doi.org/10.1109/MSEC.2018.2888779]

[7]   D. Bruschi, and N. Diomede, *A framework for assessing AI ethics with applications to cybersecurity.* AI Ethics, 2022.
        [http://dx.doi.org/10.1007/s43681-022-00162-8]

[8]   P. McDaniel, N. Papernot, and Z.B. Celik, "Machine Learning in Adversarial Settings", *IEEE Secur. Priv.,* vol. 14, no. 3, pp. 68-72, 2016.
        [http://dx.doi.org/10.1109/MSP.2016.51]

[9]   M. Kumar, and K. Dutta, "LDAT: LFTM based data aggregation and transmission protocol for wireless sensor networks", *Journal of Trust Management,* vol. 3, no. 1, p. 2, 2016.
        [http://dx.doi.org/10.1186/s40493-016-0023-y]

[10]   H. Xia, W. An, J. Li, and Z. Zhang, "Outlier knowledge management for extreme public health events: Understanding public opinions about COVID-19 based on microblog data", *Socio-Economic Planning Sciences,* vol. 80, pp. 1-13, 2022.

[11]   J. Sipior, "Considerations for development and use of AI in response to COVID-19", *International Journal of Information Management,* vol. 55, pp. 1-7, 2020.

[12]   K.C. Santosh, "COVID-19 Prediction Models and Unexploited Data", *J. Med. Syst.,* vol. 44, no. 9, p. 170, 2020.
[http://dx.doi.org/10.1007/s10916-020-01645-z] [PMID: 32794042]

[13]   H. Greenspan, R. San José Estépar, W. Niessen, E. Siegel, and M. Nielsen, "Position paper on COVID-19 imaging and AI: From the clinical needs and technological challenges to initial AI solutions at the lab and national level towards a new era for AI in healthcare", *Medical Image Analysis,* vol. 66, pp. 1-12, 2020.

[14]   M. Alazab, M. Alazab, A. Shalaginov, A. Mesleh, and A. Awajan, "Intelligent mobile malware detection using permission requests and API calls", *Future Gener. Comput. Syst.,* vol. 107, pp. 509-521, 2020.
[http://dx.doi.org/10.1016/j.future.2020.02.002]

[15]   A. Ismael, and A. Şengür, "Deep learning approaches for COVID-19 detection based on chest X-ray images", *Expert Systems with Applications,* vol. 164, pp. 1-12, 2021.

[16]   L. Wang, Z.Q. Lin, and A. Wong, "COVID-Net: a tailored deep convolutional neural network design for detection of COVID-19 cases from chest X-ray images", *Sci. Rep.,* vol. 10, no. 1, p. 19549, 2020.
[http://dx.doi.org/10.1038/s41598-020-76550-z] [PMID: 33177550]

[17]   T. Ozturk, M. Talo, E.A. Yildirim, U.B. Baloglu, O. Yildirim, and U. Rajendra Acharya, "Automated detection of COVID-19 cases using deep neural networks with X-ray images", *Comput. Biol. Med.,* vol. 121, p. 103792, 2020.
[http://dx.doi.org/10.1016/j.compbiomed.2020.103792] [PMID: 32568675]

[18]   G. Jain, D. Mittal, D. Thakur, and M.K. Mittal, "A deep learning approach to detect Covid-19 coronavirus with X-Ray images", *Biocybern. Biomed. Eng.,* vol. 40, no. 4, pp. 1391-1405, 2020.
[http://dx.doi.org/10.1016/j.bbe.2020.08.008] [PMID: 32921862]

[19]   R. Jain, M. Gupta, S. Taneja, and D.J. Hemanth, "Deep learning based detection and analysis of COVID-19 on chest X-ray images", *Appl. Intell.,* vol. 51, no. 3, pp. 1690-1700, 2021.
[http://dx.doi.org/10.1007/s10489-020-01902-1] [PMID: 34764553]

[20]   M.J. Horry, S. Chakraborty, M. Paul, A. Ulhaq, B. Pradhan, M. Saha, and N. Shukla, "COVID-19 detection through transfer learning using multimodal imaging data", *IEEE Access,* vol. 8, pp. 149808-149824, 2020.
[http://dx.doi.org/10.1109/ACCESS.2020.3016780] [PMID: 34931154]

[21]   Y. Pathak, P.K. Shukla, A. Tiwari, S. Stalin, S. Singh, and P.K. Shukla, "Deep Transfer Learning Based Classification Model for COVID-19 Disease", *IRBM,* vol. 43, no. 2, pp. 87-92, 2022.
[http://dx.doi.org/10.1016/j.irbm.2020.05.003] [PMID: 32837678]

[22]   P. Afshar, S. Heidarian, F. Naderkhani, A. Oikonomou, K.N. Plataniotis, and A. Mohammadi, "COVID-CAPS: A capsule network-based framework for identification of COVID-19 cases from X-ray images", *Pattern Recognit. Lett.,* vol. 138, pp. 638-643, 2020.
[http://dx.doi.org/10.1016/j.patrec.2020.09.010] [PMID: 32958971]

[23]   J. Somasekar, P. Pavan Kumar, A. Sharma, and G. Ramesh, "Machine learning and image analysis applications in the fight against COVID-19 pandemic: Datasets, research directions, challenges and opportunities", *Mater. Today Proc.,* vol. •••, pp. 777-780, 2020.
[http://dx.doi.org/10.1016/j.matpr.2020.09.352] [PMID: 32983909]

[24]   A. Sufian, A. Ghosh, A.S. Sadiq, and F. Smarandache, "A survey on deep transfer learning to edge computing for mitigating the COVID-19 pandemic", *J. Systems Archit.,* vol. 108, p. 101830, 2020.

[http://dx.doi.org/10.1016/j.sysarc.2020.101830]

[25]   C. Iwendi, A.K. Bashir, A. Peshkar, R. Sujatha, J.M. Chatterjee, S. Pasupuleti, R. Mishra, S. Pillai, and O. Jo, "COVID-19 patient health prediction using boosted random forest algorithm", *Front. Public Health,* vol. 8, p. 357, 2020.
[http://dx.doi.org/10.3389/fpubh.2020.00357] [PMID: 32719767]

[26]   L. Wynants, B. Van Calster, G. S. Collins, R. D. Riley, G. Heinze, E. Schuit, and M. van Smeden, "Prediction models for diagnosis and prognosis of covid-19: systematic review and critical appraisal",

[27]   S. Lalmuanawma, J. Hussain, and L. Chhakchhuak, "Applications of machine learning and artificial intelligence for Covid-19 (SARS-CoV-2) pandemic: A review", *Chaos Solitons Fractals,* vol. 139, no. 110059, p. 110059, 2020.
[http://dx.doi.org/10.1016/j.chaos.2020.110059] [PMID: 32834612]

[28]   L. Liu, J. Lin, P. Wang, L. Liu, and R. Zhou, "Deep Learning-Based Network Security Data Sampling and Anomaly Prediction in Future Network", In: *Discrete Dynamics in Nature and Society,* 2020.
[http://dx.doi.org/10.1155/2020/4163825]

[29]   E.E.D. Hemdan, M.A. Shouman, and M.E Karar, "Covidx-net: A framework of deep learning classifiers to diagnose covid-19 in x-ray images",

[30]   I. D. Apostolopoulos, and T. A. Mpesiana, "Covid-19: automatic detection from x-ray images utilizing transfer learning with convolutional neural networks", *Physical and engineering sciences in medicine,* vol. 43, no. 2, pp. 635-640, 2020.
[http://dx.doi.org/10.1007/s13246-020-00865-4]

[31]   A. Narin, C. Kaya, and Z. Pamuk, "Automatic detection of coronavirus disease (COVID-19) using X-ray images and deep convolutional neural networks", *Pattern Anal. Appl.,* vol. 24, no. 3, pp. 1207-1220, 2021.
[http://dx.doi.org/10.1007/s10044-021-00984-y] [PMID: 33994847]

[32]   Y. Song, S. Zheng, L. Li, X. Zhang, X. Zhang, Z. Huang, J. Chen, R. Wang, H. Zhao, Y. Chong, J. Shen, Y. Zha, and Y. Yang, "Deep learning enables accurate diagnosis of novel coronavirus (COVID-19) with CT images", *IEEE/ACM Trans. Comput. Biol. Bioinformatics,* vol. 18, no. 6, pp. 2775-2780, 2021.
[http://dx.doi.org/10.1109/TCBB.2021.3065361] [PMID: 33705321]

[33]   X. Xu, X. Jiang, C. Ma, P. Du, X. Li, S. Lv, L. Yu, Q. Ni, Y. Chen, J. Su, G. Lang, Y. Li, H. Zhao, J. Liu, K. Xu, L. Ruan, J. Sheng, Y. Qiu, W. Wu, T. Liang, and L. Li, "A deep learning system to screen novel coronavirus disease 2019 pneumonia", *Engineering (Beijing),* vol. 6, no. 10, pp. 1122-1129, 2020.
[http://dx.doi.org/10.1016/j.eng.2020.04.010] [PMID: 32837749]

[34]   A. Kumar, P.K. Gupta, and A. Srivastava, "A review of modern technologies for tackling COVID-19 pandemic", *Diabetes Metab. Syndr.,* vol. 14, no. 4, pp. 569-573, 2020.
[http://dx.doi.org/10.1016/j.dsx.2020.05.008] [PMID: 32413821]

[35]   A. Zeroual, F. Harrou, A. Dairi, and Y. Sun, "Deep learning methods for forecasting COVID-19 time-Series data: A Comparative study", *Chaos Solitons Fractals,* vol. 140, p. 110121, 2020.
[http://dx.doi.org/10.1016/j.chaos.2020.110121] [PMID: 32834633]

[36]   O.S. Albahri, A.A. Zaidan, A.S. Albahri, B.B. Zaidan, K.H. Abdulkareem, Z.T. Al-qaysi, A.H. Alamoodi, A.M. Aleesa, M.A. Chyad, R.M. Alesa, L.C. Kem, M.M. Lakulu, A.B. Ibrahim, and N.A. Rashid, "Systematic review of artificial intelligence techniques in the detection and classification of COVID-19 medical images in terms of evaluation and benchmarking: Taxonomy analysis, challenges, future solutions and methodological aspects", *J. Infect. Public Health,* vol. 13, no. 10, pp. 1381-1396, 2020.
[http://dx.doi.org/10.1016/j.jiph.2020.06.028] [PMID: 32646771]

[37]   A. Ali, J. Qadir, A. Sathiaseelan, A. Zwitter, and J. Crowcroft, "Big data for development: applications and techniques", *Big Data Analytics,* vol. 1, 2016no. 1, pp. 1-24. https://www.google.org/

flutrends/about/
[http://dx.doi.org/10.1186/s41044-016-0002-4]

[38]   D. Checa, and A. Bustillo, "A review of immersive virtual reality serious games to enhance learning and training", *Multimedia Tools Appl.,* vol. 79, no. 9-10, pp. 5501-5527, 2020.
[http://dx.doi.org/10.1007/s11042-019-08348-9]

[39]   A. Zwitter, "Big Data ethics", *Big Data Soc.,* vol. 1, no. 2, 2014.
[http://dx.doi.org/10.1177/2053951714559253]

[40]   N. Sharma, J. Dev, M. Mangla, V.M. Wadhwa, S.N. Mohanty, and D. Kakkar, "A heterogeneous ensemble forecasting model for disease prediction", *New Gener. Comput.,* vol. 39, no. 3-4, pp. 701-715, 2021.
[http://dx.doi.org/10.1007/s00354-020-00119-7] [PMID: 33424081]

CHAPTER 5

Currency Trend Prediction using Machine Learning

Deepak Yadav[1] and **Dolly Sharma**[1,*]

[1] *Department of Computer Science, Amity University, Noida, India*

Abstract: The field of cryptocurrency has witnessed exponential growth in popularity in recent years. Almost ten years ago, the release of Bitcoin marked the beginning of a new era of innovation in the financial sector. In this work, we outline what exactly defines a cryptocurrency, describing fundamental concepts, underlying technologies such as the blockchain, and subsequently the viability of this new digital financial asset. Building on this knowledge, we examine the infamous volatility of cryptocurrency prices, analyzing pricing data and the likelihood of these currencies, specifically Bitcoin, being in the midst of a financial bubble. We examine the prediction of prices, or rather the inability to do so, before introducing the Currency Analyzer web application developed as part of this work. Containing up to date prices, this application predicts the prices of Bitcoin using machine learning. The research, planning methodologies, technologies, and design and evaluation of this application are described in detail in this chapter, followed by a conclusion and future scope.

Keywords: Bitcoin, Blockchain, Currency Trend, Machine Learning.

INTRODUCTION

There is no method to accurately predict the prices of any cryptocurrency. However, there are certainly trends in prices, which can be examined and attempted to forecast using various new technologies. Building on the information, we will now examine the applied element of this work: an application for displaying Bitcoin prices and predicting future values of Bitcoin. The prices of crypto-currency can be extremely unstable. For example, data taken from CoinDesk on April 12th, 2018, shows that in the space of one hour (11:00-12:00 GMT) the price of Bitcoin spiked from just under $7000 to just under $8000. There are countless occurrences of this happening throughout the lifetime of Bitcoin. Another example of this volatility is when the currency reached its

---

[*] **Corresponding author Dolly Sharma:** Department of Computer Science, Amity University, Noida, Uttar Pradeshn, India; E-mail: dolly.azure@gmail.com

Vaishali Mehta, Dolly Sharma, Monika Mangla, Anita Gehlot, Rajesh Singh and Sergio Marquez Sanchez (Eds.)

highest price on December 16th, 2017, of over \$19,300, before plummeting to \$13,800 a mere five days later - a drop of almost 30%. The sheer instability of crypto-currency prices and the rate at which they change determine there will never be a dependable method of predicting prices. However, one can consider a variety of things when considering buying or selling crypto-currency to determine if the time is right. It is important to clarify that the price is solely governed by demand, but there are indeed a great number of factors that may indirectly influence the price of crypto-currency.

Price of Bitcoin

Due to its popularity, the price of Bitcoin often affects the price of other crypto-currencies. One could argue that if the price of Bitcoin is affected by the same events as other crypto-currencies, its price will change in tandem with those of other crypto-currencies. However, the size and popularity of Bitcoin lead many to look to its data when considering buying or selling any crypto-currencies. For example, consider a sudden increase in negative media content related to Blockchain technology [1]. If the majority agree with the negative content, most of the market could decide to sell their investments. Bitcoin, with an estimated market dominance of 40-45%, also the majority, would subsequently decline in price. If most of the majority sold their Bitcoin, owners of other crypto-currencies would be likely to sell due to the majority of the market decline. By comparing graphed data of the prices of a given cryptocurrency against those of Bitcoin, it becomes clear that Bitcoin activity does have a bearing on other cryptocurrency prices. See Fig. (**1**) below, detailing the prices of Bitcoin and Ethereum over one week.

Fig. (1). Bitcoin and Ethereum Prices, Apr 8 - 15 2018.

While one could consider this pure coincidence, with a week arguably not being long enough to decipher any relationships between the two, the same can also be seen for a longer period of three months. Consider Fig. (**2**) below.

Fig. (2). BTC and ETH Prices, Jan 15 - Apr 15, 2018.

In both instances, the prices of both Bitcoin and Ethereum follow roughly the same path. Bitcoin prices can be seen to be much more volatile, rising and falling more severely and in shorter spaces of time than Ethereum prices. For example, one should consider the sharp rise in the price of Bitcoin shortly after April 12th, 2018, against the slightly more dulled rise of Ethereum. This can also be observed in the rise and fall of the prices from February to March 2018; the price of Bitcoin is seen to be more erratic, detailing many sudden increases and decreases. Ethereum follows the same general path with less sharp changes, implying that Bitcoin leads to increased buying or selling of Ethereum.

Background Information

The beginning of the rise of crypto-currency can be pinpointed in 2009 when the first major crypto-currency was released to the public. Much like traditional currency, any crypto-currency is an asset, designed to be traded in exchange for goods and services. Crypto-currency is based on cryptography, the study of breaking or creating codes and ciphers to either encrypt plain text or decrypt the ciphertext, to keep the exchange of digital information safe and secure. Based on Coin Market Cap figures, one of the most widely used websites for tracking the size and price of various crypto-currencies, there are currently just over 1500 cryptocurrencies in existence today, with some of the most popular being Bitcoin, Ethereum, Litecoin, and Ripple. When compared to the relatively small number of the 180 traditional currencies in circulation throughout the world, one might think that cryptocurrencies are more popular than traditional currencies. This is not the case, however, mostly since, anyone can develop and release a crypto-currency into the virtual world with the help of Blockchain Technology.

Focus on Bitcoin

The arrival of modern crypto-currency can be pinpointed in 2009 when the first major crypto-currency was released to the public. The concept of this first crypto-currency, Bitcoin, was introduced in a paper published in 2008 by authors under the supposed pseudonym of Satoshi Nakamoto. 16 In their paper, Nakamoto proposes the idea of a peer-to-peer electronic cash system based on digital signatures and independent of any financial institution or government. Nakamoto also outlines a solution to verifying transactions, preventing "double-spending" using a proof-of-work method. This would involve time-stamping transactions, adding them to a chain of hash-based proofs, which cannot change one transaction without redoing all previous entries in the proof-of-work. To change any entries in the chain, a single CPU would have to redo all entries before any new entries are added, which would require phenomenal computing power. Nakamoto also adds that this means the system is safe from threat as long as "honest" nodes collectively hold more CPU power than any group of attacking nodes.

The Price of Bitcoin

The first 50 coins were mined and released by Nakamoto in 2009 when the price per coin was estimated to have been a mere $0.001 US dollars. Bitcoin can be traded on various exchanges, Trading Crypto-currency, but what had been considered the first real-world transaction of Bitcoin occurred in 2010, long before most of these exchanges existed. This transaction of Bitcoin occurred when programmer Laszlo Hanyecz posted on a Bitcoin Forum, offering 10,000 Bitcoin in exchange for someone to order a pizza to his home in Florida. The post still exists today, containing comments from various users at the time as well as more recent comments lightheartedly highlighting the rise in the price of Bitcoin. The currency stayed at very low prices until late 2010 when the price rose to $0.36 per coin. The price began rising in February 2011 and peaked at $1.06, reaching "dollar parity", a much sought-after milestone. The price of Bitcoin continued to rise, fueled by media coverage, and spiked to over $100 and in 2013. Still rising, prices reached over $900 at the end of 2013, eventually settling between $400 - $800 for most of 2014, 2015, and 2016. 2017 saw Bitcoin prices soar from just under $1000 to a staggering $17,500. One cannot help but be reminded of those two pizzas Hanyecz spent 10,000 Bitcoin on, now worth a staggering $175 million. In 2018, the price of Bitcoin fell by roughly 60% and had hovered consistently between $5000 and $7000 since. Even so, this is still exceptionally higher than any other crypto-currency. Ethereum, the second most expensive coin, has averaged in the last month at around $400-$700 per coin, a mere 10% of the price of a Bitcoin.

Decentralized System

The simple explanation for a decentralized system is to say it is owned and managed by the public, instead of one single centralized entity like a bank or government. While the system varies from currency to currency, most implement this idea by using time-stamps or unique serial numbers on each transaction. These unique transactions are recorded in a global ledger, a copy of which is kept in one very currency owner's machine. Any anomalies in a transaction will be made obvious when checking the global ledger, avoiding the need for a trusted third party to verify transactions. This feature makes it virtually impossible to forge transactions into an account.

Blockchain Technology

While there are many different technologies behind various crypto-currencies, arguably the most renowned and important is the concept of blockchain. Modern Crypto-currency is the global ledger in which all transactions of a cryptocurrency are recorded. Blockchain technology was first proposed by Nakamoto, and thus in this section, we will be discussing blockchain technology concerning Bitcoin. As outlined by Nakamoto, the blockchain consists of multiple blocks added to the chain in chronological order. Each block consists of several transactions, which are stored in the block as hashed items. So that a new block to be added, it must be verified through the mining process. When a miner joins the Bitcoin network and downloads the software for validating and relaying transactions, a copy of the blockchain is also automatically downloaded Mining of Cryptocurrency, involves solving a complex computational problem and requires immense processing power. Once a block has been validated, it is added to the chain and the miner is rewarded. Every block containing information for every transaction, including the first "genesis" block, can be viewed either on a local copy of the blockchain or on sites such as Blockchain.info. The Blockchain website provides details for any given block, such as block number, number of transactions within the block, block time-stamp, and block reward. Most importantly, each block also stores the hashed key of the previous and next block in the chain, linking all blocks together.

Comparing Traditional Currency and Crypto-Currency

There are many similarities and differences to be found between traditional currencies and cryptocurrencies. Firstly, traditional currencies rely on centralized banks and governments to regulate and verify all transactions. This means that one person or group could destroy any proofs of transactions or change any account balances simply by breaking into or hacking one location. In contrast, cryptocurrencies are decentralized, meaning any potential threat would have to hack into every user's machine to destroy records or accounts. Of course, this would be an issue if there were few or no users, but the growing number of cryptocurrency owners means the likelihood of this is very small. The decentralized nature of cryptocurrencies and their global ledger also adds to the credibility of each transaction. In contrast to the relative ease with which someone could forge a paper note, the global ledger means cryptocurrency transactions are virtually impossible to forge. Additionally, any exchange of traditional currency carried out digitally (such as online banking or credit cards) can be easily traced back to the account and person it came from. Use of wallet addresses in cryptocurrency, Anonymity, still means the source and destination of the transaction can be seen without exposing sensitive information related to any party.

Future of Bitcoin

Of course, with such a volatile asset as Bitcoin, it is hard to say if any major collapse will ever occur or if prices would ever recover from such a collapse. Any possible collapse of Bitcoin could occur for some reasons, such as the advent of quantum computers capable of compromising the blockchain or a simple sudden loss of faith in the resource. The initial years of Bitcoin saw a relatively stable increase in prices, slowly climbing to just under $1000 by the end of 2016. This price growth was fueled by the gradual, natural growth of Bitcoin's popularity, easily seen by exploring the popularity of the term in Google searches over time. For most of its life, Bitcoin had been a relatively unknown term, or at least certainly not understood by the majority. In 2017 however, the term began together momentum surpassed the $1000 mark, with prices rising exponentially for 2017. At Bitcoin's peak of $19,661.63 on 17 December 2017, prices had risen by a staggering 1870% in one single year. While no concrete calculation can be done to determine what qualifies as a bubble, the sharp, almost irrational growth of prices would be difficult to refer to as anything other than a bubble. In keeping with the characteristics of every boom-and-bust cycle, Bitcoin suddenly plummeted to $13,857.14 on 22 December 2017. In the months since, prices have continued to rise and fall toward an overall gradual decline, which could be interpreted as simply a correction of the ridiculous prices to prices that reflect more accurately the cryptocurrency's worth, as opposed to an actual crash. As very recently summarised well by Derousseau, factors such as increased interest by governments, the arrival of Bitcoin futures, and the growing number of alternative cryptocurrencies could all be leading factors in price declines. Governments have now banned Bitcoin in several countries, which of course negatively affects the market as those countries' residents sell-off their currency. Bitcoin futures, allowing investors to simply bet on whether Bitcoin prices will rise or fall, means that those interested in cryptocurrency no longer need to own that currency to profit from it, possibly leading to a decline in the market in the future. Lastly, as more cryptocurrencies are added to the market, the market space for existing currencies will reduce. While the popularity of the bigger currencies may remain steady, the addition of newer varieties is likely to steal some of the spotlights from Bitcoin as people invest early with the hopes of these new currencies eventually reaching Bitcoin prices.

Goals and Objectives of Proposed Work

The main objective of this work was to make the area of cryptocurrency more accessible to an individual with little knowledge of the field.

- *Introduce the concept of this work*: We will provide the reader with an introduction to the work, detailing its inspiration and goals.
- *Provide the reader with a rounded understanding of cryptocurrencies*: We will examine where cryptocurrency began and the concept of modern cryptocurrency in simple terms, including how to begin trading cryptocurrency and the underlying technologies. We will then analyze the overall viability of cryptocurrency as an asset based on its fundamental components.
- *Explain to the reader how volatile cryptocurrency prices can be*: Having provided the reader with an understanding of cryptocurrency, we will discuss the prices of cryptocurrency, how they are determined, and what can inadvertently affect them. We will consider predicting prices, or rather the inability to predict prices, examining any known indicators that aid in the uncertain forecasting of prices.
- *Describe in detail the applied aspect of this work*: We will examine the approach of the team to the applied work, including methodologies and technologies used and design and evaluation of the system. Any issues encountered throughout the development process will also be discussed, including how such issues were resolved and what could be done differently in the future.
- With regards to the applied component of this work, our objectives are as follows:
- *Deliver cryptocurrency prices to the user*: The web application should bring up-to-date prices for the Bitcoin currency to the user in the form of an easily interpreted graph. The user will be able to view the price in comparison to a traditional currency, such as the Euro.
- *Provide an educated guess as to future changes in prices*: Machine Learning [2] and Neural Networks [3, 4] will be integrated to provide the user with an

educated estimate of what a price will change. It should be noted that the aim is not to predict prices perfectly, as this is impossible due to the variety of factors that influence prices. However, previous price data will be used to attempt to decipher any trend and subsequently produce a price estimate, which will be relayed to the user through the web application. Natural Language Processing techniques could also be implemented to gather and analyze data on user discussions on relevant topics from sources such as Twitter and news websites. These discussions are proven to have a bearing on fluctuations in prices.

- *Work closely with the given learning outcomes for this work*: All requirements for the research and development process of this work will be strived towards by the team. This includes carrying out extensive research, applying appropriate methodologies, taking advantage of relevant new technologies, and critically evaluating the work, including identifying strengths, weaknesses, and future recommendations.
- *Metrics For Success or Failure* The metrics for the success or failure of this work undoubtedly relate closely to the fore mentioned objectives. A definitive list of metrics for success of the work as well as a web application is as follows:

- A simple, effective web application: Again, to measure this, we will ask some friends or family to use the web application for a short time and to give us their opinion of its usability and how informative it was afterward.
- Educated guesses of future cryptocurrency prices: We will measure the accuracy of our predictions against the actual data. We will carry out this examination the week before submission.
- Work: We will measure the success of our teamwork by reflecting on how we resolved any issues and how we conducted ourselves in stressful times.

LITERATURE REVIEW

The field of crypto-currency has enjoyed exponential growth in popularity in recent years [5 - 9]. Almost ten years ago, the release of Bitcoin marked the beginning of a new era of innovation in the financial sector. The launch of Bitcoin transformed the financial industry differently. Due to the success and popularity of Bitcoin, many other similar crypto-currency came into existence in the industry. There is a large market for these currencies and their scope in the near future. With such great scope, success, and popularity of these crypto-currencies, there also comes the volatility. There are many industries and people who invest or trade in these crypto-currencies, and with this comes the serious concern of the volatility of these. There is a need for a system that can show the trend of the future of these crypto-currencies such that it can help the industry and people who are involved in these crypto-currencies to get an idea of the price trend. Building on this knowledge, we examine the infamous volatility of cryptocurrency prices, analyzing pricing data and the likelihood of these currencies, specifically Bitcoin, being in the midst of a financial bubble. We examine the prediction of prices, or rather the inability to do so, before introducing the Currency Analyzer. There are certainly trends in prices, which can be examined and attempted to forecast using various new technologies. The proposed work aims to provide the past trends of the crypto-currency and along with this, it will show the current prices and project the future trend based on past trends, which can help the people have basic ideas of the future trend.

Future Scope of Technology

The future scope of this technology touches the following areas:

Machine Learning

It's an application of artificial intelligence [10]. Also, it allows software applications to become accurate in predicting outcomes. Moreover, machine learning focuses on the development of computers to learn automatically without human intervention.

There are various uses of machine learning in various fields, increasing its scope.

Improved Customer Services

Poor customer service remains one of the chief complaints among consumers, regardless of the industry. Originally, the complaints centered on slow customer service, but with the universal utilization of automated phone support, customers often get frustrated for not being able to speak to a human. Machine learning applications can understand the need of each customer by analyzing the previous account activity and help the customer to make better product selection offered by banking & financial service companies.

Risk Management

Machine learning technology can be a powerful ally in the quest for better risk management. The traditional software applications predict creditworthiness based on static information from loan applications and financial reports. But machine learning technology can go further to analyze the applicant's financial status as it may be modified by current market trends and even relevant news items.

Machine Learning can identify rogue investors working in unison across multiple accounts (practically impossible for a human investment manager) by deploying predictive analysis to huge amounts of data in real-time [11, 12].

Fraud Prevention

The greatest responsibility of any financial service provider is to prevent their client from any kind of fraudulent activity [13]. Financial frauds cost the USA $50 billion annually. Old ways of keeping clients' accounts secure are no longer good enough. With the advancement in data security, criminals have stepped up to the challenge. To protect clients' data against increasingly sophisticated threats, institutions and companies must stay one step ahead of hackers. Machine learning enables applications to thwart security breaches by outthinking the criminals [14]. Machine learning can compare each transaction against the account history. Any unusual activity like out-of-state purchase, large cash withdrawal, etc., raises the red flag that delays the transaction until user confirmation.

Network Security

Even after implementing costly and increasingly complex IT security platforms, big organizations seem defenseless against modern cyber-attacks. Machine learning technologies can perfectly identify suspicious patterns. The power of intelligent pattern analysis, combined with big data capabilities, certainly gives machine learning technology an edge over traditional, non-AI tools.

Crypto-currency trend prediction using machine learning is an initiative to predict the prices or trend in prices of a crypto-currency using machine learning so that people or investors looking forward to investing in these types of crypto-currencies, can have a view about the trend of prices which can help in better analysis of the crypto-currency.

There is a lot of scope in this field of machine learning. This prediction method can be used in various fields such as the stock market, national currencies, and many more. Even they can be used in various medical fields, agricultural fields, and in many other ways. Price predictions are attempts to predict the price for a certain period in the future. There are different methods for doing a price prediction, which vary based on whether the prediction is short-or-long-term. The most common indicators used for making a price prediction are moving averages and momentum indicators. Furthermore, resistance and support lines are used to identify a scope of possible price values in the future.

Scope of this Work

Since the machine will always be learning and accumulating data about crypto-currency prices. The model will only get smarter and more accurate with time to predict the future prices with much more accuracy. The scope of the work is enormous if identified, but it will be limited to the purpose of demonstration, beta testing, and data collection for successive results and output. Over-in-all, the scope of the system is to help the people dealing with the crypto-currency prices and get a basic idea about the future trend of the crypto-currency.

- The system can be used to show the previous trend of the currency for record and reference.
- The system can be used to show the current prices for the crypto-currency to keep a check on the prices.
- The system can be used to check the future trend of the crypto-currency based on the previous data.
- Using this system, we can create a similar system for various national currencies, different crypto-currencies, and stocks, which in the future can be very useful for investors and traders.

Investment Predictions

The machine learning technology implications in the banking and finance sector allow the traders to have an order placed on a predetermined price and, also allows for existing on predetermined selling price, which saves the traders from unbearable loss as it sells the stock automatically when the price drop down from the certain limit. The automatic trading technology makes trading easier for both large and small investors.

IMPLEMENTATION

The work proposed in this book chapter started with the preliminary research work that continued in various stages.

Research Methodology

The authors did extensive reading of the latest news items relating to cryptocurrency and researched a list of technologies, examining which would be best to include in the proposed work. Database of Prices: Based on the authors' collective experiences from the previous academic year, it was first agreed that Python 3 would be ideal for obtaining data. The authors carried out some quick searching online and found numerous free cryptocurrency APIs (Application Programming Interfaces) available, all of which stored vast amounts of records for prices of cryptocurrency against a variety of traditional currencies for increments of time, usually every minute. The authors concluded this was often enough for a web application that does not deal with trading and therefore does not need to be accurate. After refreshing collective knowledge of MongoDB documentation, the authors agreed on using a MongoDB database to save data from an API via a Python 3 script.

Application Back-End

Having decided on the details of the proposed work's database system, back-end of the application was to be worked upon. Once again, previous experiences encouraged the use of Python 3 and the Flask Framework. Application Front-End: For the front-end of the application, Vue.js and D3.js were considered. It appeared this combination would work well for creating a web application with simple yet intuitive design, as well as creating striking visual representations of our data.

Containerization

Having heard about the benefits of Containerization, Docker was researched upon, which is a leading platform in Containerization. Containerization, put simply, is the packaging of applications with all relevant libraries and dependencies. This feature eliminates issues when training applications on different machines, which may arise due to conflicts in installed software and the software the application was initially built with.

Machine Learning: With regards to attempting to decipher trends in prices, TensorFlow was explored. TensorFlow could fit in well with the overall architecture of proposed work (Fig. **3**).

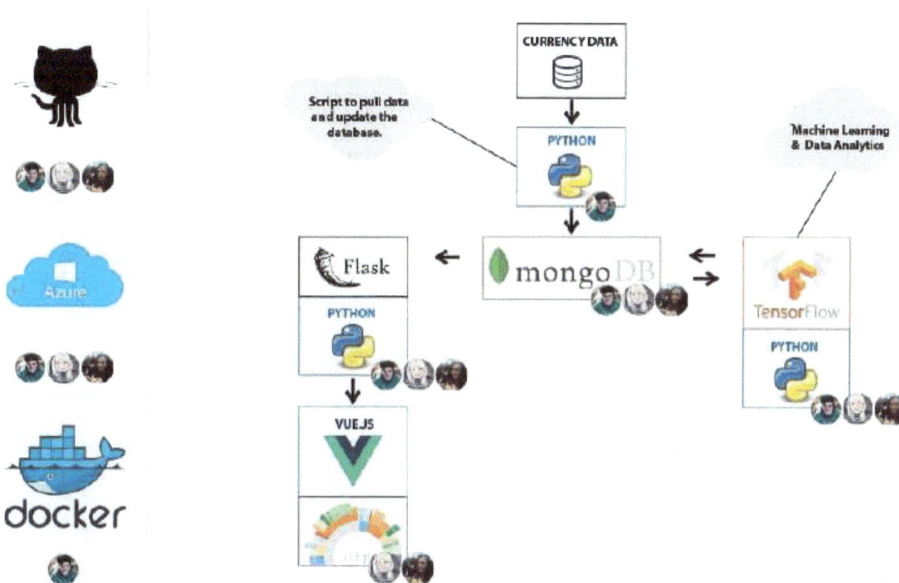

Fig. (3). Initial Expected Architecture.

Agile Development

For software development, Agile methodology was observed to be the best to follow. Agile approaches often include the division of work into short periods called sprints, often two to six weeks in length. At the beginning of each sprint, a goal for the end of the sprint is defined, such as a particular component of the proposed work to be working or some element to have been tested extensively. The life cycle followed for the proposed work was of four-week sprints, providing a definitive timeline of progress.

Testing

Metrics for Success or Failure: Testing conducted was user-driven for the most part. Based on the metrics outlined in the aforementioned section, the following tests related to each metric were conducted:

- *Metric One - Simple Web Application*: Again, it was decided that to test the simplicity of the web application, it would be best to ask those who had little or no knowledge of cryptocurrency. Similar to the above, five users would be asked to use the web application for a brief period and provide feedback on their opinions of its usability, using the same scale as above.
- *Metric Three - Future Cryptocurrency Price Estimates*: To test the accuracy of the web application's predictions, predictions were tested over one week or seven predictions. Due to TensorFlow's training and testing facilities, this test could be carried out in one sitting. The TensorFlow model would be trained, and subsequently shown seven unseen prices, and asked to predict the new price. For example, the model can be shown a price from 11 December 2017 and asked to predict the price for the following day, which can then be compared against the actual data from 12 December 2017.

Technologies Used

To carry out the proposed work, the authors used various technologies and programming languages along with other things. They are mentioned below:

Python 3

Python is a high-level, easy to read programming language, ideal for programmers with any level of skill. Python has become one of the most widely used programming languages, certainly due mostly to its simple yet powerful design. Unlike languages such as $_{Java}$ and $_C$, Python syntax is relatively uncomplicated and thus not as daunting as traditional languages. This theme carries across into

Python documentation, which remains simple and arguably easier to understand than, for example, Java documentation.

For this work, the Anaconda distribution of Python 3 was used, as it is aimed at data science and machine learning applications. Anaconda's virtual environment manager, Anaconda Navigator, is included with the open-source distribution and makes installation and updating of packages a much simpler process. There are many external libraries available in the Anaconda distribution of Python 3, including some powerful data science packages like Scikit-Learn, TensorFlow, and SciPy. For these reasons, as well as experience with Python 3, the authors chose to work with this particular distribution.

The Flask Microframework

The Flask microframework is designed for building simple web applications with a Python backend. By using the Anaconda distribution, Flask can be installed simply through Anaconda Navigator, and all Flask applications can be run on any computer and accessed via opening a browser at http://127.0.0.1:5000/. The back-end of a Flask application looks very similar to a standard Python file, with added @app.route() decorators to handle what happens at specific URLs. For example, @app.route("/") defines the home page of any web application, which in most cases simply loads the specified HTML file when the URL is called in the front-end. In short, the Flask microframework allows users to create web applications with a Python back-end quickly and easily.

Redis

While MongoDB had initially been intended for use as the store for currency data, research into Redis was carried out based on advice from the team supervisor. Redis, meaning *REmoteDIctionary Server*, is an open-source in-memory data store that supports many different data types. The use of in-memory storage as opposed to disk storage offers some advantages, mainly making retrieval of data in Redis extremely fast, capable of performing roughly 110,000 $_{SET}$ operations or 81,000 $_{GET}$ operations per second. While Redis can be used for multiple purposes, such as caching or message queues, its main purpose in this application was the storage of short-lived currency data.

Forex-Python

The Redis store of currency data within this work is updated using a Python script, which obtains the data using the forex-python library. This library contains prices for most traditional currencies, as well as prices for Bitcoin obtained through CoinDesk's Bitcoin [16 - 18] Price Index API.

MongoDB

MongoDB is an open-source document-based database. As mentioned in the above section, MongoDB was initially considered for the storage of currency data, subsequently replaced with Redis. However, the machine learning data and predicted prices of Bitcoin also needed to be stored somewhere. While Redis is suitable for short-lived currency data, it would not be suitable for storing any data related to the machine learning element of the proposed work. It was decided by the team that due to previous knowledge of MongoDB, it would make sense to use it in this respect.

Within a separate Python script, data is obtained from the forex-python library and saved into a MongoDB document. As the machine learning model does not need to be retrained regularly, this is done at a much lesser frequency than that of the Redis script.

Vue.js

Vue.js is a JavaScript framework for building user interfaces, designed to be capable of integration into the proposed work at any stage. While Vue.js was initially difficult to adapt to, the wide variety of tutorials and documentation available online greatly helped. Ultimately, Vue.js proved to be a powerful tool.

Chart.js

Chart.js allows developers to display data in several differently formatted graphs, all of which are capable of animation and customization. Using the simple HTML5 <**canvas**> tag, Chart.js was much easier to adapt to than D3.js. Following brief research and some online tutorials, the authors opted for the simplicity of Chart.js. Considering the graphs in this work did not need to do anything extraordinary, Chart.js was perfectly suited to this application.

TensorFlow

TensorFlow is an open-source framework designed to allow high-performance numerical computation for machine learning purposes. The software can be used with several languages such as C and C++, with the most popular and well-documented language being Python.

TensorFlow is based upon data flow graphs. Simply put, data flow graphs detail an input, some operations often on multiple levels, and an output. Regarding TensorFlow, each node in a graph represents a mathematical equation to be performed on the given edges that contain data (often multidimensional data arrays, described as tensors) that flow between them.

TensorFlow can be used in many applications, such as type prediction, value prediction, and image recognition; this application of TensorFlow within this work concerns value prediction. Data is loaded in, manipulated into the correct format to work with a specific model, and fed to that model. The model is first trained using historical data, in this case, previous prices of Bitcoin, until it computes the correlation between actual and predicted values. Once trained, the model can be given unseen data to be tested. TensorFlow was deemed the most suitable technology for the machine learning aspect of this work, due to its extensive documentation and tutorials available online.

System Design

Throughout the development life cycle, there were some changes regarding technologies and the overall design of the web application. Having initially intended to follow the architecture, many problems and events ultimately led to some changes.

The restructuring of this application was not major but did greatly benefit the proposed work, seeing the addition of new technologies and removal of those that were deemed unnecessary.

Currency Data

The API populates data to be returned using background workers, which are used to pull data at scheduled intervals of $_n$ seconds. These workers also pull data of n days to train the machine learning model with the previous day's result and predict the end price for the current day. Initially, the API was to act as the database handler or *DAO (Data Access Object)*, controlling and encapsulating actual communications to MongoDB. The scripts would publish the new values and the API listener threads would handle the data received.

However, during the implementation of this concept for handling data, we came upon the realization that the API would be dealing unnecessarily with MongoDB. The web application only deals with the most recent data, and thus can be optimized by pre-formatting any data to suit the web application's requirements. The data from the API is requested and refreshed by the web application constantly for the most recent currency data. Consequentially, it would be cumbersome to query the MongoDB database and reformat the query result with every request. The scripts were already communicating with the API via Redis, thus it seemed optimal that the scripts handle MongoDB and use Redis solely to share the most recent data with the API. This would subsequently simplify the code and reduce the dependencies the scripts have on one another, *e.g.* the worker relies on the web application to save the data published, or the worker needs to run to allow a clean shutdown of the web application. The web application's Heroku CPU allocation is no longer competing with listener threads, and the management of MongoDB will be abstracted from the API rather than delegated to it Fig. (**4**).

Furthermore, as the machine learning implementation developed, it was realized that it would no longer require the live currency data, meaning it was no longer necessary to save real-time currency data to the MongoDB database. Now, this data will solely be used for live currency data displayed on the web application.

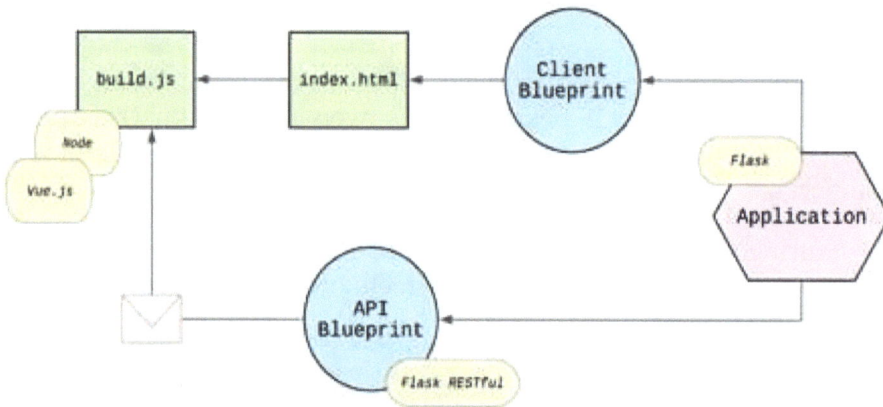

Fig. (4). Diagram of Application Design.

Machine Learning

The machine learning element of this application was built using Python 3 and TensorFlow. Machine learning is the use of statistics and computation to give systems the ability to "learn" and improve from experience without being explicitly programmed to do so. Artificial neural networks, inspired by the biological networks within our brains, are the strain of machine learning used within this work.

The *Long Short Term Memory* or LSTM algorithm [22], and efficient gradient-based model introduced by Hochreiter and Schmidhuber in 1997, was used in the building of the neural network model for this system. *Recurrent Neural Networks* attempt to address memory issues in traditional neural networks by adding loops within them, allowing information to persist. A reasonable analogy is to envision recurrent neural networks as numerous copies of the same network, each passing a message to a parent. This chain like nature resembles the behavior of sequences and lists, making them naturally suited to the architecture of a neural network.

Unfortunately, recurrent neural networks are burdened with the problem of handling long-term dependencies. As the neural network grows, gaps between past relevant data grow, and the recurrent neural network model becomes unable to learn to connect the information. In theory, recurrent neural networks are capable of handling this issue. Some are! Long Short-Term Memory is an extension or type of recurrent neural network capable of being very efficient on a large variety of problems, including timeline data [22], and is now widely used to solve these problems. LSTM models have an additional loop learning what data to forget and what data to remember; they still have the aforementioned chain-like structure, but with four different layers communicating in a certain way.

Final Architecture

In conclusion, the final architecture differs somewhat from that originally planned. A diagram of the complete final architecture for the system is detailed below in Fig. (**5**).

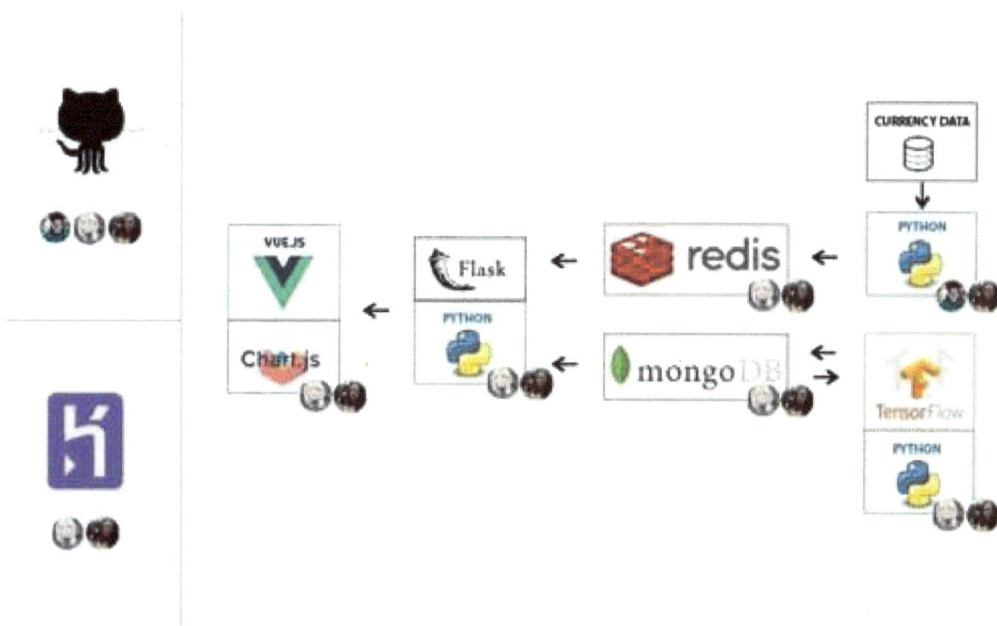

Fig. (5). Final Architecture.

RESULT

Based on the objectives outlined above, the following tests were carried out to gain insight into the success and robustness of this application.

Usability Testing

Undoubtedly, a large portion of this work surrounds explaining to the reader the fundamentals of cryptocurrency. To measure the success of these goals, it was decided that the best way to do so was to ask others with varying levels of knowledge to read one or many chapters, briefly use the web application, and gather feedback from them. A survey through Google Forms was created and sent to those who had kindly offered to read this work. All information other than the number of chapters read was on a scale of one to five. The form asked participants five questions; their initial level of knowledge of cryptocurrency, which chapters they had read, how easy they felt the terminology was to understand, how much the reading had improved their knowledge of cryptocurrencies, and how easy they felt corresponding web application was to use. Identity remained anonymous, as it was deemed not required for the survey. The link was only sent to those who had agreed to participate, and thus the form's results would not be skewed by anyone who had not participated.

Fig. (6). Bitcoin Price Over Time.

A summary of the results is detailed below:

Based on these results (Table **1**), we can conclude that while those with expert levels of initial knowledge did not learn much more, those with moderate or beginner levels of knowledge did increase that level of knowledge (Fig. **6**).

Table 1. Survey Results April 2020.

Previous Knowledge	Chapters Read	Terminology Used	Improvement of Knowledge	Use of Web Application
2	1, 2	4	4	4
5	1, 2, 3	5	2	5
4	All	3	4	5
1	1, 2	3	5	4
2	1, 2, 3	2	5	4
3	1, 2, 3	4	4	5

CONCLUSION

Reflecting on the objectives, the following is a condensed initial list of objectives for applied aspects of this work:

Objectives of this work:

1. Introduce the concept of Bitcoin.

2. Provide the reader with a rounded understanding of cryptocurrencies.

3. Explain to the reader how volatile cryptocurrency prices can be.

4. Describe in detail the applied aspect of this work.

Implementation of Proposed Work:

1. Create a simple web application that is easy to use and clear to understand.

2. Deliver cryptocurrency prices to the user.

3. Provide an educated guess as to future changes in prices.

4. Work closely with the given learning outcomes for this work.

5. Conduct work as a team in a professional manner akin to what is expected in the industry.

Evaluation of Objectives

Following the objectives discussed above, the remaining objectives of the proposed work were evaluated in the following ways:

Deliver Cryptocurrency Prices to the User

Cryptocurrency prices were delivered to the user in the form of Bitcoin prices in Euros, plotted on a graph contained on the web application home page. The data is obtained using the forex-python library, which is queried every thirty seconds for the latest Bitcoin price. The graph is updated to include this new value, with graph polling of data occurring every three seconds. This ensures that the prices are as up to date as can be.

Provide an Educated Guess as to Future Changes in Prices

Using machine learning, estimating the following day's closing price of Bitcoin has been achieved and implemented within the application. Due to the limitations of the system's prediction model, the estimate of the close price is only applicable on a day-to-day basis and cannot be used for long term predictions thus the system is retrained once per day on updated currency data. The predictions are delivered to the user via a graph, displaying previous predictions versus actual close prices. Unfortunately, natural language processing techniques were not implemented in this work, offering an opportunity for future development.

Work Closely with the given Learning Outcomes for this Work

The expected learning outcomes for this work included applying appropriate research and development methodologies, demonstrating awareness of innovative technologies, and incorporating them into the model where relevant, and the ability to critically evaluate the work and any potential for future work. Preliminary Research and throughout the commencement of this work, the team conducted extensive research into a variety of different technologies and methodologies before beginning the work. While most of the work relies on faithful technologies such as Python, an effort was made to integrate newer technologies such as TensorFlow for Machine Learning, where it was deemed important to take advantage of the newest innovations in the field.

FUTURE WORK

While the work achieved its initial objectives in some capacity or another, the point at which any work is complete and unable to be improved upon is difficult to pinpoint.

The preliminary planning of this work inevitably meant most of the technologies chosen were chosen for the right reasons and if not, were quickly replaced by more appropriate technologies. Afterall, there is, of course, opportunity for improvement of extra features in the web application.

Wider Variety of Cryptocurrencies

Of course, it would be ideal to have all the major cryptocurrencies such as Ethereum, Litecoin, Ripple, and the recently developed Bitcoin Cash implemented in and being predicted by this application. Due to time constraints and memory constraints with Heroku, it was deemed suitable to focus our efforts on the cryptocurrency with the largest market capitalization, Bitcoin.

Natural Language Processing

Natural language processing can and has previously been used to determine fluctuations in the prices of cryptocurrency. This work could greatly benefit from such technology by implementing a component that would search given sites for negative or positive discussions on cryptocurrencies. This information could be used to predict an incoming change of price or simply display the changing popularity of given cryptocurrencies from day today.

Long Term Predictions

In addition to natural language processing, a neural network model for long-term prediction could also be implemented. Unfortunately, the current application only estimates short-term values effectively, and the addition of a long-term estimate using both machine learning and natural language processing would make this application more attractive to those considering a long-term investment in cryptocurrency.

Docker

As outlined in *Research Methodology*, Docker was initially considered for its Containerization capabilities. The technology was not crucial and, due to time constraints, was not implemented to facilitate more which can be taken up as future work by readers.

CONSENT OF PUBLICATION

Not applicable.

CONFLICT OF INTEREST

The author declares no conflict of interest, financial or otherwise.

ACKNOWLEDGEMENTS

Declared none.

REFERENCES

[1]   F. Mai, Z. Shan, Q. Bai, X.S. Wang, and R.H.L. Chiang, "How Does Social Media Impact Bitcoin Value? A Test Of The Silent Majority Hypothesis", *J. Manage. Inf. Syst.,* vol. 35, no. 1, pp. 19-52, 2018.
[http://dx.doi.org/10.1080/07421222.2018.1440774]

[2]   P. Louridas, and C. Ebert, "Machine Learning", *IEEE Softw.,* vol. 33, no. 5, pp. 110-115, 2016.
[http://dx.doi.org/10.1109/MS.2016.114]

[3]   J. Le, *A Gentle Introduction to Neural Networks for Machine Learning.* https://www.codementor.io/ @james_aka_yale/a-gentle-introduction-to-neural-networks-for-machine-learning-hkijvz7lp

[4]   E. Gelenbe, and Y. Yin, ""Deep learning with random neural networks 2016",", *International Joint Conference on Neural Networks (IJCNN),* pp. 1633-1638, 2016.
[http://dx.doi.org/10.1109/IJCNN.2016.7727393]

[5]   "CoinMarketCap. Cryptocurrency Market Capitalizations. Last accessed on 6 Apr", https://coinmarketcap.com/

[6]   "Gdax: The Most Trusted Digital Asset Exchange. Last accessed on 6 Apr", https://www.gdax.com/

[7]   S. Nakamoto, *Bitcoin: A peer-to-peer Electronic Cash System.,* 2008.https://bitcoin.org/bitcoin.pdf

[8]   L. Hanyecz, *Bitcoin Forum Post: Pizza For Bitcoins?,* 2010.https://bitcointalk.org/index.php? topic=137.0

[9]   B. Wallace, *The rise and fall of bitcoin.,* 2011. https://www.wired.com/2011/11/mf_bitcoin/

[10]   K. Bakshi, and K. Bakshi, *IEEE Aerospace Conference,* pp. 1-9, 2018.
[http://dx.doi.org/10.1109/AERO.2018.8396488]

[11]   D. Zomer, *Using machine learning to predict future bitcoin prices..*https://towardsdatascience.com/ using-machine-learning-to-predict-future-bitcoin-prices-6637e7bfa58f

[12]   S. McNally, J. Roche, and S. Caton, "Predicting the Price of Bitcoin Using Machine Learning 2018", *26th Euromicro International Conference on Parallel, Distributed and Network-based Processing (PDP),* pp. 339-343., 2018.
[http://dx.doi.org/10.1109/PDP2018.2018.00060]

[13]   "Comparative analysis of machine learning techniques for detecting insurance claim fraud", https://www.wipro.com/analytics/comparative-analysis-of-machine-learning-techniques-for-detectin/ Last Accessed on Jun, 2020.

[14]   "Fraud Detection: How Machine Learning Systems Help Reveal Scams in Fintech, Healthcare, and eCommerce. AlexSoft. URL:", https://www.altexsoft.com/whitepapers/fraud-detection-how-mach-ne-learning-systems-help-reveal-scams-in-fintech-healthcare-and-ecommerce/ Last Accessed on Jun 17, 2020.

[15]   "Coinbase. Buy And Sell Digital Currency. Last accessed on 6 Apr", URL:, https://coinbase.com/

[16]   "Coindesk: Bitcoin USD Price. Last accessed on 7 Apr", URL:, https://www.coindesk.com/price/

[17]   M. Swan, "Blockchain 1.0: Currency in Blockchain: Blueprint for a New Economy", *O'Reilly Media Inc.,* pp. vii-xvi, 2015.

[18]   J. Donnelly, https://www. coindesk.com/making-sense-bitcoins-halving/

[19]   "Bitcoin core source code. Last accessed on 8 Apr", URL:, https://github.com/bitcoin/bitcoin

[20]   O. Bowcott, and A. Hern, *Facebook, and Cambridge Analytica Face Class Action Lawsuit.,* 2018.https://www.theguardian.com/news/2018/apr/10/cambridge-analytica-and-facebook--ace-class-action-lawsuit

[21]   Merriam-Webster Incorporated, *Bubble; noun.*.https://www.merriam-webster.com/dictionary/

[22]   S. Hochreiter, and J. Schmidhuber, "Long short-term memory", *Neural Comput.,* vol. 9, no. 8, pp. 1735-1780, 1997.
[http://dx.doi.org/10.1162/neco.1997.9.8.1735] [PMID: 9377276]

CHAPTER 6

A Bibliometric Analysis of Fault Prediction System using Machine Learning Techniques

Mudita Uppal[1,*], **Deepali Gupta**[1] and **Vaishali Mehta**[2]

[1] *Chitkara University Institute of Engineering and Technology, Chitkara University, Punjab, India*

[2] *Panipat Institute of Engineering & Technology, Samalkha, Panipat, Haryana, India*

Abstract: Fault prediction in software is an important aspect to be considered in software development because it ensures reliability and the quality of a software product. A high-quality software product consists of a few numbers of faults and failures. Software fault prediction (SFP) is crucial for the software quality assurance process as it examines the vulnerability of software products towards failures. Fault detection is a significant aspect of cost estimation in the initial stage, and hence, a fault predictor model is required to lower the expenses used during the development and maintenance phase. SFP is applied to identify the faulty modules of the software in order to complement the development as well as the testing process. Software metric based fault prediction reflects several aspects of the software. Several Machine Learning (ML) techniques have been implemented to eliminate faulty and unnecessary data from faulty modules. This chapter gives a brief introduction to SFP and includes a bibliometric analysis. The objective of the bibliometric analysis is to analyze research trends of ML techniques that are used for predicting software faults. This chapter uses the VOSviewer software and Biblioshiny tool to visually analyze 1623 papers fetched from the Scopus database for the past twenty years. It explores the distribution of publications over the years, top-rated publishers, contributing authors, funding agencies, cited papers and citations per paper. The collaboration of countries and co-occurrence analysis as well as over the year's trend of author keywords are also explored. This chapter can be beneficial for young researchers to locate attractive and relevant research insights within SFP.

Keywords: Analysis, Bibliometric, Fault Prediction, Machine Learning, Scopus, Software engineering, Software metrics, Testing.

INTRODUCTION

Software engineering is concerned with discovering and implementing engineering methods in the development of effective and reliable software. The Institute of Electrical and Electronics Engineers (IEEE) describes software

---

[*] **Corresponding author Mudita Uppal**: Chitkara University Institute of Engineering and Technology, Chitkara University, Punjab, India; E-mail: mudita@chitkara.edu.in

Vaishali Mehta, Dolly Sharma, Monika Mangla, Anita Gehlot, Rajesh Singh and Sergio Marquez Sanchez (Eds.)

engineering as "the application of a systematic, disciplined, quantifiable approach to the development, operation, and maintenance of software; that is, the application of engineering to software" [1].

The increased demand for software systems has also increased the demand for good quality software. So, testing is a crucial stage of the software engineering process that assures a high-quality software product [2]. Software testing can depict the presence of errors in the software rather than showing its absence [3]. Testing software is a costly process as about one one-third to one one-half of the expense is spent on developing a project. Software testing plays a significant role in Software Development Life Cycle (SDLC).

The interests of software engineers in tasks of quality assurance like testing, verification, validation, fault tolerance and fault prediction are increasing in the domain of software engineering [4]. The software testing field has various issues, such as the generation of effective test cases and their prioritization, that needs to be tackled. These problems require time, effort and cost of the testing phase which can be tackled by different proposed techniques and methodologies. Out of the total, 6% of the respondents agreed that test automation can fully replace manual testing, while 45% of the total practitioners believe that modern test automation tools offer a poor fit for their demands [5].

Testing is done either manually or automatically with the help of testing tools and it is discovered that automated software testing is better than the testing of software manually and on the other hand, very few tools of test data generation are commercially available today [6]. The automatic generation of test data or test cases is done by various techniques such as neural networks, genetic programming, fuzzy logic, or evolutionary computation.

The modification of faulty modules requires more effort and cost once the software is developed. So, predicting the faulty modules at an early stage is beneficial as it reduces overall software costs [7]. The faults present in the software degenerate its reliability and quality, thus, leading the system towards failure. So, SFP is considered an important aspect because it enhances the software quality and efficiency to reduce cost and time. In SFP, the actions required to tackle the faulty module are developed before. The consequences may disrupt the original result of the software if the major faults are not solved for a long period [8]. SFP uses approximately 50% of the resources of software system development [9]. Therefore, fault detection is emerging as an essential prospect for cost and time estimation of the development process at an early stage.

Many strategies are available to predict whether the model is faulty or not. Among them, the most popular strategies are statistical strategies and machine learning strategies. Machine learning strategies are more preferred than traditional statistical strategies because they give better results. Approaches to fault prediction are needed when the software company requires delivering a complete product well on time and within budget after testing it. Also, in the before-mentioned circumstances, recognizing and testing the faulty components of the system are reasonable. The prediction models are used for improving the quality of software by utilizing available resources. So, the basic aim of SFP is to increase the quality of the test process to detect fault-prone modules by reaching a state of highly dependable system [10].

Artificial Intelligence for Software Testing Association (AISTA) conducted a survey in 2017 to emphasize the demand for data specialists and AI engineers in the development as well as testing teams. At that moment, only 22% of the members of AISTA knew AI or ML technologies. Also, at the same moment, 76% of the members believed that AI can have consequences on manual testing in the upcoming three years [11]. ML will transform software testing as it makes judgments quicker based on more data. Also, no part of software testing will be left unaltered by ML [12].

Machine learning algorithms play an essential part in software testing by getting more accurate results and saving cost and time. ML-driven testing will commence a new age of quality assurance in the future. The product quality can be enhanced by using AI/ML techniques in the software development life cycle [13]. ML has many algorithms and techniques that can be used in the process of software testing. These techniques and algorithms are different from one another in terms of their working, implementation of mathematical and statistical models, features, assumptions, accuracy, advantages and disadvantages, and solving categories as if they resolve classification, clustering, regression, or other problems.

The cost and time of the testing phase can be reduced by fault prediction methodology. ML techniques can be used in SFP to make fast decisions on larger datasets. Techniques like Artificial Neural Network (ANN), Logistic Regression (LR), Decision Tree (DT), Genetic Algorithm (GA) and many more have been used to predict faults within the software. These techniques use software metrics like weighted methods per class, depth of inheritance tree, number of children, *etc.* Some probabilistic graphical models are used for optimization and prediction, such as Bayesian Networks (BN), Naive Bayes, Markov models with their extensions in dynamic BNs, Tree augmented Naive Bayes, *etc.* These models are used in monitoring product and system quality, predicting fault and identifying the faulty module within the software [14].

As machine learning is an emerging domain, so, the objective behind this bibliometric analysis is to explore the work done on ML techniques in the field of SFP, revealing the trends from 2000 till now. 1623 research papers were analyzed from different reputed publishers and journals.

The remaining chapter is organized as follows: Section 2 includes some related literature. Section 3 represents a comparative analysis of work done by several researchers in the field of SFP using ML techniques. Section 4 shows the results and discussion of the bibliometric analysis in the graphical representation and Section 5 concludes the chapter.

REVIEW OF LITERATURE

A comprehensive review of the literature contains papers and publications associated with ML techniques used in SFP are carried out. Some of the discussions on fault prediction based on different ML techniques are made here.

Kanmani *et al.* [15] implemented two approaches in which the neural network-based approach using Object-Oriented metrics performed better than statistical approaches. Their results were compared using 5 attributes of quality and observed that the Neural Networks (NN) gave better results. Between the 2 NN, the Probabilistic NN outperforms in the prediction of fault proneness of the developed object-oriented classes.

Singh *et al.* [16] compared Logistic Regression (LR) and Artificial Neural Networks (ANN) methods that determine the consequences of software metrics on fault proneness. The study used data collected from the public domain NASA data set. The performance of the fault proneness models was evaluated using Receiver Operating Characteristic (ROC) analysis. The areas covered under the ROC curves were 0.78 for the LR and 0.745 for the ANN model. The models yielded good AUC using ROC analysis using both LR and ANN methods. It also affirms that the creation of ANN is feasible and helpful in the prediction of fault-prone modules.

Sandhu *et al.* [17] proposed a study that aims to investigate whether requirement metrics (used in the early lifecycle) can be joined with code metrics (available in the late lifecycle) to identify the faulty modules with the help of GA. This strategy had been examined with real-time defect projects of NASA datasets. The results prove that the combination of both metrics can be used as the most suitable prediction model for the detection of fault as compared to the only code-based model.

Catal *et al.* [18] examined the performance of different evaluation metrics and classified them into two groups. In the first group, the estimation of the performance of the prediction system was done and based on the confusion matrix and balance metrics, modules were classified as faulty or non-faulty. In the second group, the system performance was estimated by predicting the faults in each module of the system with the help of the coefficient of multiple determination (R2), average relative error and average absolute error metrics. The results proved that the bigger the value of *R2*, the higher the accuracy of the prediction model.

Hall *et al.* [19] examined the quality of methodology in SFP studies using ML. They evaluated the ML methodology applied in twenty-one fault prediction papers with the help of NASA datasets. They concluded that the quality of ML techniques can be enhanced for software faults prediction.

Sharma *et al.* [20] developed techniques for software fault prediction at an early stage with the help of two metrics. These two metrics are complexity metrics and object-oriented metrics that detect the faulty modules. The results discovered that high accuracy can be attained by several metrics.

Radjenović *et al.* [21] identified the relevancy of software metrics in SFP. 106 papers were analyzed from 1991 to 2011 and inferred that the object-oriented metrics (49%) had been applied approximately twice in comparison to traditional process metrics (24%) or source code metrics (27%). The Chidamber and Kemerer (CK) metrics were the most often utilized object-oriented metrics. The post-release faults were predicted better with process metrics as compared to static code metrics.

Suresh *et al.* [22] used two techniques for the prediction of faults: statistical techniques and ML techniques. SFP was carried out by coding in a MATLAB environment. They concluded that out of six CK metrics, the Weighted Method per Class (WMC) seems to be most valuable in predicting the faults.

Singh *et al.* [23] developed a fault prediction model using a cluster-based approach with the help of the NASA MDP dataset that increases the probability of defect detection. It results in more reliable and test-effective software. It demonstrated an 83.3% probability of detection compared with standard methods of defect prediction. Furthermore, it manages the balance rates to 68.5%.

Marinescu *et al.* [24] analyzed the abilities in terms of recall and precision of Genetic Programming for predicting defect and change proneness of object-oriented classes. One of the newest applications of Genetic Programming is Symbolic regression. The results confirm that Symbolic Regression can forecast the changes with a precision of 0.7506 and a recall of 0.99. Also, it forecast defects with a precision of 0.0859 and a recall of 1.

Paramshetti *et al.* [25] surveyed several ML techniques for the prediction of software defects and observed that it enhances the software development process quality and lessens cost and time.

He *et al.* [26] conducted a survey on thirty-four releases of ten open source projects accessible on the repository of PROMISE. The result proves that Within-Project Defect Prediction (WPDP) models achieve more precision than Cross-Project Defect Prediction (CPDP) models. It also showed that a prediction model could provide satisfactory performance with a minimal subset of software metrics.

Madeyski *et al.* [27] used data from 12 open-source projects from the repository of PROMISE. The result proved that the number of distinct committers and number of modified lines metrics have a significant correlation with fault proneness, but the number of revisions and number of defects in the previous versions exhibited no significant correlation with fault prediction. It concluded that the process metrics consist of various sources of information as compared to product metrics.

Rathore *et al.* [28] presented a technique that predicts the faults in a software system with the help of GP. Data sets of 10 software projects available in the repository of PROMISE were used. The performance of the proposed approach was evaluated by the recall, error rate, and completeness parameters and concluded that GP-based models show significant results in predicting faults in software.

Reena *et al.* [29] reviewed genetic feature selection to predict defects. The research plan was to develop a GA that could work on feature selection. The bagging technique is applied to cope up with the problem of class imbalance. It leads to the conclusion that the field of GA applications is growing fast. Some systems can be used and reused in different types of GA. Also, the combination of GA and bagging techniques gives an effective improvement in the performance of prediction for most of the classifiers.

Mundada *et al.* [30] emphasize software fault prediction techniques based on ANN with the Back Propagation (BP) learning algorithm. ANN is helpful in predicting the faulty modules. ANN trained with the help of resilient BP yields better results in comparison to the conventional BP algorithm.

Sethi *et al.* [31] concluded that the ANN approach is more efficient as compared to the fuzzy logic approach. The authors proposed an ANN method that gives more accurate and precise values as compared to the classical fuzzy logic approach. Also, it can be used as a hybrid approach for better performance on a large dataset.

Haveri *et al.* [32] used the datasets taken from the PROMISE, ANT and CAMEL. The software faults can be predicted during an initial stage of the development process *via* techniques like ANN, GA and DT. GA has an estimated accuracy rate of 85.02% with ANT and 88% with CAMEL, whereas ANN with BP has obtained 81.16% accuracy with ANT and 80.28% accuracy rate with CAMEL. Also, optimizing NN using GA exhibits better efficiency and accuracy as compared to the BP technique.

Rathore *et al.* [33] presented a Recommendation System (RS) based on the logic of a decision tree that helps in choosing an appropriate technique for building a fault prediction model. Some case studies were presented that prove the effectiveness and usability of the proposed RS. Also, a prototype system was implemented.

Sharma *et al.* [34] focus on ML techniques and their accomplishments for SFP model development. They presented some software issues related to fault prediction and upcoming research. They also presented conventional techniques and aimed to describe the problem of fault proneness.

Rathore *et al.* [35] predicted the software system faults with the help of process and object-oriented metrics. The basic idea of different elements was presented that are involved in the fault prediction method and also revealed its associated problems. This survey is divided into three groups: data quality issues, software metrics and fault prediction processes. The impact of quality on techniques of fault prediction differs for different datasets.

Kokane *et al.* [36] investigated and studied suspension faults. The approaches to detect suspension faults were also reviewed and the faults were examined through different sets of ML algorithms and methods. They proposed analytics and the Internet of Things (IoT) based online model for the detection of suspension faults.

Manjula *et al.* [37] proposed a hybrid method for the prediction of defects that is a blend of GA and Deep Neural Network (DNN) schemes. The performance of classification schemes like Naïve Bayes, SVM, DT, and KNN is compared with the proposed hybrid approach in terms of sensitivity, accuracy, precision, specificity and recall. The outcome of the experimental analysis proved that the accuracy of the proposed hybrid method on the CM1 dataset is 97.59%, 97.82% on the KC1 dataset and PC4 dataset, it is 98.0% that, is superior to existing approaches.

Kumar *et al.* [38] proposed a methodology that determines the feasibility of genetic-based ML methods for the prediction of fault proneness in software using object-oriented metrics. These techniques can be utilized to build a prediction model of software having object-oriented data. Also, these techniques can be applied to predict the fault proneness in the beginning stages of the development of any software [39].

Li *et al.* [40] investigated the efficiency of unsupervised ML techniques in the prediction of a software defect. This analysis reveals that the supervised models can be compared with unsupervised models for cross-project and within-project defect prediction. Fuzzy C-Means and Fuzzy SOMs performed best among the other fourteen families of the unsupervised model.

Ahmed *et al.* [41] proposed an automated model for software defect predictive development (SDPD). The abilities of six supervised machine learning classifications techniques were evaluated to predict the defect in software modules using three National Aeronautics and Space Administration (NASA) datasets. The results of the experiment with different attributes showed the capability and efficiency of the SDPD model to identify the fault and improve the quality of software.

Qasem *et al.* [42] investigated 2 deep learning algorithms, namely, Multi-layer Perceptrons and Convolutional Neural Network. The parameters that influenced the performance of these two algorithms were discussed in this chapter. The author proved that altering factors had a significant impact on the forecast of the performance and obtained a higher rate in comparison to the ML algorithms. The results concluded that the rate of fault detection might increase or decrease by the estimated factors.

Rhmann *et al.* [43] used software change metrics for defect prediction. For experimental purposes, an android project and Git repository is used. GFS-logit boost had shown the best performance in terms of recall and precision. Friedman's statistical test was applied to evaluate the performances of different techniques and check whether they were statistically different or not. The authors concluded that several techniques applied to defect prediction were statistically alike in relation to their performance.

DATA AND METHODOLOGY

Bibliometrics has been a standard tool for research management in the past few decades. The research question that led to this research was: "What is the present scenario of ML techniques in SFP?" This led to the search on the Scopus database using "software fault prediction", "software testing", "software metrics" and "machine learning" as major research criteria with "AND" Boolean operator. The literature search was refined to incorporate papers published between 2000 and 2020 with variables as authors, publishers, sources, country, document type, keywords and the affiliations of the authors. All the papers that were made part of the research were in the English language only. We have considered only the top-rated publishers for analyzing the papers. Statistical analysis was performed using the biblioshiny R package of R-Studio software [44] and the VOSViewer tool [45]. VOSviewer is used for mapping and clustering of co-citation network analysis. It is also used to cluster the citation terms and represent them in different colors and the frequency of the occurrence of data is represented by the size of the circle. The search string, scope and selection criteria are described in Fig. (**1**).

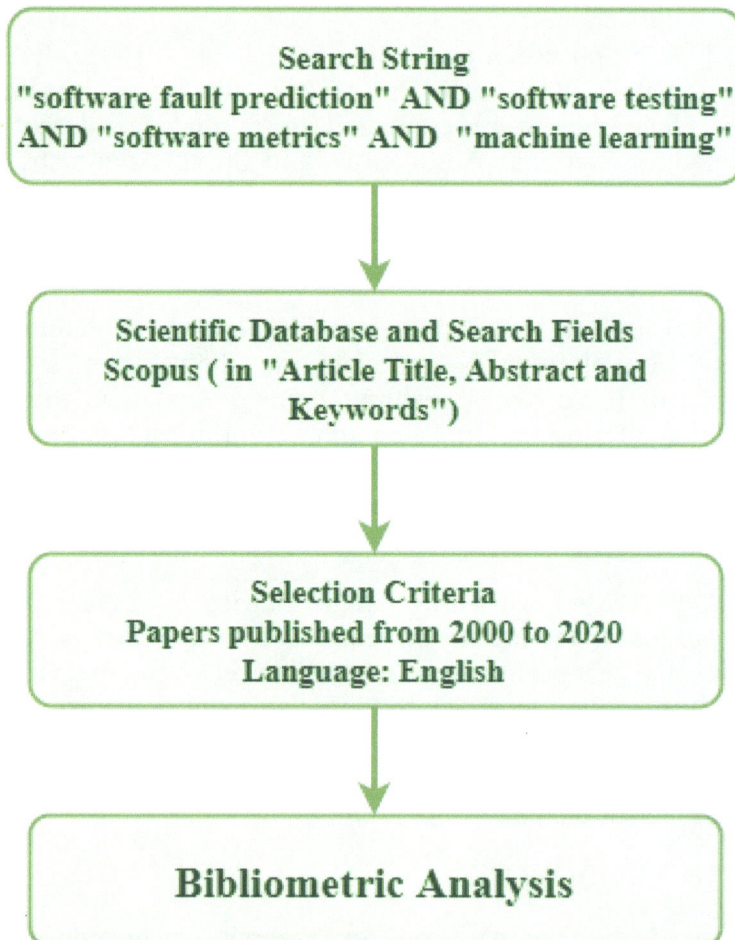

Fig. (1). Search strategy and extraction of data.

The search was carried out using the parameters as shown above. 1623 publications out of 60,830 papers were considered to be most appropriate for further analysis in the bibliometric phase. The electronically available documents were retrieved and evaluated during this analysis, so no institutional review board consent was required.

BIBLIOMETRIC ANALYSIS

A bibliometric analysis of a total of 1623 documents was performed in this study that was authored by 3233 authors with 1.99 authors per document index as shown in Fig. (**2**). The mean citation received per document was 9.74 and the document per author index is 0.502.

Description	Results
Documents	1623
Period	2000 to 2020
Sources (Journals, Books, etc)	813
Average citations per documents	9.742
Average citations per year per document	1.049
References	35696
Keywords Plus (ID)	6438
Author's Keywords (DE)	3004
Authors	3233
Author Appearances	4567
Single-authored documents	274
Documents per Author	0.502
Authors per Document	1.99
Co-Authors per Documents	2.81
Collaboration Index	2.26

Fig. (2). Description of Bibliometric Analysis of 1623 documents.

Among all the papers, Conference Paper (69%) has the highest count, followed by Article (24%), Conference Review (4%) and Book Chapter (3%). Table **1** shows the distribution of document types retrieved from Scopus.

Table 1. Document types.

Type	Documents	Percentage
Conference Paper	1113	69%
Article	390	24%
Conference Review	68	4%
Book Chapter	52	3%

A. Annual Trend of Publications

All 1623 publications chosen for the bibliometric analysis were separated by publication year and represented in the time series with an exponential trendline, as shown in Fig. (**3**). The annual growth rate is 1.8%.

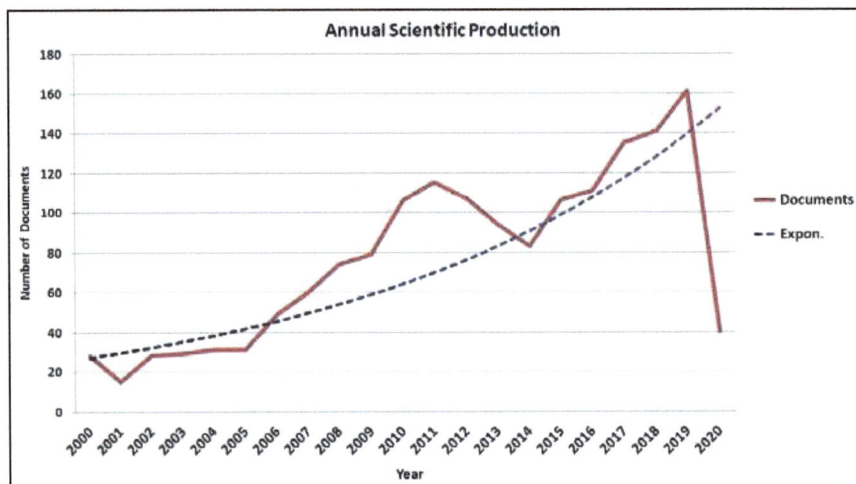

Fig. (3). Number of papers (1623) published in the year (2000-2020).

B. Top authors, organizations and funding agencies working in SFP

The authors, institutions and funding sponsors are mentioned in the bibliometric. The most contributing authors with the maximum number of publications (n) are J.C. Maldonado (n = 16), followed by T.M. Khoshgoftaar (n = 14) and O. Taipale (n = 12), as shown in Fig. (**4**).

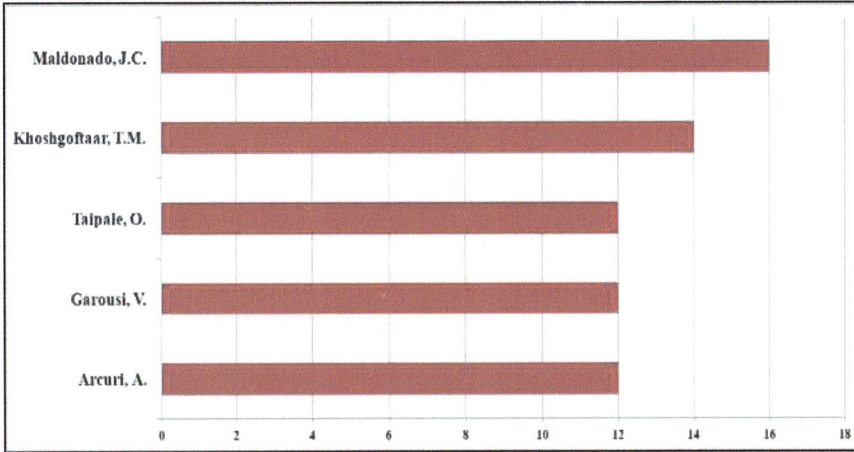

Fig. (4). Authors with Highest Publications.

Fig. (**5**) represents the top 5 institutions that published maximum research papers in the SFP domain. Among these, the two institutions are of India with 30 papers and the other three are of China and Brazil.

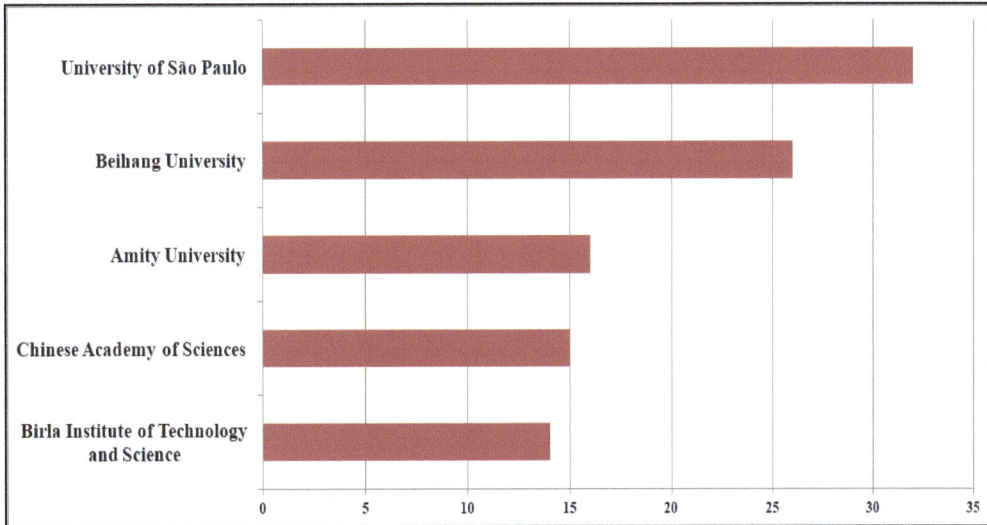

Fig. (5). Organizations with Highest Publications.

Fig. (**6**) represents the top 5 funding agencies raising the maximum number of funds. The top agency is from China with 38 research funding, followed by the USA with 17 research funding.

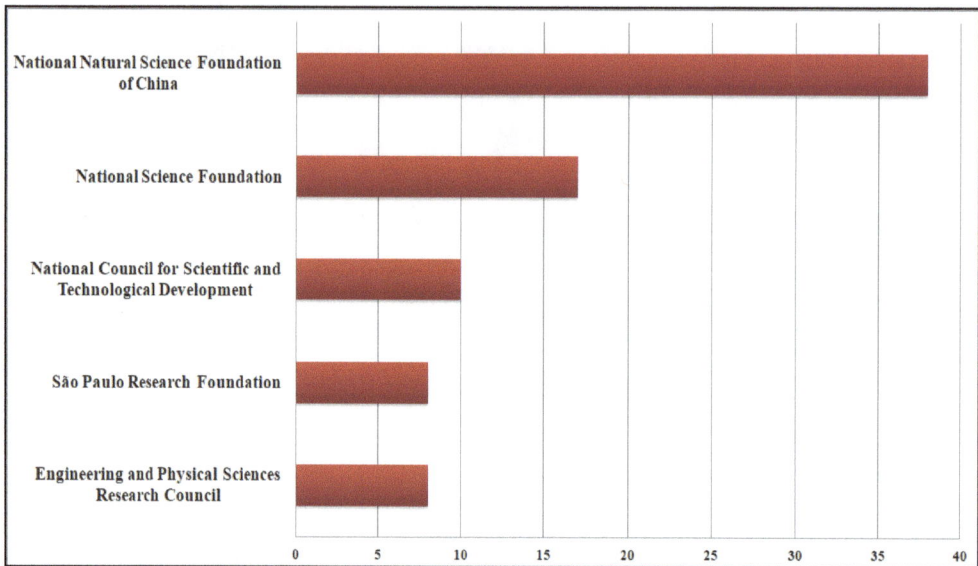

Fig. (6). Top 5 Funding Agencies.

C. Percentage of Publishers

An accurate analysis is received from high-quality literature as good resources are necessary. As shown in Fig. (**7**), IEEE is the most well-recognized publisher having a majority of 23% followed by Springer (10%) and ACM (6.3%)The other publishers like Elsevier, IGI Global, CEUR-WS and Inderscience publishers are having 2.8%, 1.4%, 1.3%, and 0.5% of publications respectively.

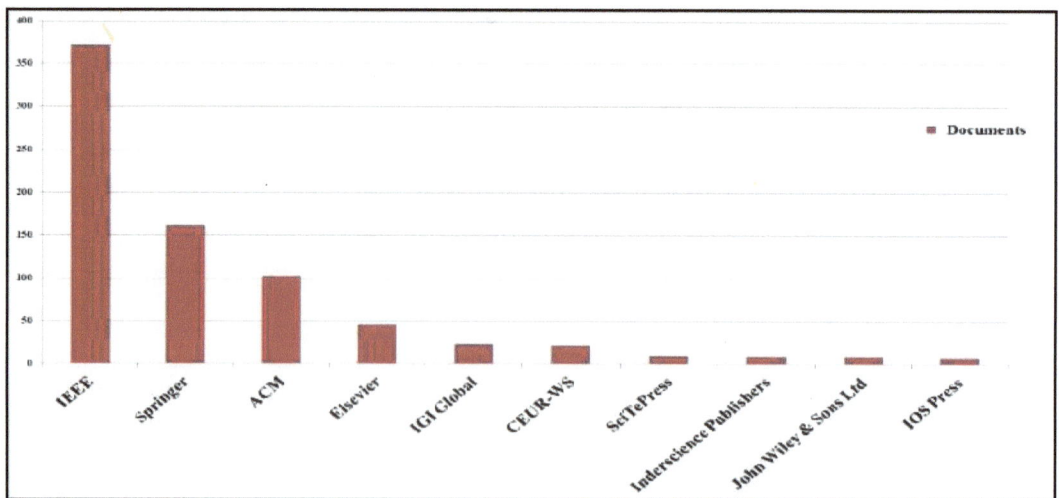

Fig. (7). Top 10 Publishing Venues.

D. Country Distribution Analysis

Fig. (**8**) represents that the USA had the maximum publications, *i.e.*, 271 (16.7%) followed by India with 234 (14.4%) papers and then by China, Brazil, UK and Canada with 219 (13.5%), 90 (5.5%), 74 (4.5%) and 61 (3.8%) publications respectively.

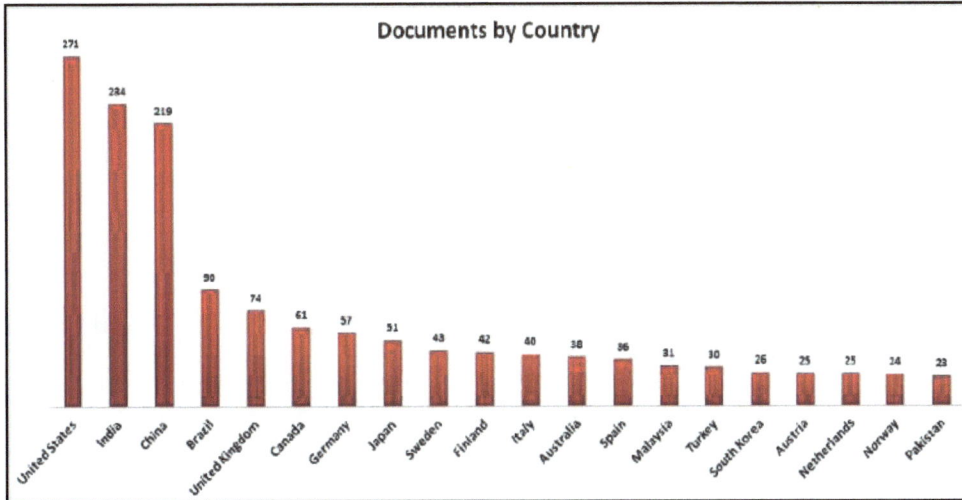

Fig. (8). Number of papers (1623) published by country (2000-2020).

The global collaboration network among 35 countries with at least 10 papers per country is shown in Fig. (**9**). Each country's colour signifies the number of average citations per document received by them. The size of each and every node depicts the number of papers that have been published by that particular country. 7 clusters were formed based on association strength between documents and countries.

- Cluster 1- India, Iran, Ireland, Japan, Jordan, Malaysia, Saudi Arabia, Turkey.
- Cluster 2- United Kingdom, Russia, Indonesia.
- Cluster 3- United States, Israel.
- Cluster 4- Austria, Germany, Italy, Poland, Serbia, Slovenia, Switzerland.
- Cluster 5- Australia, China, Pakistan, Hong Kong, New Zealand, South Korea.
- Cluster 6- Brazil, Canada, Egypt, France, Norway.
- Cluster 7- Finland, Netherlands, Spain, Sweden.

E. Keywords Analysis

In this analysis, an overlay visualization of the co-occurrence of author keywords was made. A threshold of at least ten occurrences of a keyword was fixed to recognize the most frequently used author keywords mentioned in the literature and it gave a total of 45 keywords.

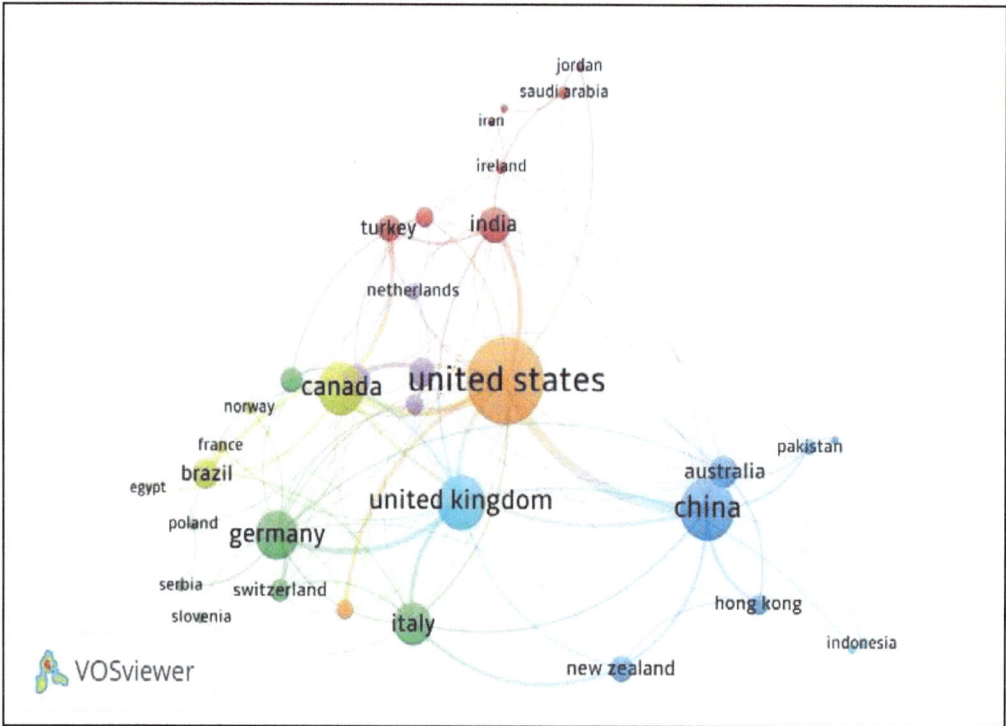

Fig. (9). Network visualization of the distribution of the country's co-authorship relationship.

The top five co-occurring keywords were "software testing" (n = 404), "software metrics" (n = 180), "software fault prediction" (n = 65), "software quality" (n = 58) and "machine learning" (n = 55) as shown in Fig. (**10**). A total of 45 keywords out of all 3007 keywords were inserted into the network and they were clustered year-wise that are shown in different colors. The total link strength of software testing is 204 followed by 118 software metrics.

F. Publication Sources

Most of the papers are published in Lecture Notes in Computer Science, with about 5.7% of total publications, followed by the Association for Computing Machinery, having a share of 2.5%. At the same time, IEEE Transactions on

Software Engineering got the maximum citations and has the most number of citations per paper (CPP) as 112 followed by the Journal of Systems and Software (35.5 CPP) and IEEE Software (34 CPP) as shown in Fig. (**11**). The two journals having the lowest citations in the top 15 publication sources list are CEUR Workshop Proceedings with 1.2 citations per paper and Advances in Intelligent Systems and Computing with 1.5 CPP.

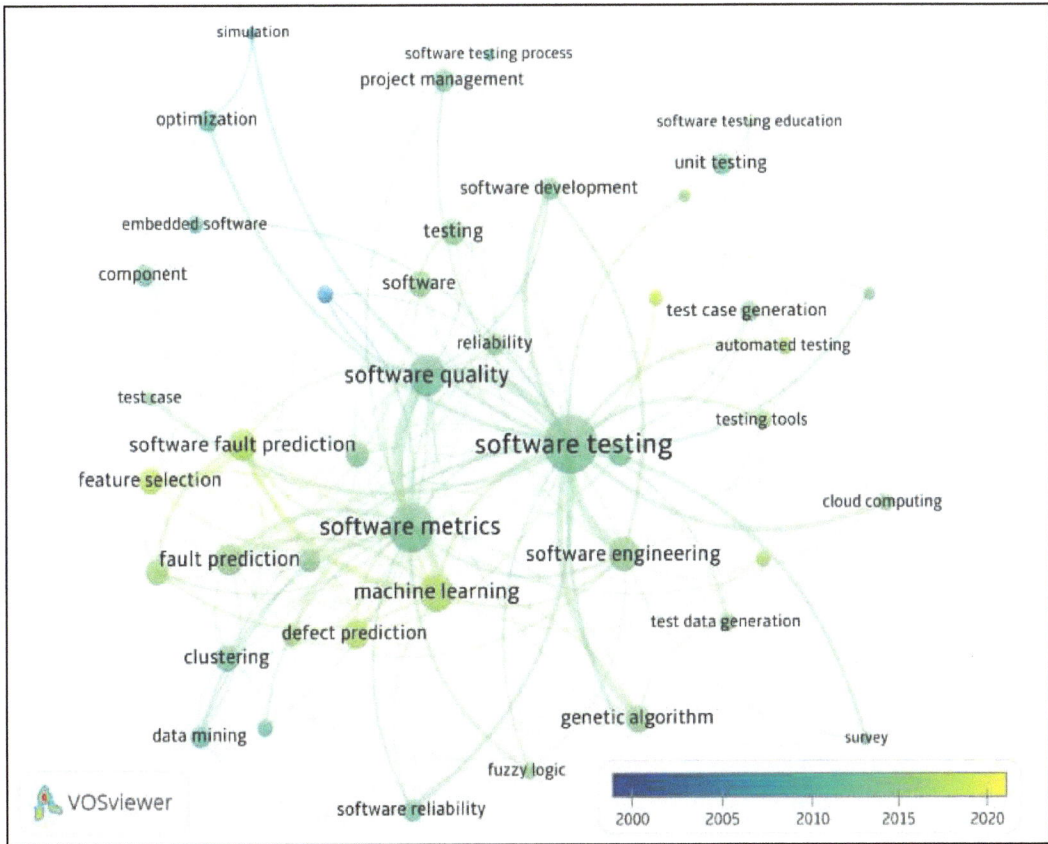

Fig. (10). Overlay visualization of co-occurrence of author keywords.

The three-field plot is designed by applying the clustering technique on data records to correlate different parameters like keywords, countries, and affiliations. The three-field plot shown in Fig. (**12**) uses a similar concept as applied earlier, but the difference is in the visualization of how the keywords are connected with the different countries and organizations.

Sources	Papers	%	Citations	CPP
Lecture Notes in Computer Science	87	5.34%	502	5.7
ACM International Conference Proceeding Series	53	3.25%	134	2.5
Proceedings - International Conference on Software Engineering	44	2.70%	748	17
Communications in Computer and Information Science	33	2.02%	76	2.3
Advances in Intelligent Systems and Computing	31	1.90%	47	1.5
CEUR Workshop Proceedings	26	1.60%	33	1.2
Journal of Systems and Software	24	1.47%	852	35.5
Information and Software Technology	18	1.10%	480	26.7
Proceedings - International Computer Software and Applications Conference	14	0.86%	86	6.1
Proceedings of The ACM Symposium on Applied Computing	13	0.80%	96	7.4
IEEE Transactions on Software Engineering	12	0.74%	1345	112
IEEE Software	11	0.67%	373	34
International Journal of Software Engineering and Knowledge Engineering	11	0.67%	80	7.3
Software Quality Journal	10	0.61%	102	10.2
Proceedings of The International Conference on Software Engineering and Knowledge Engineering	10	0.61%	31	3.1

Fig. (11). Top 15 sources and their publications, citations and CPP.

DISCUSSION

A bibliometric analysis assists in the evaluation of historical references and research trends in any desired domain which has been gone through scientific evolution throughout the long term. The topmost five trending topics from analysis of publications are software testing, software metrics, software fault prediction, software quality and machine learning from 2000 to 2020. Exponential growth over the years is also represented which proves that ML is an emerging technique in SFP. The top 5 authors, institutions and funding sponsors revealed that India has a good contribution to this domain. IEEE has the maximum amount of papers published, followed by Springer. *USA, India* and *China* are the top 3 countries involved in the research of ML techniques for software fault prediction. The co-authorship relationship between countries is represented *via* network visualization that differentiates countries on the basis of the work done by different countries into clusters. Besides, keyword analysis is done through the co-occurrence of author keywords over a span of 20 years. The highest number of research papers are published in Lecture Notes in Computer Science followed by ACM International Conference Proceeding Series. *IEEE* Transactions on

Software Engineering has the maximum number of citations among other publishers. The association of keywords with different countries and organizations showed the trends of research done. Furthermore, it can be concluded that the maximum number of research works are implemented using ML algorithms. Looking forward to the advancements in ML techniques for SFP shows good potential for future research in this field.

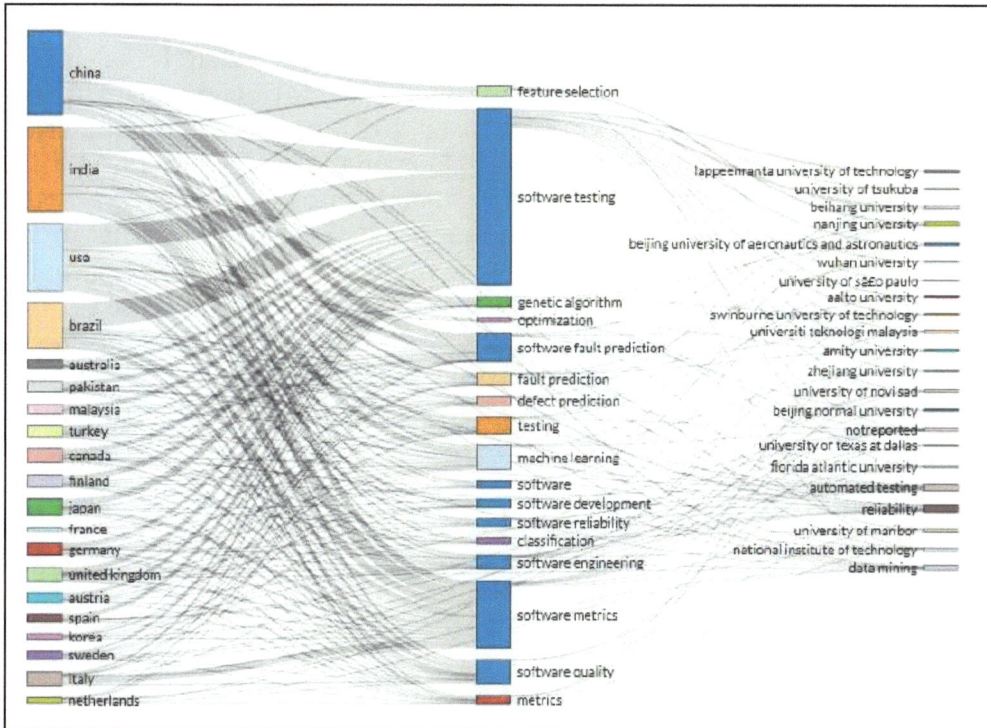

Fig. (12). 3-field plot of classification by country, affiliations and author keywords from data records.

CONCLUSION & FUTURE WORK

Software fault prediction using ML techniques is observed as the most efficient method of software performance determination. This chapter explores the 20 years of publications indexed by Scopus. The fault prediction in software at an early stage of the development process can be made by using techniques such as ANN, DT, GA, *etc.* It helps in enhancing the quality of the software. ML analyzes complex data automatically by using smart models and algorithms and achieves better outcomes in software testing. Fault prediction in software plays a significant role in its development process because the detection of the fault-prone module at an early stage not only reduces effort or time but also reduces the overall cost of the software product. The smart automation of software testing will enhance the software quality and customer's experience by providing defect-free solutions and applications. Many different approaches have been developed by the researchers to address the issue of identifying bugs in the software. ML-based methods are considered to be the most promising techniques because of their learning mechanism. The defect prediction before the actual testing and reduction of time and cost of the software project needs some enhanced software prediction techniques. 1623 articles on ML techniques for SFP published from 2000 to 2020 were thoroughly analyzed through a bibliometric review.

This bibliometric analysis presents a picture of scientific research that helps in comparing and visualizing the research output of ML techniques in SFP. VOSviewer and Biblioshiny tools were used to illustrate and illuminate the patterns of performance and impact of work done on ML techniques on SFP. This thorough analysis revealed that the maximum amount of work is done on public datasets using process or object-oriented metrics. This chapter presents insights into the development and aspect of the most cited publications in the domain of SFP. With the help of bibliometric tools, interesting analysis and visualizations of the research associations between different parameters were presented. These research outcomes can serve as the starting point or be used as background literature for further studies on ML techniques for the prediction of software faults.

CONSENT OF PUBLICATION

Not applicable.

CONFLICT OF INTEREST

The author declares no conflict of interest, financial or otherwise.

ACKNOWLEDGEMENTS

Declared none.

REFERENCES

[1]   L. Tripp., "IEEE Standards Collection Software Engineering", In: *Institute of Electrical and Electronics Engineers*New York, NY, 1994.
[http://dx.doi.org/10.1109/IEEESTD.1994.121429]

[2]   P. Bourque, and R.E. Fairley, "Guide to the software engineering body of knowledge (SWEBOK (R)): Version 3.0", https://cs.fit.edu/~kgallagher/Schtick/Serious/SWEBOKv3.pdf

[3]   P.C. Jorgensen, "12.2 Software Testing", *Computers, Software Engineering, and Digital Devices,* 2018.

[4]   G. Abaei, and A. Selamat, "A survey on software fault detection based on different prediction approaches", *Vietnam Journal of Computer Science,* vol. 1, no. 2, pp. 79-95, 2014.
[http://dx.doi.org/10.1007/s40595-013-0008-z]

[5]   D.M. Rafi, K.R.K. Moses, K. Petersen, and M.V. Mäntylä, "Benefits and limitations of automated software testing: Systematic literature review and practitioner survey", In: *2012 7ᵗʰ International Workshop on Automation of Software Test (AST)*. IEEE, 2012, pp. 36-42.

[6]   M. Alzabidi, A. Kumar, and A.D. Shaligram, "Automatic Software structural testing by using Evolutionary Algorithms for test data generations", *International Journal of Computer Science and Network Security*, vol. 9, no. 4, pp. 390-395, 2009.

[7]   A. Mockus, and D.M. Weiss, "Predicting risk of software changes", *Bell Labs Tech. J.*, vol. 5, no. 2, pp. 169-180, 2000.
        [http://dx.doi.org/10.1002/bltj.2229]

[8]   A. Arora, A. Sikka, and L. Ramanathan, A Systematic Literature Review on Software Fault Prediction and Fault Tolerance in Software Engineering. 2017.

[9]   P.R. Srivastava, and T. Kim, "Application of genetic algorithm in software testing", *Int. J. Softw. Eng. Appl.*, vol. 3, no. 4, pp. 87-96, 2009.

[10]   C. Catal, and B. Diri, "Investigating the effect of dataset size, metrics sets, and feature selection techniques on software fault prediction problem", *Inf. Sci.*, vol. 179, no. 8, pp. 1040-1058, 2009.
        [http://dx.doi.org/10.1016/j.ins.2008.12.001]

[11]   T. M., King, J. Arbon, D. Santiago, D. Adamo, W. Chin, and R. Shanmugam, "AI for testing today and tomorrow: industry perspectives", In: *2019 IEEE International Conference On Artificial Intelligence Testing (AITest)* IEEE, 2019 , pp. 81-88.

[12]   J. Arbon, "AI for Software Testing", In: *Pacific NW Software Quality Conference. PNSQC*, 2017.

[13]   Mudita Uppal, and D. Gupta, "The Aspects of Artificial Intelligence in Software Engineering", *Journal of Computational and Theoretical Nanoscience*, vol. 17, no. 9/10, pp. 4635-4642, 2020.

[14]   D. Rodriguez, J. Dolado, and J. Tuya, "Bayesian concepts in software testing: an initial review", *Proceedings of the 6th International Workshop on Automating Test Case Design, Selection and Evaluation.*, pp. 41-46, 2015.
        [http://dx.doi.org/10.1145/2804322.2804329]

[15]   S. Kanmani, V.R. Uthariaraj, V. Sankaranarayanan, and P. Thambidurai, "Object-oriented software fault prediction using neural networks", *Inf. Softw. Technol.*, vol. 49, no. 5, pp. 483-492, 2007.
        [http://dx.doi.org/10.1016/j.infsof.2006.07.005]

[16]   Y. Singh, A. Kaur, and R. Malhotra, "Predicting software fault proneness model using neural network", In: *International Conference on Product Focused Software Process Improvement* Springer: Berlin, Heidelberg, 2008, pp. 204-214.
        [http://dx.doi.org/10.1007/978-3-540-69566-0_18]

[17]   P.S. Sandhu, S. Khullar, S. Singh, S.K. Bains, M. Kaur, and G. Singh, "A study on early prediction of fault proneness in software modules using genetic algorithm", *International Journal of Computer and Information Engineering*, vol. 4, no. 12, pp. 1891-1896, 2010.

[18]   C. Catal, "Performance evaluation metrics for software fault prediction studies", *Acta Polytech. Hung.*, vol. 9, no. 4, pp. 193-206, 2012.

[19]   T. Hall, and D. Bowes, "The state of machine learning methodology in software fault prediction", In: *2012 11ᵗʰ International Conference on Machine Learning and Applications* IEEE, 2012.
        [http://dx.doi.org/10.1109/ICMLA.2012.226]

[20]   R. Sharma, N. Budhija, and B. Singh, "Study of predicting fault prone software modules", *Int. J. Adv. Res. Comput. Sci. Softw. Eng.*, vol. 2, no. 2, pp. 1-3, 2012.

[21]   D. Radjenović, M. Heričko, R. Torkar, and A. Živkovič, "Software fault prediction metrics: A systematic literature review", *Inf. Softw. Technol.*, vol. 55, no. 8, pp. 1397-1418, 2013.
        [http://dx.doi.org/10.1016/j.infsof.2013.02.009]

[22]   Y. Suresh, L. Kumar, and S.K. Rath, "Statistical and machine learning methods for software fault prediction using CK metric suite: a comparative analysis", *Int. Sch. Res. Notices,* 2014.

[23]   P. Singh, and S. Verma, "An efficient software fault prediction model using cluster based classification", *Int. J. Appl. Inf. Syst.,* vol. 7, no. 3, pp. 35-41, 2014.

[24]   C. Marinescu, "How good is genetic programming at predicting changes and defects?", *In 2014 16th International Symposium on Symbolic and Numeric Algorithms for Scientific Computing,* IEEE, p. 544-548, 2014.
[http://dx.doi.org/10.1109/SYNASC.2014.78]

[25]   P. Paramshetti, and D.A. Phalke, "Survey on software defect prediction using machine learning techniques", *Int. J. Sci. Res.,* vol. 3, no. 12, pp. 1394-1397, 2014.

[26]   P. He, B. Li, X. Liu, J. Chen, and Y. Ma, "An empirical study on software defect prediction with a simplified metric set", *Inf. Softw. Technol.,* vol. 59, pp. 170-190, 2015.
[http://dx.doi.org/10.1016/j.infsof.2014.11.006]

[27]   L. Madeyski, and M. Jureczko, "Which process metrics can significantly improve defect prediction models? An empirical study", *Softw. Qual. J.,* vol. 23, no. 3, pp. 393-422, 2015.
[http://dx.doi.org/10.1007/s11219-014-9241-7]

[28]   S.S. Rathore, and S. Kumar, "Predicting number of faults in software system using genetic programming", *Procedia Computer Science,* vol. 62, pp. 303-311, 2015.

[29]   R. Reena, and R. T. Selvi, "A survey of genetic feature selection for software defect prediction", *i-Manager's Journal on Software Engineering,* vol. 10, no. 3, p. 20, 2016.

[30]   D. Mundada, A. Murade, O. Vaidya, and J.N. Swathi, "Software fault prediction using artificial neural network and Resilient Back Propagation", *Int. J. Comput. Sci. Eng.,* vol. 5, no. 03, 2016.

[31]   T. Sethi, "Improved approach for software defect prediction using artificial neural networks", *In 2016 5th International Conference on Reliability, Infocom Technologies and Optimization (Trends and Future Directions)(ICRITO),* IEEE, pp. 480-485, 2016.
[http://dx.doi.org/10.1109/ICRITO.2016.7785003]

[32]   A. Haveri, and Y. Suresh, "Software Fault Prediction Using Artificial Intelligence Techniques", In: *2017 2nd International Conference on Computational Systems and Information Technology for Sustainable Solution (CSITSS)* IEEE, 2017, pp. 1-5.
[http://dx.doi.org/10.1109/CSITSS.2017.8447615]

[33]   S.S. Rathore, and S. Kumar, "A decision tree logic based recommendation system to select software fault prediction techniques", *Computing,* vol. 99, no. 3, pp. 255-285, 2017.
[http://dx.doi.org/10.1007/s00607-016-0489-6]

[34]   D. Sharma, and P. Chandra, "Software fault prediction using machine-learning techniques", *Smart Computing and Informatics.,* Springer: Singapore, pp. 541-549, 2018.

[35]   S.S. Rathore, and S. Kumar, "A study on software fault prediction techniques", *Artif. Intell. Rev.,* vol. 51, no. 2, pp. 255-327, 2019.
[http://dx.doi.org/10.1007/s10462-017-9563-5]

[36]   P. Kokane, and P.B. Sivakumar, "Online Model for Suspension Faults Diagnostics Using IoT and Analytics", In: *International Conference on Advanced Computing Networking and Informatics* Springer: Singapore, 2019, pp. 145-154.
[http://dx.doi.org/10.1007/978-981-13-2673-8_17]

[37]   C. Manjula, and L. Florence, "Deep neural network based hybrid approach for software defect prediction using software metrics", *Cluster Comput.,* vol. 22, no. 4, pp. 9847-9863, 2019.
[http://dx.doi.org/10.1007/s10586-018-1696-z]

[38]   A. Kumar, and A. Bansal, "Software fault proneness prediction using genetic based machine learning techniques", *2019 4th International Conference on Internet of Things: Smart Innovation and Usages*

(IoT-SIU), pp. 1-5, 2019.
[http://dx.doi.org/10.1109/IoT-SIU.2019.8777494]

[39] D. Gupta, A.S. Brar, and P.S. Sandhu, "Modeling Of Fault Prediction Using Machine Learning Techniques", *Proceedings of 2nd National Conference on Challenges & Opportunities in Information Technology (COIT-2008)*, 2008.

[40] N. Li, M. Shepperd, and Y. Guo, "A systematic review of unsupervised learning techniques for software defect prediction", *Inf. Softw. Technol.*, p. 106287, 2020.
[http://dx.doi.org/10.1016/j.infsof.2020.106287]

[41] M.R. Ahmed, M.A. Ali, N. Ahmed, M.F.B. Zamal, and F.M.J.M. Shamrat, "The Impact of Software Fault Prediction in Real-World Application: An Automated Approach for Software Engineering", *Proceedings of 2020 the 6th International Conference on Computing and Data Engineering*, pp. 247-251, 2020.
[http://dx.doi.org/10.1145/3379247.3379278]

[42] O. Al Qasem, M. Akour, and M. Alenezi, "The Influence of Deep Learning Algorithms Factors in Software Fault Prediction", *IEEE Access*, vol. 8, pp. 63945-63960, 2020.
[http://dx.doi.org/10.1109/ACCESS.2020.2985290]

[43] W. Rhmann, B. Pandey, G. Ansari, and D.K. Pandey, "Software fault prediction based on change metrics using hybrid algorithms: An empirical study", *Journal of King Saud University-Computer and Information Sciences*, vol. 32, no. 4, pp. 419-424, 2020.
[http://dx.doi.org/10.1016/j.jksuci.2019.03.006]

[44] M. Aria, and C. Cuccurullo, "bibliometrix: An R-tool for comprehensive science mapping analysis", *J. Informetrics*, vol. 11, no. 4, pp. 959-975, 2017.
[http://dx.doi.org/10.1016/j.joi.2017.08.007]

[45] N.J. Van Eck, and L. Waltman, "Software survey: VOSviewer, a computer program for bibliometric mapping", *Scientometrics*, vol. 84, no. 2, pp. 523-538, 2010.

CHAPTER 7

COVID-19 Forecasting using Machine Learning Models

Vishal Dhull[1,#], Sumindar Kaur Saini[1,*, #], Sarbjeet Singh[1] and Akashdeep Sharma[1]

[1] *University Institute of Engineering and Technology, Panjab University, Chandigarh, India*

Abstract: The global pandemic due to the novel coronavirus (2019-nCoV) is responsible for millions of deaths worldwide. It has been caused by a syndrome related to respiratory organs, namely Coronavirus 2 (SARS-CoV-2), believed to have originated in Wuhan. Pattern analysis of the spread of COVID-19 is critical to provide proper guidelines to the public for their safety and health. The epidemiological dataset of coronavirus is used to forecast a future number of cases using various machine learning models and validated concerning the complete count of globally present cases. The dataset has been compiled using different datasets from Johns Hopkins University, National Health Commission, and the World Health Organization (WHO). The prediction has been able to observe the total cases in 222 nations globally. This paper presents a comparative study of the existing forecasting machine models used on the COVID-19 dataset to predict worldwide growth cases. The machine learning models, namely polynomial regression, linear regression, and Support vector regression (SVR), were applied to the dataset that was outperformed by Holt's linear and winter model in predicting the worldwide cases. However, Facebook's Prophet Model gave the best results. The value of the Root means square error (RMSE) was observed to be 5387.741339, with the Mean absolute percentage error (MAPE) value and correlation coefficient calculated to be 0.0020933 and 0.99998, respectively. Hence, Facebook's Prophet Model is the most promising approach and this prediction of COVID-19 cases can be used for the risk evaluation and safety measures to be taken in corresponding areas globally.

Keywords: Confirmed Cases, COVID-19, Coronavirus, Forecasting, Pneumonia.

INTRODUCTION

The outbreak in December 2019 of a deadly virus similar to pneumonia leads to a life threat globally. The main cause was identified as the seventh member of Ortho Coronaviridae subfamily different in structure from the SARS-CoV and

---
* **Corresponding author Sumindar Kaur Saini**: University Institute of Engineering and Technology, Panjab University, Chandigarh, India; E-mail: sumindarkaursaini@gmail.com
\# These authors have equal contribution.

Vaishali Mehta, Dolly Sharma, Monika Mangla, Anita Gehlot, Rajesh Singh and Sergio Marquez Sanchez (Eds.)

MERS-CoV called coronavirus (2019- nCoV) [1]. On 12, December 2019, the Chinese Center for Disease Control and Prevention (CDC) recognized a recently developed pneumonia structure with the help of cell cultures and molecular techniques followed by testing that concluded that it was a non-SARS nCoV. This newly developed Coronaviridae family is responsible for causing colds and diseases such as diarrhea as it consists of big-sized, single as well as plus-stranded RNA viruses [2, 3]. The first case of coronavirus was reported in Wuhan's wet market, a province in Hubei, China, in December 2019, and the number of cases is increasing rapidly globally since then [4], causing the virus to spread from one human to another [5, 6]. The deadly virus was renamed Coronavirus disease (COVID-19), and the world-renowned World Health Organization (WHO) gave this name and on March 11, 2020, it was declared a global pandemic. The WHO released the situation report-106 on May 5, 2020, according to which there are 3,517,345 COVID- 19 cases and 243,401 deaths globally. There were nearly 84404 cases and 4643 deaths in China. With an increasing number of cases every day, WHO has declared COVID-19 as a global pandemic; hence it is vital to analyze the data and patterns to forecast the spread of the virus in a particular region and globally. This will help create awareness among the people, and the governments can take strategic measures to avoid its spread on a larger scale. It can lead the health and security officials to research more in this area to mitigate the lifetime effects of COVID-19. The total number of confirmed cases of COVID-19 from 29 April 2020 to 5 May 2020 have been highlighted in Fig. (**1**) [7].

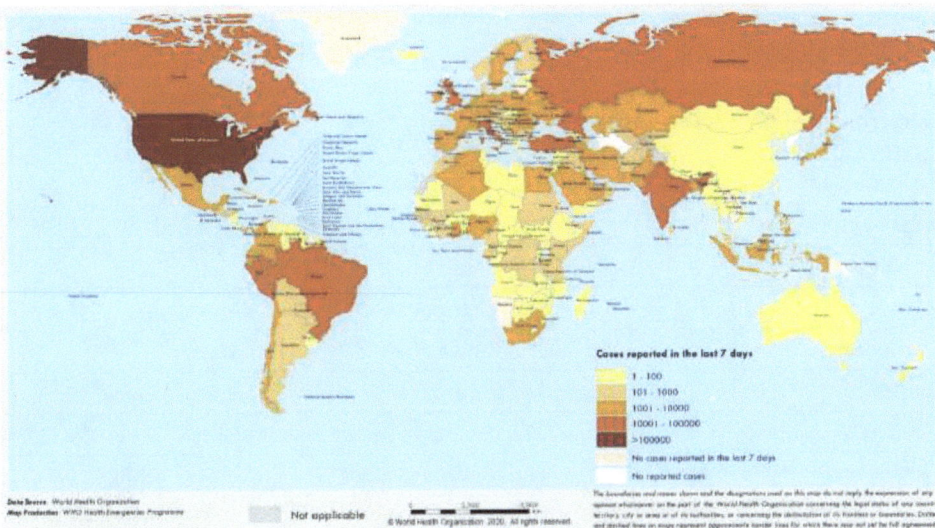

Fig. (1). Confirmed COVID-19 cases from 29 April 2020 to 5 May 2020 [7].

The term forecasting refers to a technique dependent on historical information for predicting the outputs to find out trends for the future. It is an essential task in data science. A particular company's goals or disease prevention depends on knowledge used for better forecasts [8]. A significant part of forecasting is to properly observe the time series for making reliable predictions enough for a better consideration of confirmed COVID-19 cases.

The following section describes the dataset of 222 nations used for the forecasting and various methodologies used to foretell the count of COVID-19 cases worldwide.

Dataset Description

The time prediction using the models of machine learning was observed using an open dataset of 2019-nCoV that has been contributed by Johns Hopkins University as a dashboard. It gathered nearly 222 nations' information and represented it in the form of 8 columns, and 21866 rows and graphs of total confirmed COVID-19 cases, recovery cases, deaths, mortality, and recovery rate. The university has also made this data accessible to the public in the form of Google sheets that have timely updates on the different cases [9]. The researchers could utilize this data for the analysis of the pattern through which the novel coronavirus spread. The prediction algorithms used the dataset from 22 January 2020 to 5 May 2020 for training. The dataset has been taken from the following link: https://doi.org/10.1016/S1473-3099(20)30120-1. Table **1** represents the column-wise description of the novel coronavirus dataset used for the prediction of COVID-19 cases.

Table 1. Description of the novel coronavirus dataset.

S.No.	Index Number
Observation Date	Date of the observation of COVID-19 cases
Province	Province/Location of observation
Country	Country or region of COVID-19 observation
Last Update	Time at which the data is last updated
Confirmed	Count of cases that are confirmed for a province or country.
Deaths	The number of deaths for a province.
Recovered	The number of recovered cases for a province or country.

Literature Review

Several pieces of literature in writing have suggested the utilization of machine learning models for COVID-19 pandemic forecast [10 - 18]. Tandon *et al.* [10] analyze the exhibition of seven distinctive time series models; ARIMA (An autoregressive integrated moving average), SES (Simple exponential smoothing), Holt's linear trend, moving average, S-curve pattern, quadratic pattern, and linear pattern. The consequences of the examination show that ARIMA has the best performance among all the thought about models. Elmousalami and Hassanien [11] assess and think about the presentation of the moving normal, weighted moving normal, and SES models for the worldwide COVID-19 diseases. The author infers that the SES is the most precise model for the COVID-19 estimate. Petropoulos and Makridakis [12] assess the performance of Holt's straight pattern model to Fig. the worldwide affirmed cases. The exhibition of LSTM is assessed by [13] to conjecture the COVID-19 transmission in Canada. Yonar *et al.* [14] gauges and conjectures the quantity of COVID-19 plague instances of G8 nations utilizing ARIMA and Brown/Holt direct remarkable smoothing strategies. Jiang *et al.* [15] assess the exhibition of ARIMA and earthy colored straight pattern models to anticipate the transmission of COVID-19 in China. Panda [16] gauges the quantity of COVID-19 diseases with 95% certainty stretch for various states in India utilizing Holt-Winters' Additive and ARIMA models.

A study analyzing the effects of COVID 19 based on Likely Positive Cases and fatality in India during and after the lockdown period from 24 March 2020 to 24 May 2020 by Vatsal Tulshyan, Dolly Sharma, Mamta Mittal [19] infers that the Prophet model performs better as far as the accuracy on the genuine information is concerned. Forecast portrays that the absolute cases were rising during the lockdown, however in a controlled way with an exactness of 87%. After the unwinding of lockdown controls, the forecasts have demonstrated an obnoxious circumstance with a precision of 60%.

A fundamental econometric model is proposed by Benvenuto D, Giovanetti M, Vassallo L, Angeletti S, and Ciccozzi M. *et al.* [20], which might be entirely significant for anticipating the spread of COVID-2019. They did autoregression incorporated moving average (ARIMA) model expectation on Johns Hopkins epidemiological data to foresee the epidemiological model of the predominance and occurrence of COVID-19. For additional examination or future thought, the case definition and data grouping must be looked after consistently (Benvenuto *et al.* 2020). By Duan X and Zhang X. *et al.* [21], the recently affirmed instances of COVID-19 in Japan and South Korea from January 20, 2020, to April 26, 2020, are assembled every day. We know about the way that programmed relapse coordinated moving normal (ARIMA) models, examined two snippets of data, gathered and anticipated that there would be new affirmed cases each day during the 7 days from April 27, 2020, to May 3, 2020. Essentially, the assurance result and two kinds of data assortment are likewise given (Duan and Zhang 2020). Ilie OD, Cojocariu RO, Ciobica A, Timofte SI, Mavroudis I, and Doroftei B [22]. proposed an autoregressive incorporated moving normal (ARIMA) model was set up and used to foresee the epidemiological examples of COVID-19 in the three nations of Ukraine, Romania, the Republic of Moldova, Serbia, Bulgaria, Hungary, the USA, Brazil, and India. To improve the precision, the principle day by day data of COVID-19 from March 10, 2020, to July 10, 2020, was gathered from the official locales of the Romanian government (GOV.RO), the World Health Organization (WHO), and the European Center for Disease Control and Prevention (ECDC) site. Patil *et al.* [17] gauged the pinnacle COVID-19 cases utilizing direct pattern and SSM models for Brazil, the US, and India. Ahmar and Val [18] proposed the sutte-ARIMA model for gauging COVID-19 cases in Spain and contrasted the exhibition and that of ARIMA.

Methodology

Various methodologies can be used to forecast COVID-19 cases with increased accuracy compared to the state-of-the-art. The section given below focuses on various paradigms used to predict confirmed COVID-19 cases globally.

Linear Regression (LR)

Sir Francis Galton proposed linear regression in 1894. This method establishes a relationship between a dependent variable, a scalar response, and one or multiple independent variables known as explanatory variables. There are certain linear predictor functions used to model the parameters from the dataset that leads to the formation of linear models. The conditional mean, median, or some other quantile is used to observe the values of independent variables. It is based on the conditional probability distribution of the results obtained in the prediction. It is similar to a statistical test applied on a definite dataset and allows control over the effect of the variables in understanding the relationship between them, unlike Fisher's exact test, Chi-square, analysis of variance (ANOVA), and t-test making it useful in biomedical research. The risk factors for a particular disease can be evaluated accurately using physical and biological situations [23]. The analysis of correlation measures the strength of dependency between the required variables. It consists of a dimensionless number "r", which gives a value of -1 if the relationship is negative and gives +1 if the relationship is positive.

$$Y = mx + c \qquad \qquad (1)$$

The linear regression analysis is represented by equation 1 where a dependency between the x, an independent variable, and y, a dependent variable, has been given by the line of best fit.

The Fig. (**2**) represents the line of linear regression among the data points that have been drawn in comparison of the independent variable with the dependent variable on the x and y-axis, respectively.

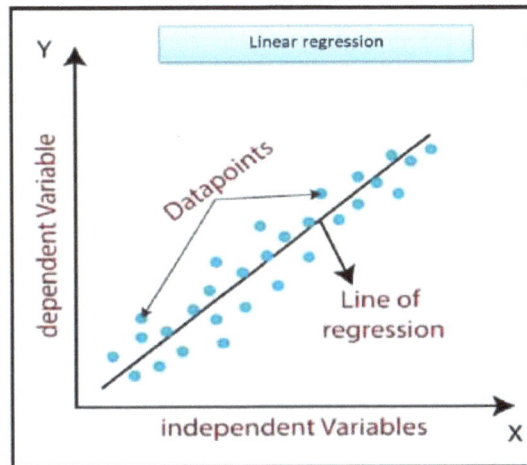

Fig. (2). The plot of linear regression.

Polynomial Regression (PR)

Polynomial regression represents the association between the x and y representing the non-dependent and dependent value, respectively, concerning the representation of nth degree polynomial in x. Hence it is an example of the analysis of polynomial regression. It can fit a relationship whose nature is non-linear and is given as the output of x and its mean value corresponding concerning y, represented by E(y|x). It works linearly in the statistical estimation problem as the regression function $E(y|x)$ represents the output as linear for unknown features whose estimation occurs with respect to the initial information. The polynomial regression is regarded as one of the special cases of multiple linear regression [24]. Equation 2 represents.

$$y = a + b_1x + b_2x^2 + \ldots + b_nx^n + e \qquad (2)$$

Here y is the dependent variable, a is intercept at y, e is the error rate and b is the slope.

Fig. (**3**) shows polynomial regression among the data points between the dependent and independent variables on the y and x-axis, respectively.

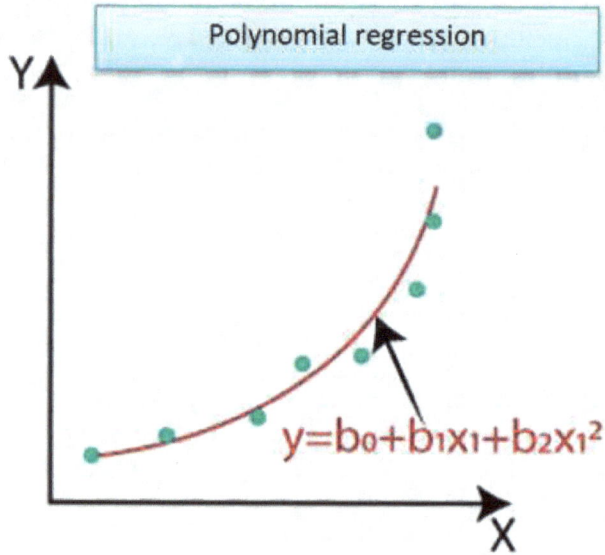

Fig. (3). The plot of polynomial regression.

Holt's Linear Model Prediction

In 1957, Holt gave a method to predict the data according to features using exponential smoothing. It used a forecast equation as represented in equation 3 along with the two smoothing equations, the first one was for the level as represented in equation 4 followed by another equation for trend as represented in equation 5.

$$\text{Forecast equation: } y_{t+h\,|t} = L_t + hb_t \qquad (3)$$

$$\text{Level equation: } L_t = y_t + (1-\alpha)\,(L_{t-1} + b_{t-1}) \qquad (4)$$

$$\text{Trend equation: } b_t = \beta^*(L_t - L_{t-1}) + (1-\beta^*)\,b_{t-1} \qquad (5)$$

In these equations, L_t represents the measurement of the forecasting series for the time at a particular time represented by t, b_t represents the trend estimation (given by the slope) of a particular forecasting series at a particular time given by t is considered to be the smoothing parameter for the level, and its value should lie between 0 and 1 inclusively, whereas β * represents the trend parameter for smoothening and its value also lies in the range [0,1] inclusively.

As per the equation, Lt is the weighted average value given by y_t, and L_{t-1}+ bt-1 represents the one-step-ahead training forecast for the required time t. According to the trend equation, the bt is the weighted average of the estimated trend at the time "t" hence this factor value is based on the L_t- Lt-1 and bt-1. The forecast function represents the trending and the h-step-ahead forecast is the same as the last level that is estimated and added to the h times the last estimated trend value [25 - 27]. The forecast equation is a linear function of "h" as represented in Fig. (**4**).

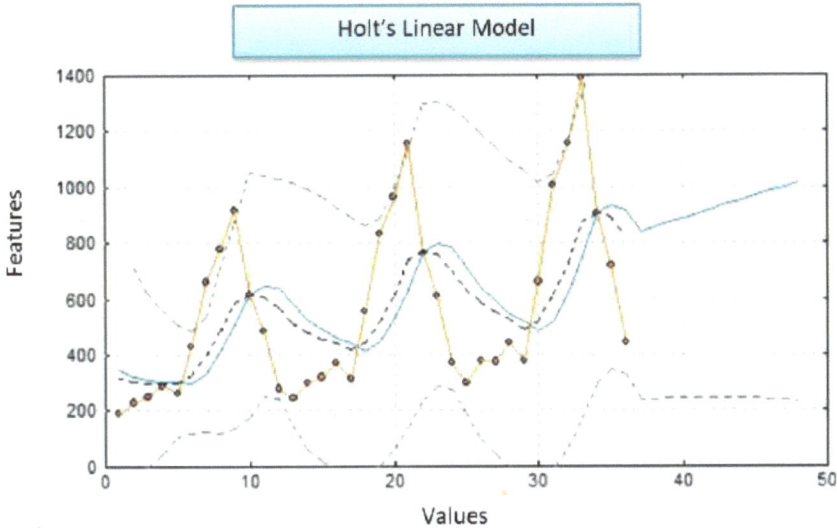

Fig. (4). The general depiction of Holt's Linear Model where the solid yellow line represents the "Level", the solid blue represents the forecast of the model and the dotted blue line represents the limiting level set as 95.0% of the model.

Holt's Winter Model Prediction

The methodology of Holt was extended by Holts and Winters in 1957 and 1960 respectively to observe the results according to seasonality. This methodology consisted of the forecast equation and another three smoothing equations - the first was for the level L_t, the second was for the trend $b$and the third was for the seasonal component $s$and they had three smoothing parameters-t t α, $\beta^*$and γ. The seasonality frequency referred to the total number of seasons was represented by m. This methodology has two variations, namely additive paradigm and multiplicative paradigm. The additive paradigm represents that throughout the observed series, variations (seasonal) are constant and the multiplicative paradigm represents a proportional change in series levels. The seasonal parameter is observed in the format of absolute terms in the scale of observed series whereas the series is adjusted seasonally by subtraction of seasonal component given in the level equation that forms a part of the additive methodology, whereas, in the multiplicative paradigm, there is a relative representation of the seasonal feature where there is an adjustment in the observed series according to the result of the division by the calculated seasonal component. Each year, this season component adds up to approximately give a value m.

$$y_{t+h|t} = L_t + hb_t + s_{t+h-m(k+1)} \tag{6}$$

$$L_t = \alpha(y_t - s_{t-m}) + (1-\alpha)(L_{t-1} + b_{t-1}) \tag{7}$$

$$b_t = \beta^*(L_t - L_{t-1}) + (1-\beta^\square)b_{t-1} \tag{8}$$

$$s_t = \gamma(y_t - L_{t-1} - b_{t-1}) + (1-\gamma)s_{t-m}, \tag{9}$$

The component form of the additive method is represented in equations 6,7,8 and 9 where the k represents the integer part of $(h-1)/m$, that is important as it is responsible for estimating the seasonal indices that are used for forecasting by calculating the values from the samples of the final year. The weighted average between the non-seasonal forecast and the seasonally adjusted observation for a particular time t is represented by the level equation. The weighted average between the seasonal index of the same season of the previous year and the current seasonal index [27 - 29].

Autoregressive (AR) Model

As per the AR model, the output variable is dependent linearly on older values and on some imperfect terms that is predictable. The autoregressive (AR) model equation is in the form of a stochastic difference equation wherein a recurrence relation explains the relation between the input and output variables [30, 31]. The autoregressive model of order m, namely AR(m), has the general form which is represented in equation 10.

$$Z_t = \varphi_t + \varphi_1 Z_{t-1} + \varphi_2 Z_{t-2} + \cdots + \varphi_m Z_{t-m} + \varepsilon_t \tag{10}$$

Here, Z = Response variable at time t,

$Z_{t-1}, Z_{t-2}, \cdots, Z_{t-m}$ = Response variable at time lags t-1,t-2....until.., t-m, respectively,

$\varphi_0, \varphi_1, \varphi_2, \cdots, \varphi_m$ = Coefficients to be estimated, and

ε_t = Error term at time t.

Moving-average Model (MA model)

This model defines dependency among the variables wherein the output variable is linearly dependent on the current and previous values of an imperfectly predictable term that is referred to as the stochastic term [30, 32]. A moving average model of order n, namely MA(n), which has the general form, is represented in equation 11.

$$Y_t = \mu + \varepsilon_t - \theta_1\varepsilon_{t-1} - \theta_2\varepsilon_{t-2} - \cdots - \theta_n\varepsilon_{t-n} \qquad (11)$$

Where,

Y_t = Response (dependent) variable at time t,

μ = Constant mean of the process,

$\theta_1, \theta_2, \cdots, \theta_n$ = Coefficients to be estimated,

ε_t = Error term at time t,

$\varepsilon_{t-1}, \varepsilon_{t-2}, \cdots, \varepsilon_{t-n}$ = Error terms at different previous time period that are assimilated in the response variable Y

ARIMA Model

Denoted by ARIMA (m, d, n), it is a model used for forecasting *via* time series, also known as the "Autoregressive Integrated Moving Average Model". It provides various complementary approaches to the problem. These models describe the autocorrelations in the data. In the ARIMA (m, d, n), m indicates the order of the autoregressive part, d represents the amount of difference, and n indicates the order of the moving average part. According to it, when the original series value is stationary,*i.e.*d=0 then the corresponding ARIMA models get reduced to the Autoregressive–moving-average(ARMA) models [30, 33]. It is an automatic process that is capable of identification of the optimal parameters for appropriate evaluation by the ARIMA model. The difference linear operator (Δ), is defined in equation 12.

$$\Delta Y_t = Y_t - Y_{t-1} = Y_t - BY_t = (1 - B)Y_t \qquad (12)$$

The stationary series W_t is obtained as the dth difference (Δd) of Y_t as represented in equation 13.

$$W_t = \Delta^d Y_t = (1 - B)^d Y_t \qquad (13)$$

The general form of the ARIMA (m, d, n) is represented in equation 14.

$$\varphi_m(B)\,(1 - B)^d Y_t = \mu + \theta_n(B)\varepsilon_t \qquad (14)$$

$$\text{or } \varphi_m(B)\, W_t = \mu + \theta_n(B)\varepsilon_t \qquad (15)$$

SARIMA Model

ARIMA methodology cannot support seasonality, leading to the advent of the SARIMA (Seasonal ARIMA) model that is dependent on seasonal differencing, which is close to regular differencing. In this methodology, the required value is subtracted from the previous season instead of subtracting the consecutive terms. This model is represented as SARIMA(m,d,n) x (M, D, N), where M, D, and N are SAR, in order of differencing (seasonal) and SMA terms, respectively, and 'x' is referred to as the series frequency [30, 34].

SVM Model

Support Vector Machines (SVM), is a type of machine learning model capable of proposing the decrease in the structural risk inductive principle to generalize the limited learning patterns. The Structural risk minimization (SRM) minimizes the empirical risk using the simultaneous attempts and the VC (Vapnik–Chervonenkis) dimension. SVM is a learning system that recognizes the subtle patterns in complex datasets using discriminative classification learning. It consists of two main categories *i.e.*, support vector regression (SVR) and support vector classification (SVC). It makes use of a feature space that is high dimensional and gives the results of functions responsible for prediction with an expansion over the subset created by the collection of the support vectors. The SVM model depends on the subset only that consists of training data and hence ignores all the points within the threshold ε [35]. Training an original SVR means solving as represented in equation 16.

$$\text{minimize } 0.5 * \|w\|^2$$
$$\text{subject to } |y_i - <w,x_i> - b| \leq e \tag{16}$$

x_i is an independent or training feature with a dependent value. The $<w, x_i> + b_i$ gives the value of the model's prediction for a given particular sample whereas, e is a threshold being a free feature. All predictions are in the given range e to give results as the prediction. The slack variables are added, allowing for approximations and errors if the above problem is infeasible. Here, Fig. (5) represents SVR's idea, where the inner green line is the hyperplane, with the outer two red lines being the decision boundaries. The main aim of SVR is to consider all points that are between these two decision boundary lines, and the hyperplane represents the line for best fit, having the maximum number of points [36].

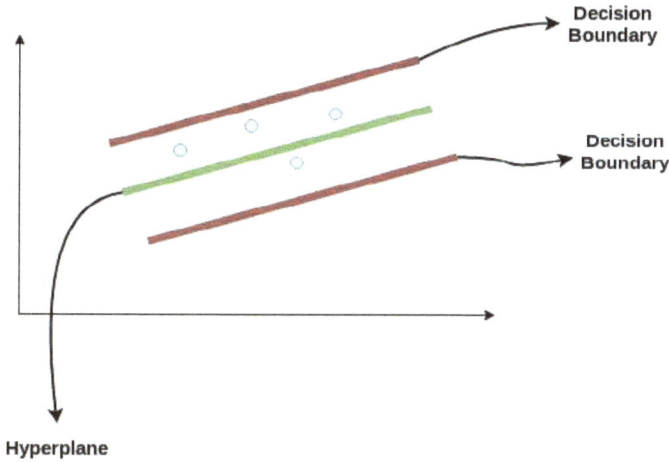

Fig. (5). The plot of SVM Regression Model.

Facebook's Prophet Model

It is used to address different issues to forecast the required output at a scale. It automates the business features of a dataset with simple and tunable paradigms. Also, it provides different backgrounds that can be used by the data analyst to predict the future with greater accuracy. The Prophet model forecasts the Time series data by calculating the additive model's output. The trends are non-linear and fit according to the yearly, monthly, weekly, and daily seasonality and holiday effect. A more extensive historical data and seasonal string effects are responsible for better results. A time-series forecast model is decomposable, given by Peters and Harvey in 1990 had three major parameters: seasonality, holidays, and trend. The performance is measured using the given equation 17.

$$y(t) = ghi(t) + s(t) + h(t) + \epsilon_t \qquad (17)$$

Here ghi(t) gives the trend function that models the changes which are non-periodic as per the values given by the time series. Facebook's prophet model utilizes two trend models, the first is a saturating growth model, and the second is a piecewise linear model that depends on the type of forecasting problem. The s(t) represents the periodic changes (*e.g.*, weekly and yearly seasonality) concerning the Fourier series, and h(t) represents the effects of holidays that occur on potentially irregular schedules over one or more days such as new product launch, Black Friday, Superbowl. The irreducible error term t represents any idiosyncratic changes that the model could not accommodate [37].

RESULTS AND DISCUSSION

Experimental Setup

The forecasting of COVID-19 was practically implemented in python 3.7.2 and importing its libraries, including the scikit and skimage. The system used to evaluate the performance consisted of the MSI mobile workstation with the model name MS-16P6. It has an NVIDIA Quadro P1000 graphics card and Intel Core i7 8th gen with the 8750H processor. The dataset was preprocessed and analyzed using the library dependent on the python, namely pandas NumPy, scikit-learn, statsmodels, Pmdrima. The graphs were visualized using Plotly, Seaborn, and Matplotlib.

Performance Metrics

MAPE

It denotes the "mean absolute percentage error" and is used for finding forecast accuracy of a particular paradigm used for forecasting. It is the percentage of the accuracy that is defined in equation 18.

$$\text{MAPE} = (1/n) * \Sigma(|T_t - F_t| \, / \, |T_t|) * 100 \tag{18}$$

here the actual value is represented by T_t and the forecast value is represented by F_t. The difference value is calculated between T_t and F_t and the resultant is divided by the T_t again. After this calculation, the absolute value is observed that is added for every calculated forecast point followed by division with the n that is the aggregate number of fitted calculated points, and then it is multiplied by 100% to calculate the final percentage error.

PPMCC

It denotes "Pearson's correlation coefficient," or "the correlation coefficient." PPMCC measures the extent of dependence between two quantities. Mathematically, it refers to the quality of least-squares fitting to older and original data. It is calculated by calculating the ratio percentage of the covariance between two variables of the dataset. After normalization to the square root of their variances and merely dividing the covariancecalculated between the variables by the multiplication of their deviations from means.

$$r = \frac{\sum (x - \bar{x})(y - \bar{y})}{\sqrt{\sum (x - \bar{x})^2 \sum (y - \bar{y})^2}}$$ (19)

where x and y calculate the appropriate value of PPMCC [38].

RMSE

It denotes "root mean square error" and is calculated by observing the standard deviation concerning the other numbers that are errors in the output given as prediction. These errors estimate the farness of the data points using the regression line. It calculates the exact concentration of the data around the best fit line. RMSE. It is represented in the given equation 20 as to where the T_t represents the actual value, and the Ft represents the forecast value.

$$RMSE = (1/n) * \Sigma (Tt - F_t)^2$$ (20)

Performance Analysis

The given section compares the different approaches used in the prediction of confirmed cases of COVID-19 globally. The whole data was segregated as the training and testing data. The given results/metric values are of the testing dataset and not of the whole data as per which there could be no inflation and henceforth, the predictive capabilities of the models can be effectively measured. The training dataset comprises observations from 2020-01-22 to 2020-04-29, while the testing comprises observations from 2020-04-30 to 2020-05-05. Then we used these models to forecast the confirmed case values from 2020-05-06 to 2020-05-23 for which there was no labelled dataset to find the accurate reading of the model performance and the models forecasted these results.

Linear Regression Prediction

Fig. (6) represents the contrast between the actual count of confirmed cases(in solid line) and the predicted count of cases (in dotted line) using a linear regression model. This model is falling apart, representing a lousy depiction of the forecasting results of COVID-19. As it is visible that the confirmed case trend is not linear, some non-linearity is added to the equation for a better result. The next model, named Polynomial regression, was used. The calculated root means squared error (RMSE) for the given graph of linear regression was 1237577.97; hence it became more important to compare it with other existing approaches.

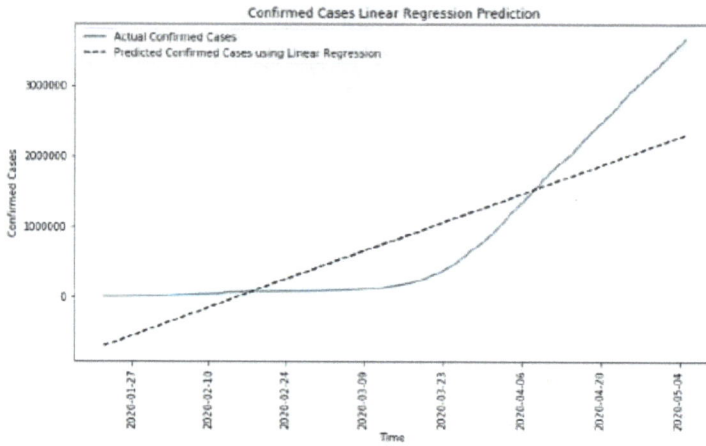

Fig. (6). Plot of confirmed cases using linear regression prediction.

Polynomial Regression Prediction

Fig. (**7**) shows the contrast between the actual count of confirmed cases (in solid line) concerning the count of cases (in dotted line) predicted using the Polynomial regression model. The linear equation was transformed into a second-degree polynomial equation by observing the linear regression model's shortcomings. The calculated root mean squared error (RMSE) for the given graph of polynomial regression was 37090.54, significantly better than the linear regression model. But RMSE value was still high, so we tried another regression technique that is SVM regression.

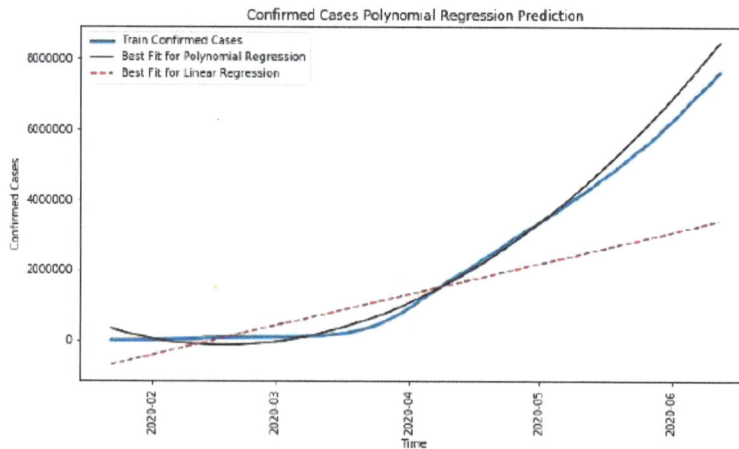

Fig. (7). Plot of confirmed cases using polynomial regression prediction.

Support Vector Machine(SVM) Regression Prediction

Fig. (**8**) shows the contrast between the actual count of confirmed cases (in solid line) and the count of cases (in dotted line) predicted using the SVM regression model. The calculated root mean squared error (RMSE) for the given graph of polynomial regression was 384166.81, which is higher than the Polynomial regression model. Since any regression model doesn't seem to minimize RMSE value, we moved to some time series models like Autoregressive and Moving-average, which are sub-parts of the ARIMA model.

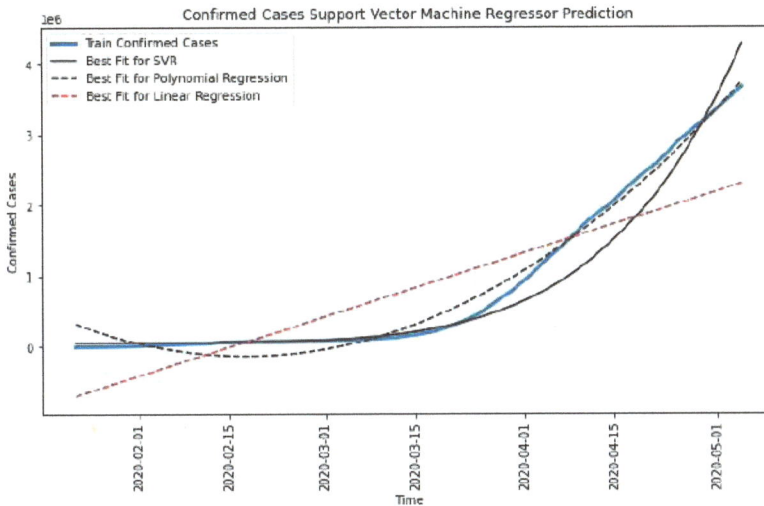

Fig. (8). Plot of confirmed cases using SVM prediction.

Auto-regressive(AR) Model Prediction

Fig. (**9**) shows the contrast of COVID-19 confirmed cases using Auto-regressive models. The blue line represents the number of cases per day, which increased exponentially from 23 March 2020 to 29 April 2020. Using it, the confirmed cases were predicted in the next days on testing data represented by the green line. It further showcases that there is an increase in these cases. The RMSE was calculated to be 26536.18, the value of MAPE was 0.007377, and the correlation in the actual and forecast value was observed to be 0.99928 for a given dataset.RMSE value decreases significantly here as compared to regression models. As the AR model only considers the older forecasts to predict future values, we moved to the MA model, which uses error terms of the previous forecasts to predict future ones.

Moving-average(MA) Model Prediction

Fig. (**10**) shows the prediction of COVID-19 confirmed cases using the Moving-average model. The blue line shows the number of cases per day, and those increased exponentially from 23 March 2020 to 29 April 2020 and using it, the confirmed cases were predicted in the next days on testing data that is represented by the green line, which showcases that there is an increase in these cases. The RMSE was calculated to be 17725.25, the value of MAPE was 0.004674, and the correlation for the actual and forecast value was observed to be 0.99939 for the given dataset. RMSE value decreases to a substantial amount in this model. Before moving to the ARIMA model, which is a combination of the AR and MA model, we evaluated the dataset concerning Holt's linear model, which uses trends in the dataset to forecast.

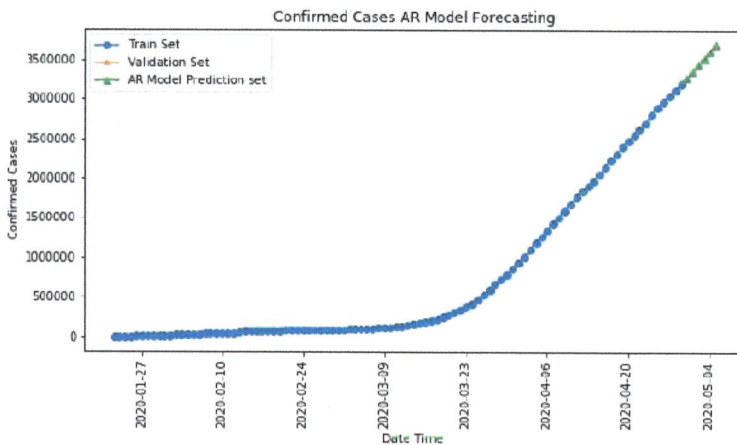

Fig. (9). Plot of confirmed cases using AR model prediction.

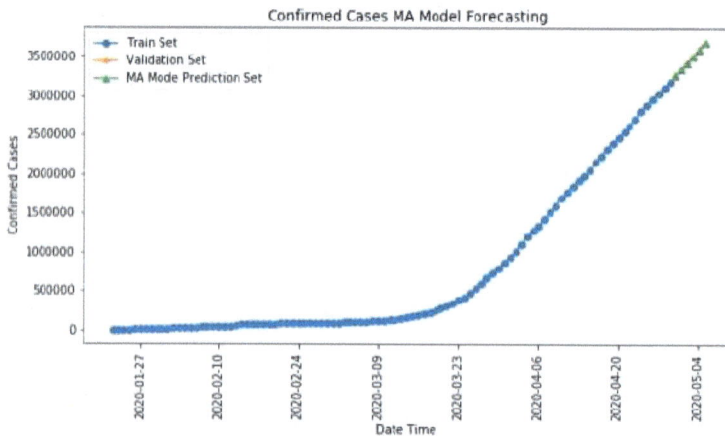

Fig. (10). Plot of confirmed cases using MA model prediction.

Holt's Linear Model Prediction

Fig. (**11**) represents the prediction of COVID-19 confirmed cases using Holt's Linear model. Blueline shows the number of cases per day. Those increased exponentially from 23 March 2020 to 29 April 2020. Using it, the confirmed cases were predicted in the next days on testing data represented by the green line that showcases an increase in these cases. The RMSE was calculated to be 17209.453044, the value of MAPE was 0.004896, and the correlation for the actual and forecast value was observed to be 0.99973 for the given dataset. RMSE value doesn't seem to decrease by a significant amount.

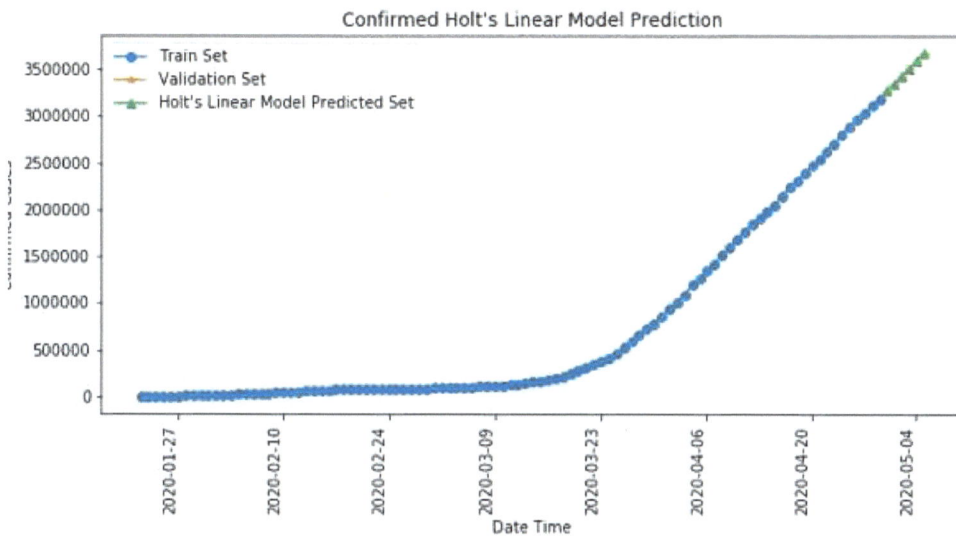

Fig. (11). Plot of confirmed cases using Holt's linear model prediction.

Holt's Winter Model Prediction

Fig. (**12**) represents the prediction of COVID-19 confirmed cases using Holt's Winter model. Blueline shows the number of cases per day, and those increased exponentially from 23 March 2020 to 29 April 2020, and using it, the confirmed cases were predicted in the next days on testing data that is represented by the green line that showcases that there is an increase in these cases. The RMSE was calculated to be 17367.85, the value of MAPE was 0.00456, and the correlation for the actual and forecast value was observed to be 0.99928 for the given dataset. Contrary to our assumption RMSE value was slightly higher than Holt's linear model, which shows a lack of seasonality in our data. So we moved to the ARIMA model, which considers both the AR and MA model factors.

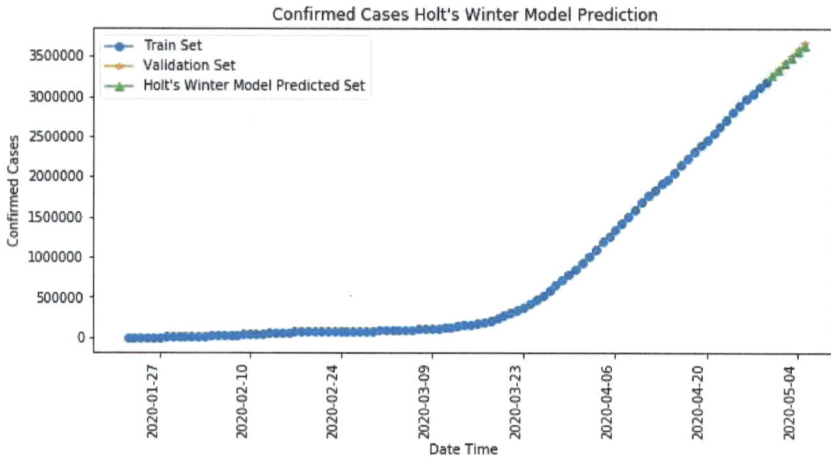

Fig. (12). Plot of confirmed cases using Holt's winter model prediction.

ARIMA Model Prediction

Fig. (**13**) represents the prediction of COVID-19 confirmed cases using the ARIMA model. The blue line shows the number of cases per day. Those increased exponentially from 23 March 2020 to 29 April 2020, and using it, the confirmed cases were predicted in the next days on testing data represented by the green line that showcases an increase in these cases. The RMSE was calculated to be 11360.64, the value of MAPE was 0.00289, and the correlation for the actual and forecast value was observed to be 0.99999 for the given dataset. As the ARIMA model result was much better than previous models, we tried another variation: the Seasonal ARIMA(SARIMA) model.

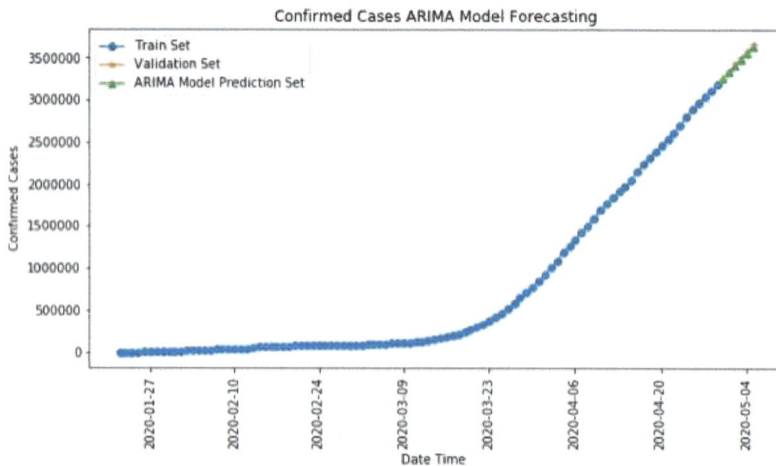

Fig. (13). Plot of confirmed cases using ARIMA model prediction.

SARIMA Model Prediction

Fig. (**14**) represents the prediction of COVID-19 confirmed cases using the SARIMA model, and the blue line shows the number of cases per day. Those increased exponentially from 23 March 2020 to 29 April 2020, and using it, the confirmed cases were predicted in the next days on testing data represented by the green line that showcases an increase in these cases. The RMSE was calculated to be 17725.25, the value of MAPE was 0.00467, and the correlation for the actual and forecast value was observed to be 0.99939 for the given dataset. RMSE value again increases, which shows a lack of seasonality in our data. Lastly, we tried Facebook's Prophet model to forecast.

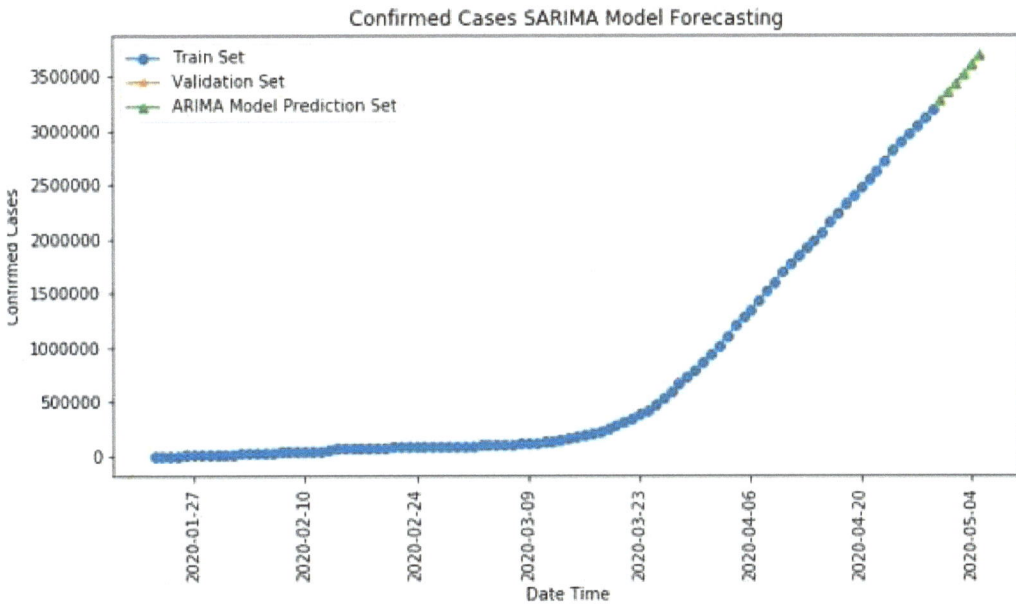

Fig. (14). Plot of confirmed cases using SARIMA model prediction.

Facebook's Prophet Model

Fig. (**15**) represents the prediction of COVID-19 confirmed cases using Facebook's Prophet model. The solid line till date 2020-05-05 represents the dataset we have taken (both training and testing), and the dotted line represents the prediction of the model on this dataset. In contrast, the graph from the date 6 May 2020 to 23 May 2020 represents the future forecast of confirmed value. The value of RMSE was 5387.74 on the testing data. The MAPE on the testing data was 0.00209, and the correlation for the actual and forecast value was observed to be 0.99998 for the given dataset. Fig. (**15**) estimated values and lower and upper bound of uncertainty interval with a faded shadow around the bold line in the graph's forecast portion where the confidence interval is 95%.

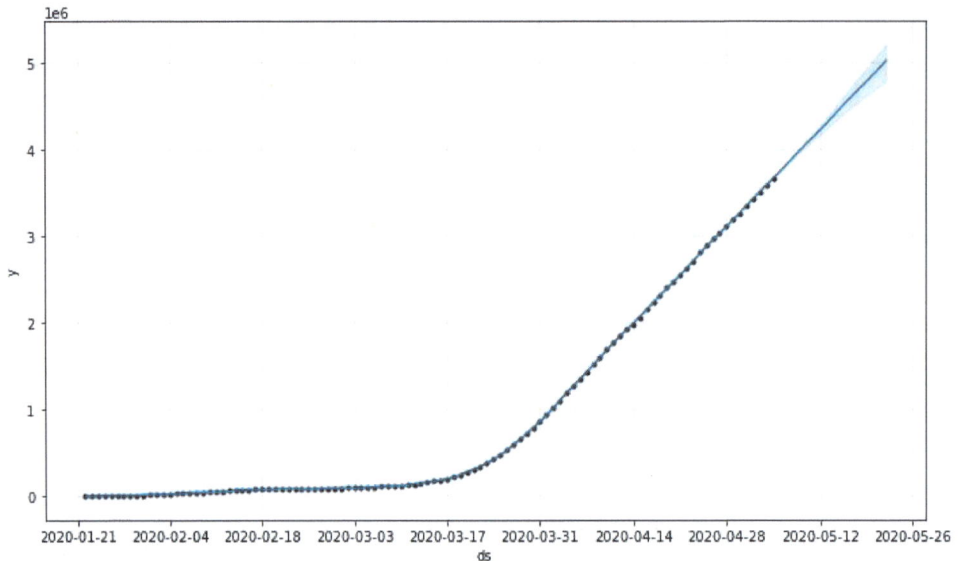

Fig. (15). Plot of confirmed cases using Facebook's Prophet model prediction.

Table **2** represents the performance metrics of machine learning models as RMSE, MAPE, and correlation coefficient. As per the RMSE values, Facebook's Prophet model shows the highest accuracy with a value of 5387.741339, followed by ARIMA and Holt's linear model with an RMSE value of 11360.649960 and 17209.453044, respectively. Also, the MAPE value of Facebook's Prophet model is the least at 0.0020933. The correlation coefficient value is the highest at 0.99998 hence making it the most optimal approach for predicting the confirmed COVID-19 cases.

Table 2. Contrast of RMSE, MAPE, and correlation coefficient for various models of machine learning.

S.No.	Model Name	Root Mean Squared Error	MAPE	Correlation Coefficient
1	Linear Regression (LR)	1237577.974585	0.35595	0.99973
2	Polynomial Regression (PR)	37090.546433	0.00784	0.99948
3	Support Vector Machine Regression (SVM)	384166.819490	0.096645	0.99871
4	Holt's Linear Model	17209.453044	0.004896	0.99973
5	Holt's Winter Model	17367.851329	0.00456	0.99928

S.No.	Model Name	Root Mean Squared Error	MAPE	Correlation Coefficient
6	Auto Regressive Model (AR)	26536.187827	0.00737	0.99982
7	Moving Average Model (MA)	17725.259671	0.00467	0.99939
8	ARIMA Model	11360.649960	0.00289	0.99990
9	SARIMA Model	17725.259671	0.00467	0.99939
10	Facebook's Prophet Model	5387.741339	0.0020933	0.99998

Table **3** represents the forecast of COVID-19 confirmed cases from 06 May 2020 to 22 May 2020 from our best model Facebook Prophet's. The table consists of Facebook Prophet's model prediction and Facebook'sProphet's upper bound, representing the uncertainty interval for this forecast.

Table 3. Prediction and upper bound of Facebook's Prophet model.

S.No.	Prophet's Prediction	Prophet's Upper Bound
2020-05-06	3745775.140590	3757012.191742
2020-05-07	3826338.855353	3840803.069866
2020-05-08	3910301.919808	3928724.501377
2020-05-09	3992235.533599	4020723.196769
2020-05-10	4070432.879944	4105565.321462
2020-05-11	4145860.667455	4196407.498191
2020-05-12	4223076.826318	4284198.750317
2020-05-13	4303202.285158	4377276.597762
2020-05-14	4383765.999921	4473180.695965
2020-05-15	4467729.064376	4567195.285497
2020-05-16	4549662.678168	4666101.938154
2020-05-17	4627860.024513	4756306.119997
2020-05-18	4703287.812024	4847705.398420
2020-05-19	4780503.970887	4946311.306752
2020-05-20	4860629.429727	5045620.131922
2020-05-21	4941193.144490	5150480.464364
2020-05-22	5025156.208945	5255454.328993

Figs. (**16 - 19**) are based on the performance of validation/testing dataset (2020-04-30 to 2020-05-05) for which there was validated/tested and supervised labeled data.

Fig. (**16**) represents the graph of RMSE values of three regression models. According to the analysis, the highest value is achieved by the linear regression model that is nearly equal to 1237577.974585 followed by Support vector machine (SVM) regression, whose value is nearly equal to 384166.819490 and the value of polynomial regression is the least according to this Fig. that is equal to 37090.546433. Hence out of these, polynomial regression presents better chances of predicting the confirmed COVID-19 cases in the future.

Fig. (**17**) represents the RMSE values of machine learning models in descending order. The AR model represents the highest value of RMSE at 26536.187827, followed by the MA model at 17725.259671 and the SARIMA model at 17725.259671. The least value of RMSE is represented by Facebook's Prophet model at 5387.741339, making it the most optimal machine learning model for time series for COVID-19 cases globally.

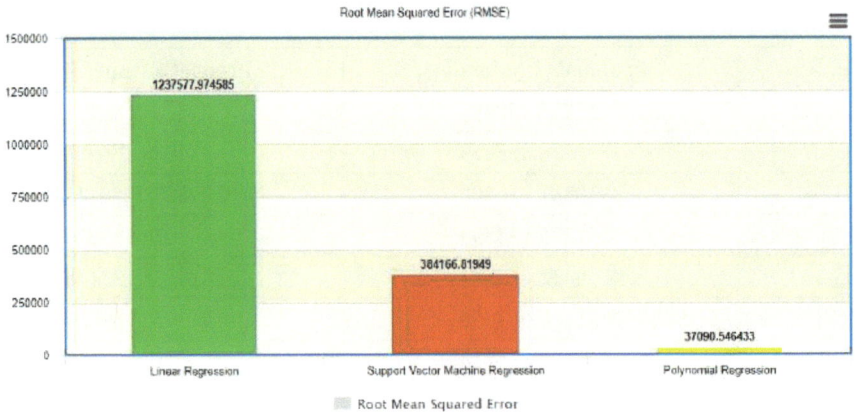

Fig. (16). Plot of RMSE of Regression models.

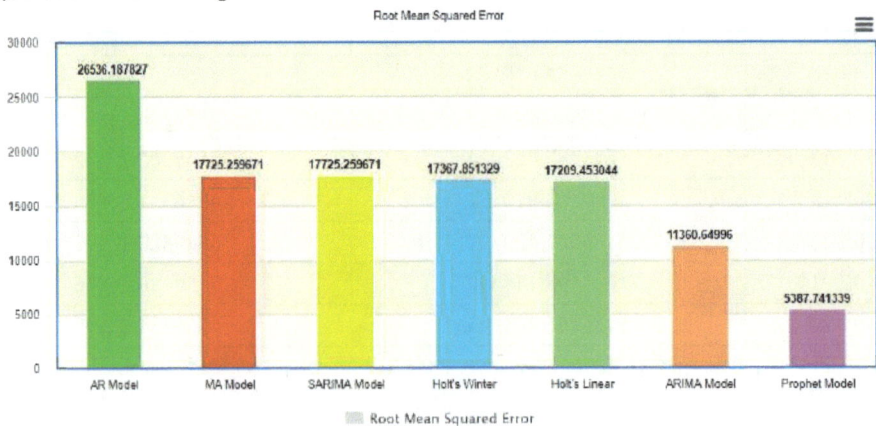

Fig. (17). Plot of RMSE of machine learning models.

Fig. (**18**) shows the comparison of MAPE values of different machine learning models. The highest value is represented by the linear regression followed by the SVM regression with 0.35595 and 0.096645. In contrast, models such as polynomial regression, AR model, Holt's linear, MA model, and SARIMA model show comparatively lesser values. However, Facebook's Prophet model shows the least value at 0.0020933, signifying that this model can achieve greater accuracy in predicting future cases according to the timeline.

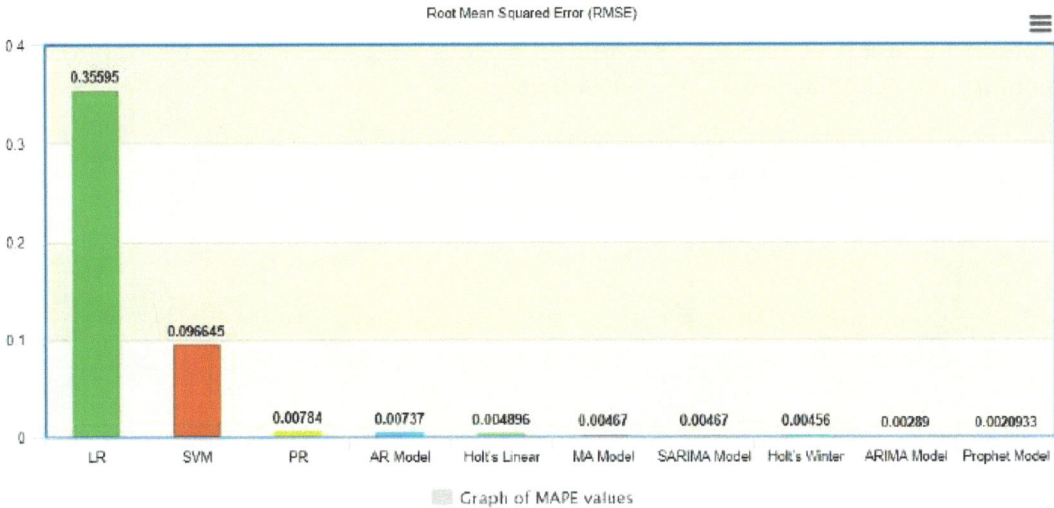

Fig. (18). Plot of MAPE values of machine learning models.

Fig. (**19**) represents the correlation coefficient values of machine learning models. According to it, the lowest value is represented by the SVM regression model at 0.99871, whereas the highest values are depicted by Facebook's prophet model at 0.99998. The other models as MA and SARIMA have the same value at 0.99939, the Holt's linear and LR have the same value at 0.99973. So, according to it, Facebook's prophet model is the most optimal machine learning model for time-based forecasting.

DISCUSSION

COVID-19 has been responsible for millions of deaths globally. The dataset used for the analysis is validated and machine learning models have been trained on it to analyze the growth and visualize the growth of coronavirus cases worldwide. The forecasting of the uprise in the cases in the future has been done using different machine learning models. The linear regression and polynomial regression were unable to predict the cases accurately and gave values of RMSE as 1237577.974585 and 37090.546433, respectively hence that led to the training of the dataset using Holt' linear and winter model followed by the AR, MA, ARIMA, and SARIMA model.ARIMA gave a better RMSE value of 11360.649960 which was better compared to the other approaches. However, Facebook's Prophet Model gave the minimum value of RMSE as 5387.741339 with MAPE and correlation coefficient as 0.0020933 and 0.99998, respectively. From the performance metrics, it has been analyzed that Facebook's Prophet Model is able to achieve the highest accuracy in predicting COVID-19 cases worldwide. This prediction helps in arousing the need for the COVID-19 pandemic controlling practices like testing, contact tracing, and quarantine in each country. These practices are essential to be followed so that there is no more new country emerging as the COVID-19 epicenter.

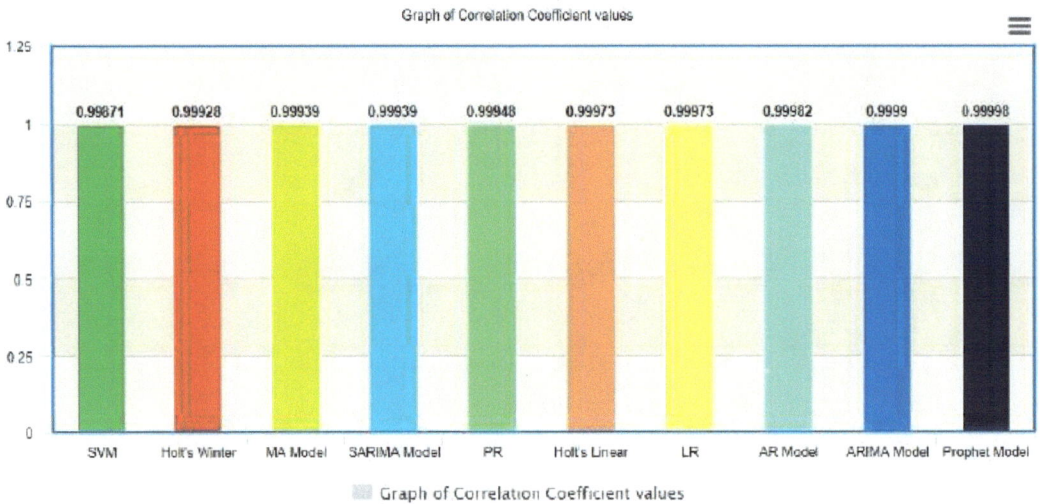

Fig. (19). Plot of correlation coefficient values of machine learning models.

CONCLUSION AND FUTURE SCOPE

COVID-19 is a global pandemic that is responsible for the increase in the mortality rate worldwide. Its spread from China to other parts of the world due to a lack of social distancing and safety measures is becoming more deadly and dangerous. Hence, the forecasting of the total count of x COVID-19 cases confirmed is necessary to take into account the different timely safety measures to be taken. This paper focuses on the comparative analysis of the different machine learning-based forecasting techniques used for the COVID-19 trend analysis. According to the results, Facebook's prophet model outperformed other machine learning models in detecting the growth of coronavirus cases globally. The time series based prediction was done based on polynomial regression(PR), linear regression (LR), Support Vector Machine Regression (SVM), Holt's Linear and winter Model, Auto-Regressive Model (AR), Moving Average Model (MA), ARIMA Model and SARIMA Model, however, the prophet model proved to increase the accuracy of detecting the total confirmed COVID-19 cases in nearly 222 nations globally. The future scope of this study is to forecast the cases using the deep learning methodologies that include recurrent neural network (RNN) and Long Short Term Memory (LSTM) networks to achieve higher accuracy for the detection of COVID-19 cases globally.

CONSENT OF PUBLICATION

Not applicable.

CONFLICT OF INTEREST

The author declares no conflict of interest, financial or otherwise.

ACKNOWLEDGEMENTS

Declared none.

REFERENCES

[1]   N. Zhu, D. Zhang, W. Wang, X. Li, B. Yang, J. Song, X. Zhao, B. Huang, W. Shi, R. Lu, P. Niu, F. Zhan, X. Ma, D. Wang, W. Xu, G. Wu, G.F. Gao, and W. Tan, "A novel coronavirus from patients with pneumonia in China, 2019", *N. Engl. J. Med.,* vol. 382, no. 8, pp. 727-733, 2020.
[http://dx.doi.org/10.1056/NEJMoa2001017] [PMID: 31978945]

[2]   C. Drosten, S. Günther, W. Preiser, S. van der Werf, H.R. Brodt, S. Becker, H. Rabenau, M. Panning, L. Kolesnikova, R.A.M. Fouchier, A. Berger, A.M. Burguière, J. Cinatl, M. Eickmann, N. Escriou, K. Grywna, S. Kramme, J.C. Manuguerra, S. Müller, V. Rickerts, M. Stürmer, S. Vieth, H.D. Klenk, A.D.M.E. Osterhaus, H. Schmitz, and H.W. Doerr, "Identification of a novel coronavirus in patients with severe acute respiratory syndrome", *N. Engl. J. Med.,* vol. 348, no. 20, pp. 1967-1976, 2003.
[http://dx.doi.org/10.1056/NEJMoa030747] [PMID: 12690091]

[3]   Y. Chen, Q. Liu, and D. Guo, "Emerging coronaviruses: Genome structure, replication, and pathogenesis", *J. Med. Virol.,* vol. 92, no. 4, pp. 418-423, 2020.
[http://dx.doi.org/10.1002/jmv.25681] [PMID: 31967327]

[4]   "World Health Organization", *Novel coronavirus—China,* 2020.

[5]   H. Lu, C.W. Stratton, and Y.W. Tang, "Outbreak of pneumonia of unknown etiology in Wuhan, China: The mystery and the miracle", *J. Med. Virol.,* vol. 92, no. 4, pp. 401-402, 2020.
[http://dx.doi.org/10.1002/jmv.25678] [PMID: 31950516]

[6]   W. Ji, W. Wang, X. Zhao, J. Zai, and X. Li, "Cross-species transmission of the newly identified coronavirus 2019-nCoV", *J. Med. Virol.,* vol. 92, no. 4, pp. 433-440, 2020.
[http://dx.doi.org/10.1002/jmv.25682] [PMID: 31967321]

[7]   World Health Organization, Coronavirus disease 2019 (COVID-19): situation report, 106.

[8]   S.J. Taylor, and B. Letham, "Forecasting at Scale", *Am. Stat.,* vol. 72, no. 1, pp. 37-45, 2018.
[http://dx.doi.org/10.1080/00031305.2017.1380080]

[9]   G. Lauren, Coronavirus COVID-19 Global Cases by Johns Hopkins CSSE. 2020.

[10]   H. Tandon, P. Ranjan, T. Chakraborty, and V. Suhag, Coronavirus (COVID-19): ARIMA based time-series analysis to forecast near future. 2020.

[11]   H.H. Elmousalami, and A.E Hassanien, Day level forecasting for Coronavirus Disease (COVID-19) spread: analysis, modeling and recommendations. 2020.

[12]   F. Petropoulos, and S. Makridakis, "Forecasting the novel coronavirus COVID-19", *PLoS One,* vol. 15, no. 3, p. e0231236, 2020.
[http://dx.doi.org/10.1371/journal.pone.0231236] [PMID: 32231392]

[13]   V.K.R. Chimmula, and L. Zhang, "Time series forecasting of COVID-19 transmission in Canada using LSTM networks", *Chaos Solitons Fractals,* vol. 135, p. 109864, 2020.
[http://dx.doi.org/10.1016/j.chaos.2020.109864] [PMID: 32390691]

[14]   H. Yonar, A. Yonar, M.A. Tekindal, and M. Tekindal, "Modeling and Forecasting for the number of cases of the COVID-19 pandemic with the Curve Estimation Models, the Box-Jenkins and Exponential Smoothing Methods", *Eurasian Journal of Medicine and Oncology,* vol. 4, no. 2, pp. 160-165, 2020.
[http://dx.doi.org/10.14744/ejmo.2020.28273]

[15]   B. Zhao, "Statistical analysis on COVID-19", *Annals of Clinical and Medical Case Reports,* vol. 3, no. 1, pp. 1-10, 2020.
[PMID: 32292527]

[16]   M. Panda, "Application of ARIMA and Holt-Winters forecasting model to predict the spreading of COVID-19 for India and its states", *medRxiv,* .
[http://dx.doi.org/10.1101/2020.07.14.20153908]

[17]   R. Patil, U. Patel, and T. Sarkar, "COVID-19 cases prediction using regression and novel SSM model for non-converged countries", *Journal of Applied Science, Engineering, Technology, and Education,* vol. 3, no. 1, pp. 74-81, 2021.
[http://dx.doi.org/10.35877/454RI.asci137]

[18]   A.S. Ahmar, and E.B. del Val, "SutteARIMA: Short-term forecasting method, a case: Covid-19 and stock market in Spain", *Sci. Total Environ.,* vol. 729, p. 138883, 2020.
[http://dx.doi.org/10.1016/j.scitotenv.2020.138883] [PMID: 32361446]

[19]   V. Tulshyan, D. Sharma, and M. Mittal, "An eye on the future of COVID-19: prediction of likely positive cases and fatality in India over a 30-day horizon using the Prophet model", *Disaster Med. Public Health Prep.,* vol. 16, no. 3, pp. 1-7, 2020.
[PMID: 33203489]

[20]   D. Benvenuto, M. Giovanetti, L. Vassallo, S. Angeletti, and M. Ciccozzi, "Application of the ARIMA model on the COVID-2019 epidemic dataset", *Data Brief,* vol. 29, p. 105340, 2020.
[http://dx.doi.org/10.1016/j.dib.2020.105340] [PMID: 32181302]

[21]   X. Duan, and X. Zhang, "ARIMA modelling and forecasting of irregularly patterned COVID-19 outbreaks using Japanese and South Korean data", *Data Brief,* vol. 31, p. 105779, 2020.
[http://dx.doi.org/10.1016/j.dib.2020.105779] [PMID: 32537480]

[22]   O.D. Ilie, R.O. Cojocariu, A. Ciobica, S.I. Timofte, I. Mavroudis, and B. Doroftei, "Forecasting the spreading of COVID-19 across nine countries from Europe, Asia, and the American continents using the ARIMA models", *Microorganisms,* vol. 8, no. 8, p. 1158, 2020.
[http://dx.doi.org/10.3390/microorganisms8081158] [PMID: 32751609]

[23]   K. Kumari, and S. Yadav, "Linear regression analysis study", *J. Pract. Cardiovasc. Sci.,* vol. 4, no. 1, pp. 33-36, 2018.
[http://dx.doi.org/10.4103/jpcs.jpcs_8_18]

[24]   J Fan, and I Gijbels, *Local polynomial modeling and its applications: monographs on statistics and applied probability 66.* CRC Press, 1996, pp. 1-360.

[25] E.S. Gardner Jr, and E. Mckenzie, "Forecasting trends in time series", *Manage. Sci.,* vol. 31, no. 10, pp. 1237-1246, 1985.
[http://dx.doi.org/10.1287/mnsc.31.10.1237]

[26] C.E. Holt, "Forecasting seasonals and trends by exponentially weighted averages (O.N.R. Memorandum No.52)", *Carnegie Institute of Technology, Pittsburgh USA,* 1957.
[http://dx.doi.org/10.1016/j.ijforecast.2003.09.015]

[27] *Encyclopedia of Production and Manufacturing Management. Springer.,* P.M. Swamidass, Ed., Online: Boston, MA, 2000, p. 274.
[http://dx.doi.org/10.1007/1-4020-0612-8_409]

[28] P.R. Winters, "Forecasting sales by exponentially weighted moving averages", *Manage. Sci.,* vol. 6, no. 3, pp. 324-342, 1960.
[http://dx.doi.org/10.1287/mnsc.6.3.324]

[29] RG Brown, *Exponential smoothing for predicting demand.*. Cambridge, Mass., Arthur d. little.

[30] R. Noche, and T. Nochai, "ARIMA model for forecasting oil palm price", *Proceedings of the 2nd IMT-GT Regional Conference on Mathematics, Statistics and applications,* pp. 13-15, 2006.

[31] T.C. Mills, *Time Series Techniques for Economists.* Cambridge University Press, 1990, pp. 1-388.

[32] W. Enders, "Stationary Time-Series Models", In: *Applied Econometric Time Series(Second ed.)* Wiley: New York, 2004, pp. 48-107.

[33] D. Asteriou, and S.G. Hall, "ARIMA models and the Box–Jenkins methodology", *Appl. Econ.,* vol. 2, no. 2, pp. 265-286, 2011.

[34] DB Percival, and AT Walden, "Spectral analysis for physical applications", *Cambridge university press,* 1993.
[http://dx.doi.org/10.1017/CBO9780511622762]

[35] D. Basak, S. Pal, and D.C.R. Patranabis, "Support Vector Regression, Neural Information Processing-Letters and Reviews",

[36] C. Cortes, and V. Vapnik, "Support-vector networks", *Mach. Learn.,* vol. 20, no. 3, pp. 273-297, 1995.
[http://dx.doi.org/10.1007/BF00994018]

[37] S.J. Taylor, and B. Letham, Forecasting at scale.PeerJPreprints5:e3190v2. 2017
[http://dx.doi.org/10.7287/peerj.preprints.3190v2]

[38] F. Galton, "Regression towards mediocrity in hereditary stature", *J. Anthropol. Inst. G. B. Irel.,* vol. 15, pp. 246-263, 1886.
[http://dx.doi.org/10.2307/2841583]

CHAPTER 8

An Optimized System for Sentiment Analysis using Twitter Data

Stuti Mehla[1,*] and **Sanjeev Rana**[1]

[1] *Department of Computer Science & Engineering, Maharishi Markandeshwar Deemed University, Mullana, Ambala, Haryana, India*

Abstract: Progression in technology and innovation increases internet users, who post their perspectives on social media platforms regarding any product or service. It brings forth significant terms, *i.e.*,"feedback of users," termed as sentiments and plays a substantial role for commercial organizations to analyze and find polarity related to their respective services. In Sentiment Analysis, the feature extraction phase is a crucial one that affects the entire process's processing. In the case of high dimensional Real-Time data, it leads to a sparse feature matrix and gives rise to steady processing. In this exploration work, we have proposed an Improved Optimized Feature Sentiment Classifier for Big Data (IOFSCBD) System, which deals with advancing the classifiers by giving improved values in each sort of dataset. Results show better execution of the Improved Optimized Feature Sentiment Classifier for Big Data system System.

Keywords: Ant Colony Optimization (ACO), BAT, Big Data, Natural Language Processing (NLP), Particle Swarm Optimization (PSO), Support Vector Machine (SVM).

INTRODUCTION

Sentiment Analysis is when clients' opinions are altogether considered and deduced to a conclusion, *i.e.*, the polarity of views. It is a significant field as it is straightforwardly or in a roundabout way related to customers and has the principal role in each NLP field, *i.e.*, marketing intelligence text classification. Sentiment Analysis combines two definitions, "Sentiment" and "Analysis."The word sentiment represents a feeling that can be euphoric, cofounding, irritating, and distracting and based on certain attitudes and opinions and abstract nature sentiments [1]. The view implies an emotion usually motivated by a person's perception. The psychologists attempt to present a multitude of emotions classified into six distinct classes: joy, love, fear, sadness, surprise, and anger. The

[*] **Corresponding author Stuti Mehla:** Department of Computer Science & Engineering, Maharishi Markandeshwar Deemed University, Mullana, Ambala, Haryana, India; E-mail: stutimehla@gmail.com

Vaishali Mehta, Dolly Sharma, Monika Mangla, Anita Gehlot, Rajesh Singh and Sergio Marquez Sanchez (Eds.)

emotions based on sadness and joy are experienced daily at different levels. We are mainly concerned with sentiment analysis detecting a positive or negative response or opinion [1]. The major significance of sentiment analysis is that every emotion linked to human perception forms an ingrained part of all humans which means that every human can generate different opinions acting as a tool for sentiment analysis. Sentiment analysis is defined as information extraction and natural language processing task to positively or negatively gain the writer's feelings based on requests, comments, and questions analyzing large datasets or documents. It means to define a writer's feeling about a specific topic based on the writer's own choice [2]. It models a branch that can provide a judgment over distinct fields. The measurement of sentiments is a biased technique with it is complex to achieve high accuracy of automated systems.

The term sentiment analysis (S.A.) is popularly known as opinion mining which is a process of emotion classification usually conveyed by a text that may be positive, negative, or neutral. The terms sentiment analysis and opinion mining can be used interchangeably [3]. This process is a part of text classification, which examines users' posts and concludes their sentiment. Positive sentiments concluded through words like 'wonderful, good', and negative sentiments concluded through 'rude and bad'. 'The Conclusion drawn by analyzing these posts can be useful for business purposes and marketing. This concept developed a unique research area for real-world text analysis problems. Lot of problems were encountered during sentiment analysis, *i.e.*, spam opinion or fake reviews, negation handling, domain independence and NLP overhead, Sarcastic or irony nature, and the last one is feature engineering. In Feature engineering, feature selection is a crucial stage where the main focus is to reduce the data dimensionality by discarding non-relevant features. In the latest research, lots of work was done using different feature selection protocols. In feature engineering, one of the significant problems is sparsity. This research work has developed a hybrid optimization system that deals with the same problem and utilizes machine learning algorithms.

LITERATURE REVIEW

The Literature review discusses the related work in the field of sentiment analysis. This section provides an insight into the origin, process, and different types of sentiment analysis, followed by the importance of social media in sentiment analysis. This section also shows the research done on semantic orientation also [4]. Sentiment analysis was introduced in 2001 when authors first used the process for finding the trend of small investors by using web sources. They designed a classification algorithm to classify the sentiments for better prediction. Some real-life categorization cases had the aim to find out the polarity. In such types of problems, non-topic-based categorization methods failed. Due to categorization methods, it can't extract the meaningful output, *i.e.*, data's polarity. Thus, the need for S.A. merges intending to remove the polarity of classified data. In this research work [5], the authors have supported the same experimentally. They have taken movie review data that gives text polarity by classification and sentiments of texts compared to the topic's sentiments. The objective was achieved using supervised techniques, *i.e.*, Naïve Bayes, Support vector machine, Maximum Entropy, and feature extraction techniques like unigram, bigram, and combinations of both used and analysis. Experimental results showed that SVM is a better classifier. After this study, S.A. termed a classification problem that uses preprocessors, classifiers, feature selectors, and many more to complete the task. After being termed as a classification problem, more other researchers define S.A.'s objectives and decide S.A.'s hierarchy, and the same is explained in the following research. One important aspect related to S.A. is its relationship with opinion mining. In this research work [6], authors dealt with the same issue and briefly described the three components of opinion mining, *i.e.*, source, evaluation, and view related to opinion. In this research work, the focus is given on the representation of text and experimentally proved that it plays a major role by changing text's overall polarity. Thus, the need for sentiment emerges to extract the polarity of categorized or classified data. The author started to use supervised learning-based Sentiment analysis techniques to access data for different applications, *i.e.*, user reviews about the movie. With the emergence of new terms and technologies, *i.e.*, Big Data, Hadoop, Machine learning, it comes into play. Many social media platforms, *i.e.*, Twitter, review the product on online shopping portals, blogs, datasets, review sites, microblogging act as a rich source of data. Researchers expand the idea of S.A. on a large scale for better classification. Many social media platforms release their APIs for researchers to carry out research. The following section discussed research work, levels, and social media used in sentiment analysis. In this research work, researchers discussed S.A. levels and termed these levels as document, sentence, and aspect [6]. In this research work, the authors described how the internet and social network came into existence and proved a rich sentiment analysis data source. A comparative analysis of different data sources is achieved by a comparative analysis explained in the following research work [7]. Researchers performed a comparison between different social media, and the result, shows Twitter emerged as the most popular one to carry out research.

Now the problem arose: collecting the data from different social media. When different social media platforms release their APIs, they can resolve this. API's provide a strong foundation by collecting massive online data. Research showsTwitter as the most popular social media platform. The following research gives a detailed study of APIs, . Twitter released three APIs termed REST API,

Search API, and Streaming API. All these APIs had different purposes, as in REST APIs, researchers and developers got data about status and information regarding the user. Simultaneously, Search APIs provided query-specific Twitter content and Streaming API collected real-time data. Experiments can't use whole large massive data because it contains meaningless spam, irrelevant opinions, and freely available like Tweet Corpus data. It contains large emoticons, and these types of features were not of any use. These issues became challenges for researchers [8 - 10]. While aiming at the issue mentioned earlier, Researchers worked using Twitter [11]. Researchers studied data sources like blogs, datasets, and review sites in this research work. Process of analysis extracted knowledge from data. In this, at different levels, analysis is done. Researchers also showed a comparative analysis of Naïve Bayes and SVM Classifiers. Authors took Dataset from Amazon containing electronic equipment reviews like cameras, laptops, and phones. This paper also discusses the importance of Twitter to get genuine results [12]. The Authors proposed a study on Twitter data, *i.e.*, mostly used social media platforms for carrying out the distinct types of analysis. Tweet-Rush helped to analyze twitter's data, and it further provides results making it useful for advertisers and marketers. Tweet Flow provides recommendations and calculated minimum and maximum values of tweet flow. It is observed how beneficial a user would be in tweet spread and obtained genuine results during analysis [13]. In this research work, researchers considered Twitter an impressive point to carry out different activities, *i.e.*, democratic event prediction, movie box-office, popularity linked with celebrities. S.A. represented one person's opinion or feelings to another domain type. In this research work, authors [13] made a review of sentiment analysis on Twitter-based data by describing and adopting various methodologies.The models reached an efficiency of about 85% to 90%.After performing lots of research on Twitter data, the semantic orientation concept comes, which is a major factor in deciding the polarity of input data. It is explained in the ensuing section [15]. When additives were added with phrases, this combination gave a different meaning: semantic orientation. The authors experimented with polarity detection using unsupervised learning algorithms. They used the dataset of movie reviews and automobiles and used two terms for positive and negative feedback of phrases, *i.e.*, recommended and not recommended, respectively. The proposed algorithm's core was the classification process that used PMI-IR (Pointwise Mutual Information-Information Retrieval) to determine the semantic orientation of phrases for giving reviews about movies and automobiles [14]. This research work provides deep knowledge of sentiment analysis. The research scope in sentiment analysis divided into two types one was data-oriented and the second was goal-oriented. In a data-oriented approach, S.A. performed on seven types of data *i.e.* related to society, security, travel industry, finance, medical industry, and entertainment industry, to find out polarity and make predictions and plans. This approach used data for different purposes like elections, education, healthcare, sales, stock market, and box office and make predictions related to terrorist attacks, disease, or climatic outbreaks. In the goal-oriented approach, S.A. is further divided into seven types according to the type of problem. The goal-oriented approach includes expertise and influential data to find out the truth by detecting spam, irony, and sarcasm nature of data, to find out emotions like stress, mood and depressions and cognitive behavior in specific domain and cross-domain. The above section gives a clear view on Sentiment Analysis as a classification problem, levels of S.A., data on which S.A. applied. In the next section, we will discuss the research and improvements done on tools and techniques used .A. Broadly techniques of S.A. are branched into three varieties machine learning techniques, lexicon-based techniques, and hybrid [15]. This section will discuss the latest research in the field of approaches applied in S.A. Machine learning techniques apply ML algorithms and linguistic features for text classification for labeled and unlabelled data. In contrast, the Lexicon-based approach uses precompiled sentiments using the dictionary-based and corpus-based approach and is generally used to find the opinion to analyze the text. The hybrid approach uses a combination of both [16]. This literature block provides a complete study and research on these three approaches. These approaches focus on predictions by using different types of concepts *i.e.* optimization, exploratory data analysis, and data mining. The basic idea of machine learning is to respond to computers' problems despite explicit programming. So there is a need to train and test the machine with the dataset and achieve intelligence from data. This approach is divided into supervised and unsupervised learning techniques. A mathematical model built using the supervised learning approach contains both inputs and outputs. Data on the applied approach is divided into two sections *i.e.*, training data and testing data. According to the objective function, data is trained. The rest of the data was tested with the objective of prediction. Supervised techniques can solve classification, regression, and active learning problems. Recommendation system, face and speaker verification, and ranking problems utilize supervised techniques. Supervised techniques work on labeled data and help the user predict patterns and relationships. There are different classifiers *i.e.* probabilistic classifier, linear classifier, decision tree, and rule-based classifier. On the contrary, Unsupervised techniques contain only input data to find the structures in data. Algorithms used in the unsupervised technique work on unlabeled data, and the basic aim is to find commonalities between data. Now, recent research work on machine learning techniques is explained below:

As S.A. is a popular method to analyze and provides insights to organizations to improve their strategies by providing deep knowledge of buyer's trends. This [17] discussed the same issue and uses the SVM classifier, based on state-of-the-art methodology, and classified into two types, where one detects the message sentiment such as SMS that presented a task at the message level and tweets. The other type detected the term-based sentiment in a task at the message level. In a competition of 44 teams, the submissions based on such a framework stood first in both classifier's tasks. The message-level task results obtained an F-score of 69.02 and 88.93 in a term-level task. The researcher simplemented a large variety of certain features such as semantic, sentiment, and surface-form features. Lexicons with two large sentiments of words were also generated. One occurred from tweets with emoticons and the other occurred from tweets with hashtags. Thus, the lexicon-based features provided5F-score points gain.Both of the systems were able to replicate using available resources freely. More research was discussed below related to business enhancement by capturing customers' sentiments. In this research, authors [18] suggested a new technique that was beneficial for organizations, having a sole purpose of reviewing the public's sentiments related to the brands. Twitter was used for carrying out the experiments. In this proposed work, lexicons explored an ensemble-based classifier. Ensemble classifier utilizes L.R., SVM, R.F., and N.B. and results show improved accuracy. In this research work [19] an approach was proposed using KNN, Naïve Bayes, and the modified version of k-means clustering. The modified version was more accurate than the KNN techniques and Naïve Bayes individually. There searchers obtained a classification accuracy of 91% overall over the 500 mobile review test-set. The algorithm running time is O(n+VlogV) for training where n represented the word number in a document and the V represents the vocabulary reduced size. It runs faster than machine learning algorithms *i.e.* Support Vector Machines and Naïve Bayes classification, which took more time in optimal converging regarding the set of weights. The accuracy level was comparable to the existing algorithms used for the classification of sentiments based on reviewing mobile. The sarcastic nature of customers also affects the overall polarity of sentiments. It plays a major role by changing the overall polarity of sentiments, so some of the research work is discussed below, aiming to the same issue. In this research, authors [20] proposed an algorithm of Machine Learning *i.e.* Naïve Bayes and it performed the analysis of customer sentiments, including sarcastic comments. It worked well for the comments of the negative type. The problems generally arose when the tweets were sarcastic or ironic had difficult context or reference. To improve the evaluation accuracy, the researchers required something to take the references and context into consideration. They further tried to build a network *i.e.* LSTM network, and the results were benchmarked as compared to the Natural Language Tool Kit machine learning implementation. Authors [21] presented an approach for sentiment classification using a classifier named k-nn classifier, and the method used for feature selection is bag-of-words. The result indicates that the k-nn approach provided a good high form of accuracy compared to sentiment classification-based polarity. The results obtained present that the k-nn classifier outperforms well for analyzing sentiments. The results have also shown that the classifier along with bag-of-words-based feature selection, outperforms well dependent over polarity-based sentiment classification. Authors [22] proposed a system that targets the extraction of tweets to classify them as negative or positive with the help of techniques based on machine learning. Finally, it is subjected to techniques based on evaluating the performance. In a television broadcast dated November 8, 2016, Prime Minister Modi declared that all the currencies of 500 and 1000 rupee notes were illegal, which was a step to curb fake notes and black money. Considering the demonetization dataset was extracted from Twitter-based data using Twitter API, Scikit-learn performed preprocessing and NLTK, which was further subjected to execute algorithms of classifiers *i.e.* Support Vector Machines, Naive Bayes, and Logistic Regression. We will be discussing different researches having different aims, but the main objective is to enhance the machine learning techniques. Authors [23] proposed a novel perspective and cast the issue of domain adaptation as a projecting task of embedding. The proposed model has taken the two mono-domain input embedding spaces and it learned the projection to a space of bi-domain type that jointly optimized in two basic ways. The one was to project across the domains and these condone was the sentiment prediction. The researchers performed the adaptation of domain type experiments on twenty source-target domain type pairs for classification of sentiment and it reported the novel type state-of-the-art resulted over eleven of the domain pairs that include the adaptation of Amazon domain datasets and the datasets of SemEval 2013 and 2016. The experiment analysis has shown that the model outperformed well compared to existing approaches. This research paper [24] proposed a design for sentiment analysis to detect the negative and positive user views. A Naïve Bayes classifier in addition to n-gram method was used. It performed the overall analysis over the whole user-based sentence. The complete work was implemented using Hadoop Ecosystem to perform the large data-parallel processing operation.

The lexical approach focus on the construction of meaningful words termed lexical chunks. It calculates the sentiments by considering the semantic orientation of words present in the text. The lexicon-based approach uses precompiled sentiments using the dictionary-based and corpus-based approaches and is generally used to find the opinion to analyze the text.

In the following section, the recent researches in the field of lexicon approaches are explained [25]. In this approach, a score was given to lexicons. Lexicons were termed as a collection of words. According to the lexicons ' score, these words were distinguished as positive, negative, and neutral. These individual scores were combined and the highest score showed the overall polarity of text. In this paper did a comparative analytical study of techniques, using SA [26]. Feature Extraction is important in S.A. ITD and ITS were two feature factors considered when weights were applied to features in this research work. ITD reflects the value that tells about a term's importance in a document and uses it to find term frequency. Researchers have used three mathematical methods which were favorable while performing retrieval of information, classification of text, and clustering in text mining. ITS stand for the importance of terms for expressing features and it was a weighting method based on a statistical approach and worked on learning. In this work, authors used ITS compared to IDF with term frequency(T.F.). Researchers defined seven statistical feature selection methods in ITS, which were as follows: first was D.F. for document frequency, the second was I.G. for information gain, third was MI for mutual information, OR for odds ratio, CHI for chi-square statistic, WLLR for Weighted Log-Likelihood Ratio and WFO for Weighed Frequency and Odds. So term weighting was important in the feature extraction phase. In this paper, the authors proposed supervised techniques using ITD and ITS and movie data for experiment purposes and scored an accuracy of 88.5%, 88.7%, and 88.0% [27]. When adverbs and adjectives were added with review, they showed different sentiment polarities. Researchers proposed a link analysis method termed propagation, which computes each adverb's strength and adjective. The propagation method was divided into two words where the positive word propagation method computes positive strength and the negative word method computes negative strength and if a word had both positive and negative word strength, then it was neutralized. Researchers used the Chinese lexicon method and collected all adverbs which affected adjectives. According to the emotion of adverbs, a score was given. If a word reflects positively then the positive score was given. Similarly for negative words and score was between +1 and-1 and the higher magnitude represented stronger sentiment either in a positive or negative direction. In this research work, the authors used a Hotel dataset which consists of 2000 each positive and negative feedback termed as reviews, and extracted adjectives and adverbs having 3947 and 100 in numbers from this Chinese lexicon. They have implemented five–scale evaluation method for giving a score. The proposed approach has two phases one was sentiment classification and the second was the five-scale evaluation method. They experimented with a five-fold cross-validation method, calculated accuracy, and then compared the scored magnitude of an adjective using the proposed approach. Researchers used two evaluation parameters, precision and distance precision, for evaluation in the five scale estimation method. Experiments show that the proposed approach was efficient and had a 5.7% precision compared to those techniques that just compute the adjective strength [28]. In this research work, researchers had proposed and implemented two approaches for classification tasks. One approach worked on binary classification, converting available information *i.e.* data, into positive and negative and another approach worked on 3-way classification by categorizing data into three categories *i.e.* positive, negative, and neutral. To implement both approaches, authors have implemented three models: unigram model, model based on feature, and model based on tree kernel. In this experiment, researchers used Twitter data. Unigram model was implemented as a baseline. In feature-based model-new, features were searched and recommended from previous work. Results show that 100 features used for data classification show better results than the unigram model using 10,000 features. Models based on tree kernel show better results as compared to both models. A combination of these models was also done for experiments, *i.e.* unigram with feature-based and unigram with tree kernel. Researchers concluded that both combinations outperform over 4% of the unigram model. In this research work, these five models were termed as Unigram Model, tree kernel model, 100senti-feature model, unigram plus senti-features, kernel plus senti-features. In experiments, results show that the tree kernel gives 2.58% and 2.66% accuracy, respectively, compared to unigram and senti-features [29]. In this research work, researchers proposed three AAC (Adverb-Adjective Combinations) Scoring methods. The first scoring method was for adjective variable termed variable scoring. The second scoring method was for adverb relevance with the adjective and termed as adjective priority scoring. The third was adverb first scoring related to adverb relevant to the adjective. The AAC method intensity is computed as an adverb of degree between 0 to1. During the experiment, I took 220 BBC news articles. The authors used comparative analysis and adjective priority scoring proved the best algorithm [30]. In this research work, Ontology engineering was experienced in Sentiment Analysis when 667 tweets were preprocessed by creating domain ontology. Researchers use the opendover12 web service to tag opinions and explore the intensity of sentiment. The proposed architecture had two versions. The first is the full-fledge ontology-based semantic system(SEM) and the second is the first without synonym augmentation. The second approach shows better results and concluded that advanced algorithms can be used in place of Opendover in the future for sentiment determination [31]. In this research work, researchers studied the diachronic phenomenon, and data were extracted from two different sources. One source was socio-political and another was sports and a combination of both sources from Google N-grams corpora. This research work based onthe word epoch delimitation was performed. Opinion change phenomenon which used covariance between two or more frequencies was analyzed. In this research work, Out of 1400 words, eight types of emotions were recognized using WNA based NRC and researchers termed it as Word Emotion Association Lexicon. Results show that the proposed methodology predicts the future between socialism and capitalism using covariance.

Hybrid approaches use both machine learning techniques as well as lexicon-based approaches. In this section, we will explain the latest research carried out in the field of hybrid techniques.

This research work [32] viewed and expected a methodology presenting a combined form of lexical-based and machine learning approaches. The hybrid approach, *i.e.* proposed approach, provides a high amount of accuracy than the classical-type of the lexical method. It helped and provided an enhanced form of redundancy rather than machine learning. The approach, *i.e.* proposed, was mainly used for opinion/sentiment mining through natural language processing (NLP), which helped extract the opinions/sentiments from the text associated with an entity [33]. In this research work, researchers proposed an unsupervised algorithm that utilizes a lexicon containing 2968 words to accomplish domain capability. A semi-supervised lexical classification algorithm and a bipartite operator graph are also proposed . As data was sparsed to overcome this problem, researchers utilized RLS classification algorithm. In the proposed approach, knowledge of sentiment was extracted from the lexicon and an RLS algorithm was utilized termed as Lexical-RLS. Proposed approach work on different types of domains containing lotus and political blogs. Lexical and semi-supervised lexical RLS were both implemented on base models. Feature extraction methods were used to improve the performance [34]. For morphological rich language, researchers proposed new algorithm subjectivity and sentiment analysis termed SSA. The dataset used for the experiment contains 2798 chat turns, 3015 Arabic tweets, and 3008 sentences. Sources of this dataset are Wikipedia Talk pages and web forum sentences. In the subjectivity analysis phase, the subjectivity and objectivity of collected sentences were evaluated manually. Then in the second phase, bipolarity classification of 3982 adjectives was done. In experiments, SVM outperformed baseline methods for subjectivity classification and yielded an accuracy of 73% for tweets and 84.36% for forums. SVM outperformed the baseline method for sentiment classification with an accuracy of 70.30% for chat turns. Error analysis and irony detection played a significant role in the improvement of accuracy [35]. In this research work, the authors perform two tasks *i.e.* classification of sentiment and detecting the changes in sentiment. In both tasks, lexicon approaches and approaches based on machine learning were used; the facebook dataset containing 3000 status messages was used for analysis purposes. Researchers developed a Lexicon approach based on Spanish Linguistic Inquiry and Word Count. For evaluation, the proposed approach employs c4.5, N.B., and SVM and results in the accuracy of 83.17%,83.13%, and 83.27%, respectively [36]. In this research work, researchers proposed two approaches, one was target-dependent and the second was context-dependent for sentiment classification. Both approaches were performed using SVM and enhanced performance using graph-based optimization. In both approaches, the PMI technique was used to select the noun's target nouns and phrases. Dataset taken for experiment purpose was Twitter data included the query related to Obama, Google, iPad, Lakers, and Lady Gaga. Researchers obtained 68.2% and 85.6% accuracy in both approaches [37]. In this research work, the authors proposed an approach for the classification of emotion by adopting the emotion cause extraction technique, which was good for eliminating irrelevant features through the chi-square method. A combination of emotional words and short phrases was collected to identify emotional words from tweets. The multi-class classification was done using SVR termed as Support Vector Regression and resulted in a precision 0f 75.07% [38]. In this research work, early detection of the Twitter trend was proposed and compared with google Trends. Researchers concluded that temporal changes were important to decide the emerging topic. This was done by detecting the polarity of tweets by using the sentiment lexica technique. For the experiment, the authors collected 4000000 tweets related to political parties during the German Parliamentary election. Sentiment Lexica technique which was used in experiments were SenticNet3 and SWN, where the focus was on finding the polarity of words by drawing a relational graph between political tweets and time.

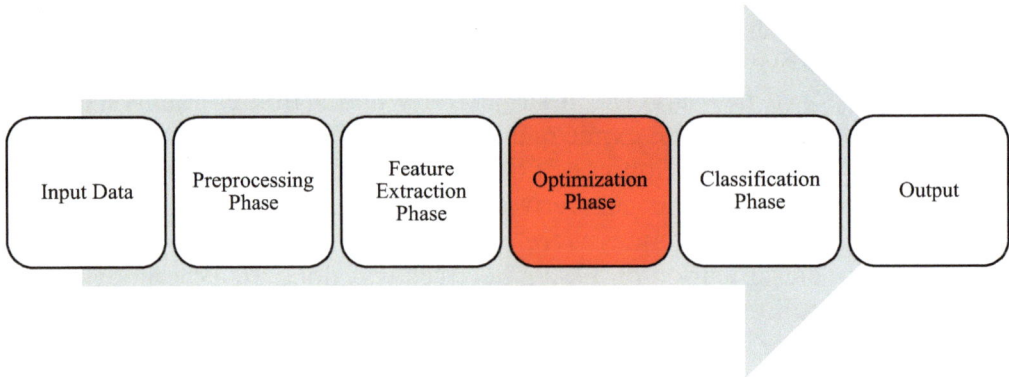

Fig. (1). System Model.

SYSTEM MODEL

The system model (Fig. **1**) describes the working of our proposed model *i.e.* IOFSCBD System. IOFSCBD works on the principle of optimizing the sparse matrix obtained after the feature extraction phase. In the case of high dimensional input data, lots of irrelevant features are added, and during the feature, extraction it results in a sparse matrix. So, there is a prerequisite to upgrade the output of this phase and it turns into the driving factor for our proposed system. This issue is resolved by reducing the data dimensionality and this is done by optimizing the sparse matrix weights. After the feature extraction phase, optimization algorithms are combined with classifiers and then implemented on Tweet Data and it shows better results as the data size is increased, which is shown in results. Presently in this section, we will clarify the various stages of the IOFSCBD System.

INPUT PHASE

In this phase, it is explained how the twitter data is collected for the following experimentation. The data set is collected through REST APIs. It is explained below:

REST APIS

The programmatic access is provided by REST APIs for reading and writing Twitter data.

1. With the use of OAuth, REST API identifies users and Twitter applications.

2. CSV format is followed for the response.

PREPROCESSING PHASE

In preprocessing phase, the first tokenization is done. In tokenization, input data is converted into tokens. Stopwords are those words that reflect no opinion, stopwords are removed in this phase. After the removal of stopwords, stemming is done, in which illogical data is removed. Input data is converted into features; features are those words that decide the polarity.

FEATURE EXTRACTION PHASE

In the feature extraction phase, weights are given to extracted features during preprocessing phase by using the Term Frequency and Inverse Document Frequency (TF-IDF) technique resulting in a dynamic array. After using the TF-IDF technique, weights are clustered into two categories *i.e.* positive and negative. As input is high dimensional, it will contain unimportant features and the feature matrix is sparse.

OPTIMIZATION PHASE

As the result of the feature extraction phase is a sparse matrix. There is a need to optimize this feature matrix. In this IOFSCBD System, we have used Particle Swarm Optimization(PSO),Ant Colony Optimization (ACO),BAT for optimization, and three of these are inspired by nature. We reduce the data dimensionality by optimizing the feature matrix and this is done by converting the feature matrix into an optimized feature matrix.

CLASSIFICATION PHASE

In the classification Phase, optimized feature matrices are classified into two categories *i.e.* positive and negative. In our research work, we have used Naïve Bayes and SVM Classifier. IOFSCBD System has six algorithms named NBPSO, NBACO, NBBAT, SVMPSO, SVMACO, and SVMBAT.

WORKING

In this section, we will be describing the algorithms of the IOFSCBD system, which are explained below:

Step 1: Input the tweets.

Step 2: In this step, tweets are pre-processed.

Step 3: In this step, extract the features TF-IDF.

Step 4: In this step, class label features are set.

Step 5: In this step, features are optimized using an optimization algorithm.

Step 6: According to the optimization algorithm, we initialize it. E.g. If the optimization algorithm is PSO then the swarm is initialized.

Step 7: After initialization fitness function is updated.

Step 8: Updated function is optimized,

if optimized then it learns the feature by the corresponding Classifieri.e Naïve Bayes, SVM, Maximum Entropy.

Else go to Step 7.

Step 9: In this step, classifier models are tested.

Step 10: When classifier models are tested, then find the precision, recall, and accuracy.

The work is described in Fig. (**2**). According to it first, we input the tweet data, then preprocess it, and then features are extracted and converted into the matrix with the help of TF-IDF and then optimize data by optimization algorithms; after that, optimized features are fed to classifiers, and performance is evaluated. For input, we have taken Twitter data.

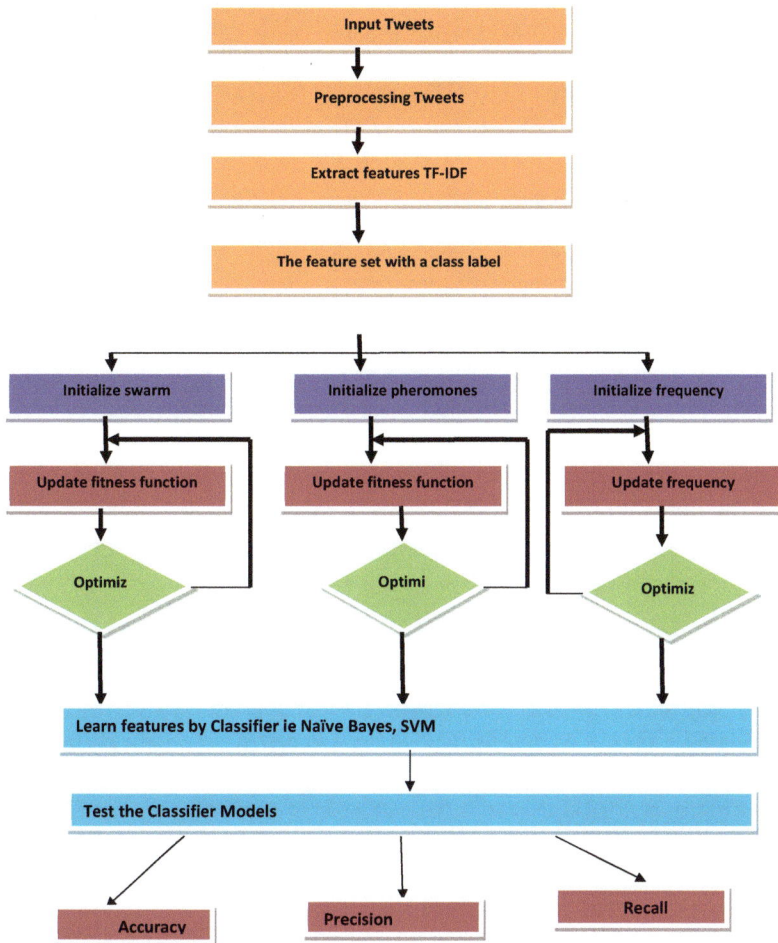

Fig. (2). Working Model.

RESULTS

This research paper has calculated values of accuracy, precision, and recall of the IOFSCBD System algorithms.

Accuracy measures the number of correct predictions done by a model out of all kinds of predictions it does. It is calculated by using the following formula:

$$Accuracy = (TP + TN)/(TP + FP + FN + TN) \qquad (1)$$

In this equation 1,TP stands for True Positive, TN stands for True Negative, FP stands for False Positive and FN stands for False Negative. Table **1** shows the values of accuracy when the data size is 1k, 2k, 3k, 5 M.B., and 5GB. In this NBPSO, NBACO, NBBAT is compared with Naïve Bayes.

Table 1. Accuracy values of Naive Bayes, NBPSO,NBACO, and NBBAT.

Techniques	1K	2K	3K	5MB	5GB
Naïve Bayes	80.234	79.98	78.2191	72.34	71.34
NBPSO	76.34	74.34	74.3857	78.21910112	82.60949558
NBACO	74.56	73.45	74.3857	74.38570369	78.27441415
NBBAT	71.34	71.23	70.2322	74.38570036	77.06441304

In Fig. (**3**), the x-axis represents the data size and the y-axis represents the parameter values of accuracy. The graph shows that NBPSO, NBACO, and NBBAT show better accuracy values as data size increases compared to the Naïve Bayes algorithm.

Table **2** shows the values of accuracy when datasize is 5MB, 3 G.B., and 5GB. In this table accuracy value of all algorithms of OFSCBD System NBPSO, NBACO, NBBAT, SVMPSO, SVMACO, and SVMBAT with different datasizes provided.

Table 2. Accuracy values of NBPSO,NBACO,NBBAT,SVMPSO, SVMACO, and SVMBAT.

Techniques	5MB	3GB	5GB
NBPSO	78.2191	78.2191	82.6095
NBACO	74.3857	74.3857	78.2744
NBBAT	74.3857	74.3857	77.0644
SVMPSO	79.5962	79.596	82.9215
SVMACO	75.8982	75.898	78.3754
SVMBAT	78.2191	78.219	81.7595

Fig. (**4**) shows the respective comparison of all algorithms of the IOFSCBD System when data size is 5MB, 3 G.B., and 5 G.B. and results show the improved accuracy values when data size increases. Fig. (**4**) x-axis represents the datasize and the y-axis represents the parameter values of accuracy.

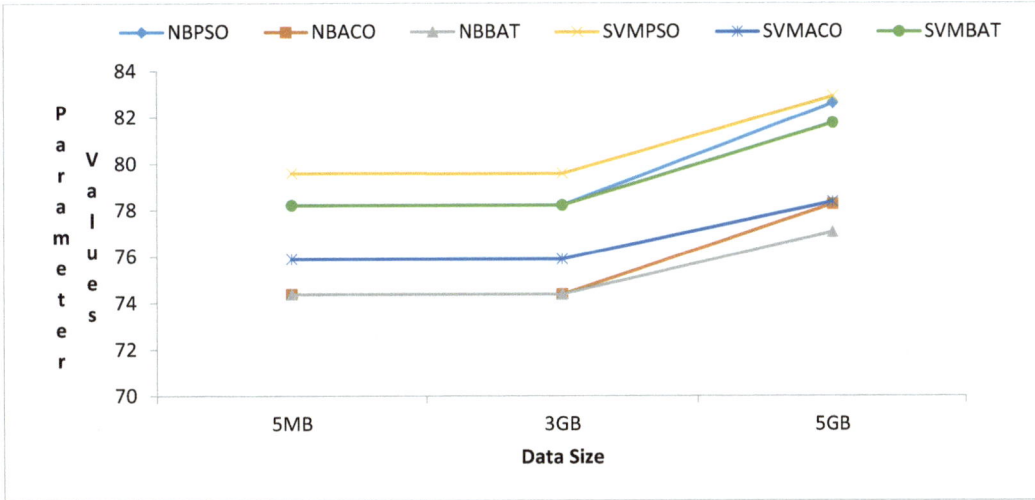

Fig. (4). Comparative analysis of NBPSO, NBACO,NBBAT,SVMPSO,SVMACO, and SVMBAT.

Precision

Precision is the ratio of correct positive predictions to the total positive predictions.

$$Precision = TP/(TP + FP) \qquad (2)$$

Table **3** gives the Naïve Bayes algorithm's precision values and proposed algorithms of theIOFSCBD System *i.e.* NBPSO, NBACO, and NBBAT when datasize is 1K,2K,3K,5 M.B., and 5GB.

Table 3. Precision values of Naive Bayes, NBPSO, NBACO, and NBBAT.

Techniques	1K	2K	3K	5MB	5GB
Naïve Bayes	83.345	78.45	79.1798	70.12	71.12
NBPSO	83.345	78.45	79.1798	79.17983	82.65469281
NBACO	80.45	71.34	72.8643	72.86432161	78.22376938
NBBAT	79.34	74.34	72.8643	72.86432161	77.01376938

Fig. (**6**) shows the precision values of Naïve Bayes decrease when data size increases. The proposed algorithms of IOFSCBD System NBPSO, NBACO, and NBBAT show better results when datasize is increased.

Table **4** indicates the values of precision of algorithms of IOFSCBD System when datasize is 5MB, 3 G.B., and 5GB.

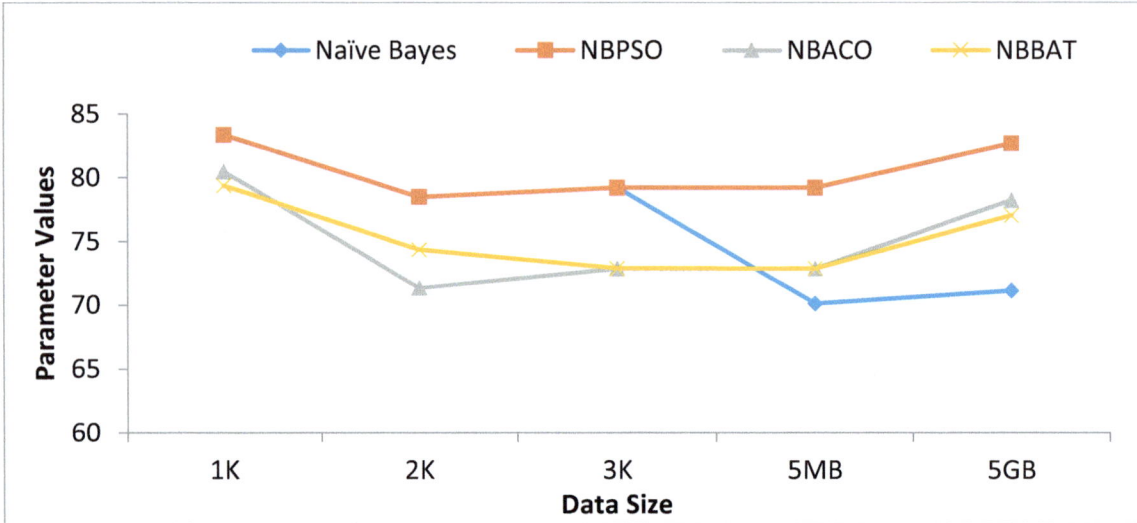

Fig. (6). Comparative analysis of Naive Bayes, NBPSO, NBACO, and NBBAT.

Table 4. Precision values of NBPSO, NBACO,NBBAT,SVMPSO, SVMACO, and SVMBAT.

Techniques	5MB	3 G.B.	5 G.B.
NBPSO	79.17983	79.1798319327731	82.65469281
NBACO	72.86432161	72.8643216080402	78.22376938
NBBAT	72.86432161	72.8643216080402	77.01376938
SVMPSO	77.89525	77.89525368	82.86413
SVMACO	74.39222042	74.392220421	78.33391806
SVMBAT	79.17983193	79.1798319327731	81.80469281

Fig. (**6**) indicates the IOFSCBD System's algorithms' performance, where the x-axis represents the data size and the y-axis represents the values of precision. Fig. (**6**) shows that when datasize increases, precision increase values, which indicates the improved performance of all algorithms.

Recall

The recall is a measure that tells us what

$$Recall = TP/(TP + FN) \qquad\qquad (3)$$

Table **5** indicates the values of recall of Naïve Bayes algorithm and proposed IOFSCBD System algorithms, *i.e.* NBPSO, NBACO, and NBBAT when data size is 1k, 2k, 3k, 5 M.B., and 5GB.

Table 5. Recall values of Naïve Bayes, NBPSO,NBACO and NBBAT.

Techniques	1K	2K	3K	5MB	5GB
Naïve Bayes	71.23	74.67	73.22	73.12	69.12
NBPSO	81.23	78.97	77.53	77.52955368	81.82955368
NBACO	76.34	74.56	75.6	75.60321716	79.59321716
NBBAT	76.56	75.78	75.6	75.60321716	78.38321716

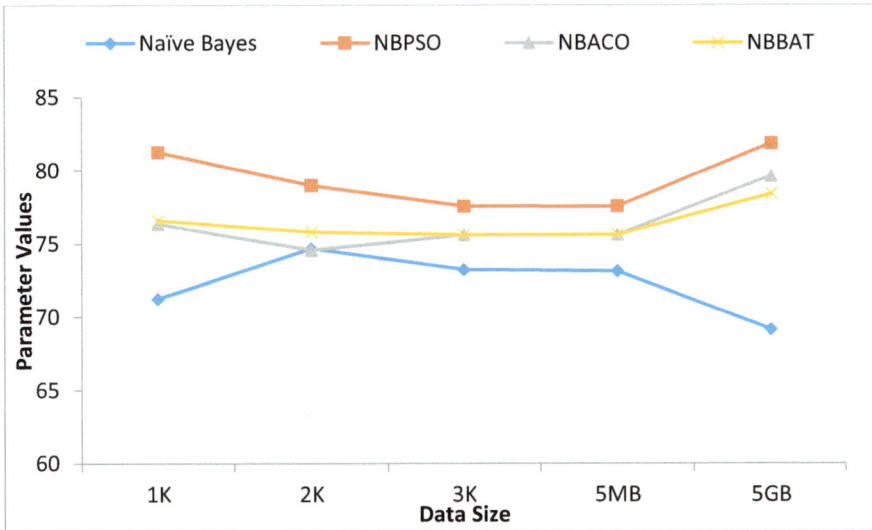

Fig. (7). Comparative analysis of Naive Bayes, NBPSO, NBACO, and NBBAT.

Fig. (**7**) indicates the values of recall of Naïve Bayes algorithm and proposed IOFSCBD System algorithms, *i.e.* NBPSO, NBACO, and NBBAT. The x-axis represents the data size and the y-axis represents the parameter values. Results show that Naïve Baye's performance degrades as data size increases, whereas proposed algorithms show better performance as data size increases.

Table **6** indicates the values of recall of all algorithms of the IOFSCBD System when data size is 5MB,3 G.B., and 5GB.

Table 6. Recall values of NBPSO, NBACO,NBBAT,SVMPSO, SVMACO, and SVMBAT.

Techniques	5MB	3 G.B.	5 G.B.
NBPSO	77.52955368	77.5295536791315	81.829553688
NBACO	75.60321716	75.6032171581769	79.59321716
NBBAT	75.60321716	75.60321715817693	78.38321716
SVMPSO	80.95300261	80.95300261096696	84.393
SVMACO	77.1556157	77.5295536791315	79.7156157
SVMBAT	77.52955368	77.1556156	80.97955

Fig. (**8**) indicates the improved performance of all the IOFSCBD System algorithms, and all these algorithms show improved performance.

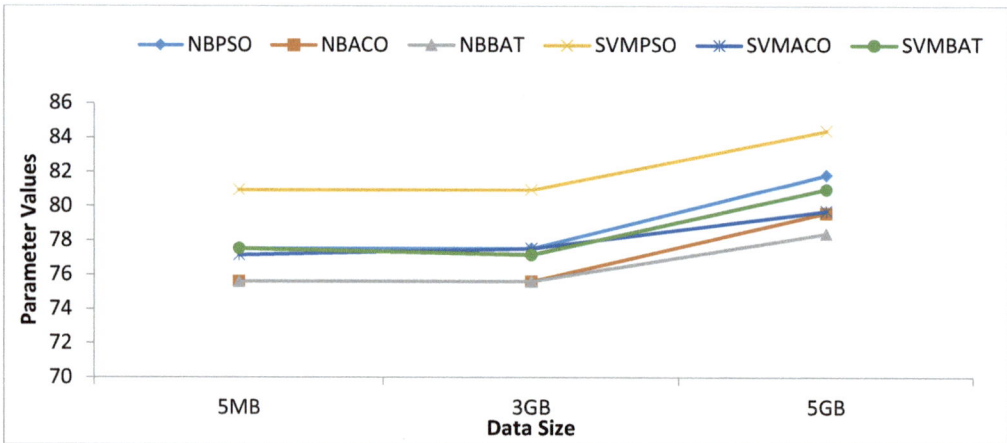

Fig. (8). Comparative analysis of NBPSO, NBACO, NBBAT,SVMPSO,SVMACO, and SVMBAT.

CONCLUSION

Since Sentiment Analysis is a research area that is beneficial for every sector, which is directly related to public opinions. In this research work, the focus is on the feature extraction phase by optimizing classifiers' weights to reduce matrices' sparsity. This system also reduces the false positive rate and enhances classifiers' performances. IOFSCBD System produces better results and deep learning techniques can enhance this system further. In this research work, optimization techniques are applied to Naïve Bayes and SVM classifiers. Now, this technique can be applied to different classifiers.

CONSENT OF PUBLICATION

Not applicable.

CONFLICT OF INTEREST

The author declares no conflict of interest, financial or otherwise.

ACKNOWLEDGEMENTS

Declared none.

REFERENCES

[1]   *T-SAF: Twitter sentiment analysis framework using a hybrid classification scheme.*, 2018.

[2]   "Efficient Twitter Sentiment Analysis System with Feature Selection and classifier Ensemble", *International Conference on Advanced Machine Learning Technologies and Applications,* 2018.

[3]   Comparison of Classification Techniques for Feature-Oriented Sentiment Analysis of Product Review Data, *Pujari, Chetana and Shetty., and Nisha P.,* Data Engineering and Intelligent Computing. Springer: Singapore, pp. 159-158, 2018.

[4]   *Yahoo!for Amazon: Opinion Extraction for Small Talk on the Web.*, 2001.

[5]   "Thumbs up? Sentiment Classi̅cation using Machine Learning", *Proceedings of the Conference on Empirical Methods in Natural,Language Processing (EMNLP), Philadelphia,* pp. 79-86, 2002.

[6]   "Mining opinion components from unstructured reviews: A review", *Journal of King Saud University – Computer and Information Sciences,* vol. 26, pp. 258-275, 2014.

[7]   "Exploiting social context for review quality prediction", *Proceedings of the 19th International Conference on World Wide Web,* pp. 691-700, 2010.

[8]   by: T. H. M. 18, "Bing Liu: The science of detecting fake reviews," content26, 22-Feb-2017. [Online]. Available:, https://content26.com/blog/bing-liu-the-science-of-detecting-fake-reviews/. [Accessed: 30-Jul-2022]

[9]   A. Mukherjee, B. Liu, N. Glance, and A. Mukherjee, "Spotting fake reviewer groups in consumer reviews", *Proceedings of the 21st, International Conference on World Wide Web, WWW '12.,* pp. 191-200, 2012.

[10]   "Stanford (2014) Sentiment", http://www.sentiment140.com/

[11]   R. S. Jagdale, V. S. Shirsat, and S. N. Deshmukh,, "Sentiment analysis on product reviews using Machine Learning Techniques", *Cognitive Informatics and Soft Computing,* pp. 639-647, 2018.

[12]   A. Diawara, "*, Archana Purwarb.TweetRush: A Tool for Analysis of Twitter Data. s.l.: I.J", *Education and Management Engineering,* vol. 2, pp. 31-40, 2018.

[13]   R.D. Desai, "Sentiment Analysis of Twitter Data", *Proceedings of the Second International Conference on Intelligent Computing and Control Systems (ICICCS 2018).*978-1-5386-2842-3.

[14]   Cummins Nicholas, Shahin Amiriparian, Sandra Ottl, Maurice Gerczuk, and Maximilian Schmitt, "Multimodal Bag-of-Words for Cross Domains Sentiment Analysis", *Proceedings of IEEE,International Conference on Acoustics, Speech, and Signal Processing (ICASSP), Calgary, Canada,* pp. 4954-4958, 2018.

[15]   P.D. Turney, "Thumbs Up or Thumbs Down? Semantic Orientation Applied to Unsupervised Classification of Reviews", *Proceedings of the 40th Annual Meeting of the Association for Computational Linguistics (ACL),* pp. 417-424, 2002.Philadelphia.

[16]   V. Mika, The evolution of sentiment analysis—A review of research topics,venues, and top-cited papers. 2017.

[17]   D. Maynard, and A. Funk, "Automatic detection of political opinions in tweets", *Proceedings of the 8th*

international conference on the semantic web, ESWC'11, pp. 88-99, 2011.

[18]   "Sentiment analysis algorithms and applications:A survey. Walaa Medhat a, *, Ahmed Hassan b, Hoda Korashy b. s.l", *Ain Shams Eng. J.,* vol. 5, pp. 1093-1113, 2014.
       [http://dx.doi.org/10.1016/j.asej.2014.04.011]

[19]   "NRC-Canada: Building the State-of-the-Art in Sentiment Analysis of Tweets", www.cs.york.ac.UK/removal-2013/task2

[20]   Tweet Sentiment Analysis with Classifier Ensembles, *Preprint submitted to Decision Support Systems,* 2014.
       [http://dx.doi.org/10.1016/j.dss.2014.07.003]

[21]   SENTIMENT ANALYSIS ON TWITTER DATA, "International Journal of Computer Science and Mobile Computing",

[22]   Sentiment Analysis, *Vol. Volume,* vol. 04, no. 12, pp. 2395-0056, 2017.

[23]   "Sentiments Analysis of Twitter Data using K- Nearest Neighbour Classifier", *International Journal of Engineering Science and Computing,* vol. 8, no. 4, 2018.

[24]   Hegde Brinda, H S Nagashree, and Prakash Madhura, "Sentiment analysis of Twitter data: A machine learning approach to analyze demonetization tweets",

[25]   "Projecting Embeddings for Domain Adaptation:Joint Modeling of Sentiment Analysis in Diverse Domains", *Proceedings of the 27ᵗʰ International Conference on Computational Linguistics, Santa Fe, New Mexico, USA,* 2018.

[26]   "Big Data: Deep Learning for financial sentiment analysis. Sahar Sohangir, Dingding Wang, Anna Pomeranets & Taghi M. Khoshgoftaar. s.l.: Springer", *J. Big Data,* vol. 5, p. 3, 2018.
       [http://dx.doi.org/10.1186/s40537-017-0111-6]

[27]   "A Comparative Study of Sentiment Analysis Techniques", *International Journal of Innovations & Advancement in Computer Science,* 2018.

[28]   "A study of supervised term weighting scheme for sentiment analysis", *Expert Systems with Applications,* 2014.

[29]   [29] Y. Lu, X. Kong, X. Quan, W. Liu, and Y. Xu, ""Exploring the sentiment strength of user reviews,"", *Web-Age Information Management,,* pp. 471-482, 2010.

[30]   Sentiment Analysis of Twitter Data, "Passonneau, Apoorv Agarwal Boyi Xie Ilia Vovsha Owen Rambow Rebecca. s.l", *Proceedings of the Workshop on Language in Social Media (LSM 2011),* vol. Vol. 2011, Association for Computational Linguistics., pp. 30-38, 2011.

[31]   " "Comparative adjectives and adverbs, and superlative adjectives and adverbs/adjetivos y adverbios comparativos y adjetivos y adverbios superlativos,"", *A Reference Grammar of Spanish,,* pp. 435-441, 2010.

[32]   "Ontology-based sentiment analysis of Twitter posts, Expert Systems with Applications. E. Kontopoulos, C. Berberidis, T. Dergiades, N", *Bassiliades.,* vol. 40, pp. 4065-4074, 2013.

[33]   "Time corpora: Epochs, opinions and changes", *Knowledge-Based Systems 69,* pp. 3-13, 2014.

[34]   "Sentiment analysis of movie review data using Senti-lexicon algorithm", *IEEE,2nd International Conference on Applied and Theoretical Computing and Communication Technology (iCATccT),* 2016.

[35]   "Document-word co-regularization for semi-supervised sentiment analysis", *Eighth IEEE International Conference on Data Mining,* pp. 1025-1030, 20082008.

[36]   SAMAR, "Subjectivity and sentiment analysis for Arabic social media. M. Abdul-Majeed, M. Diab, S. Kübler, s.l", *Comput. Speech Lang.,* vol. 28, pp. 20-37, 2014.
       [http://dx.doi.org/10.1016/j.csl.2013.03.001]

[37]   "Sentiment analysis in Facebook and its e-learning application. A. Ortigosa, J.M. Martín, and R.M. Carro. s.l", *Comput. Human Behav.,* vol. 31, pp. 527-541, 2014. [http://dx.doi.org/10.1016/j.chb.2013.05.024]

[38]   Jiang L, Yu M, and Zhou M, "Target-dependent Twitter Sentiment Classification",

CHAPTER 9

Applications of AI in Agriculture

Taranjeet Singh[1,*], Harshit Bhadwaj[2], Lalita Verma[2], Nipun R Navadia[3], Devendra Singh[1], Aditi Sakalle[4] and Arpit Bhardwaj[5]

[1] *IFTM University, Moradabad, India*

[2] *Mangalmay Institute of Engineering and Technology, Greater Noida, India*

[3] *Dronacharya Group of Institutions, Greater Noida, India*

[4] *USICT, Gautam Buddha University, Greater Noida, India*

[5] *Bennett University, Greater Noida, India*

Abstract: AI based applications are used for farm-based advisories regarding sprays, forecasting, usage of drones within the farms, infrastructure for humidity and temperature updates to the farmers, *etc.* Thanks to this, the losses of farmers have begun to decline. Therefore, considering the aims of the government regarding doubling the farmers' income, the losses of the farmers must be minimized using AI practices. AI intervention has the potential to boost the social and economic well-being of farmers within the medium to long run. The adoption of AI is useful in agriculture as it can bring industrial revolution and explosion in agriculture to feed the growing human population of the world. The study highlights that AI based farm advisory systems are playing an immense role in solving the problems of the farmers by enabling them to require proactive decisions on their respective farms. Various applications of Artificial Intelligence (AI in harvesting, plant disease detection, pesticide usage, AI based mobile applications for farmer support *etc.*) have been discussed in this survey in detail. Finally, the overview of Deep Learning and its application in agriculture is given.

Keywords: Agriculture, Artificial Intelligence, Deep Learning, Machine Learning, Pretrained Models, Transfer Learning.

1. INTRODUCTION

The worldwide population will be more than nine billion by 2050, requiring growth in horticultural creation by approx —70% to satisfy the needs. Nearly 10% growth in creation may be originated from accessing new terrains & for the remaining 90%, we need to improve our current creation. In this scenario, utilizing the most recent innovating trends for making cultivation more productive

* **Corresponding author Taranjeet Singh:** IFTM University, Moradabad, India;
E-mail: taranjeetsingh.cse@gmail.com

Vaishali Mehta, Dolly Sharma, Monika Mangla, Anita Gehlot, Rajesh Singh and Sergio Marquez Sanchez (Eds.)

remains probably our most specific need. Using artificial intelligence, we can develop smart farming to reduce farmers' losses and supply them with high submissions. Using computing, one can gather significant amounts of information from government and public websites or real time monitoring of varied data using the IoT (IoT) [1]. The term "Artificial Intelligence" (AI) is a buzzword nowadays for several sectors, service, manufacturing, and agriculture.

It is noted that the service and manufacturing sectors have begun to adopt AI practices and are ready to solve several challenges in this competitive environment. However, the agriculture sector is still within the evolving phase of using such AI practices. The agriculture sector's concerns are a low-income generation for the farmers, climatic dependence, lack of awareness among farmers, *etc*. But developed nations in Europe and the USA can reap rich dividends thanks to AI intervention in agriculture. Such AI-based applications are used for farm-based advisories regarding sprays, forecasting, drone usage within the farms, infrastructure for humidity and temperature updates to the farmers, *etc*. Thanks to this, farmers' losses have begun to decline [2]. Therefore, considering the government's aims regarding doubling the farmers' income, the farmers' losses must be minimized using AI practices. The industrial revolution of the last two centuries, which was driven by fossils and fuel-powered mechanization of mining, manufacturing, and its rapid expansion in other areas, has brought societal changes, mostly good yet with unintended consequences like urbanization and increase, the challenge remained a way to feed and clothe the growing population unless agriculture production and productivity could keep step.

In the last 50 years, approximately, the world population doubled. With the technological advances and agronomic advances, cereal assembly like wheat, rice, and maize got tripled with a touch increase in a cultivated area. In the last 20 years, the introduction of genetically modified seeds has reduced the usage of chemical pesticides and herbicides in vital crop, which has helped crop efficiency besides helping sustainability. Technology and agriculture research keep evolving, the same time the global population keeps increasing at a faster rate than agriculture production, the pace remains on, and it's predicted that by 2050, the planet population will be around 9.8 billion, 30% over today's level and this increase will come from developing countries like India. Those countries' income levels will keep rising; hence, the challenge is to feed huge, urban, and affluent mouths where the food habits, lifestyle, and environmental challenges are much more intense. In the rapid urbanization era, the mounting challenge is: will climate challenges and industrialization feed the globe of 2050 [3]. Will we need a 2nd green revolution? The answer is undoubtedly – Yes, but this revolution should be a smarter one – must provide scope, for the effective and efficient agronomy solution, judicious use of inputs, more informed agriculture decisions, a quantum jump in productivity, more crop per drop, more produce from the field and a sustainable income to the grower. Better plant and varieties are one aspect of technology, which were feasible through improved farm machinery and agronomy management driven through information technology, IoT, real-time data, predictive farm advisory, machine learning can bring farm automation, farm management and walk delivery efficiency, can only be driven by "Artificial Intelligence" [4]. Demographically agriculture is the broadest economic sector, and it plays an excellent role in India's socio-economic fabric. India contains a large and diverse arable land of 159.7 million hectares, but the yield level of most of the crops is much lesser than the world average; this is often largely thanks to unsustainable agriculture practices. Thanks to the lack of quality extension services, data delivery, and data transfer regarding plant protection, nutrient management, and marketing [5]. The complex operation of agriculture needs a pool of knowledge that is too timely and farmers to rely on diverse sources for this ranging from their own experiences, fellow farmers, agriculture specialists, advisors, input suppliers, and input dealers, the relevance and usefulness of all this information remain worthful if it is available on time, which always remain a limitation. To beat this can be an "Expert System" to create available information, advice [6]. This is often where computer science orientation comes into play. The agriculture sector in India is moving against tides; it is a sort of agriculture emergency because of lack of attention, land reforms, inefficiency in agriculture commerce, disorganized agriculture extension system, access to information and technology critical for higher cognitive process, farmer income is under tremendous stress and falling year after year [7]. The visible information and knowledge gaps make agriculture less profitable and attractive. To concur with this issue, the way of doing agriculture should be made intelligent. The adoption of technology like computer science (AI) based advisory systems by the farmers may be beneficial and might help scale back their losses. The AI techniques have contributed to assorted areas in the last twenty years, including agriculture. The term 'artificial' in AI are often taken as non-biological, and 'intelligence' as a capability to accomplish complex activities and actions Tongue Processing (NLP), Robotics, Machine Learning (ML), Automated Reasoning, Knowledge Representation, Expert Systems, Computer Vision, Speech Recognition, Automated Data Analytics, video game, Augmented Reality, Internet of Things (IoT), Cloud Computing, Statistical Computing, Deep Learning, *etc.* are some major sub-areas of AI having huge potential in solving complex problems of agriculture, of this technology is effectively leveraged for providing information to growers on soil management, time of sowing, spray schedule of various pesticides and knowledge on congenial conditions for pest infestations [8-10]. This can help farmers to be informed decisions and ensure better management and efficiency in agronomy [11]. It will also help the planet counter the emerging challenges in farming through efficient and innovative farming. National Sample Survey Organization (NSSO) has mentioned in its report in 2012 that 40% of the farmers would quit farming if they had a choice. This statement suffices the gravity of Indian farming's turbulent time and the state of agrarian crisis Indian farmers are in [12].

NITI Aayog has recently released a discussion paper wherein it envisions AI solutions for key sectors, including agriculture. There is a good potential for AI machines in agriculture to supply information to farmers on soil standards, when to sow, where to spray herbicide, and where to expect infestations [13]. Thus, if AI systems can advise farmers on best practices, India could see a farming revolution. However, such a futuristic scenario incorporates a formidable challenge of scaling it up to hide the whole value chain with factors like capacity expansion and price reduction in mind. The role of AI is evolving in three main categories (a) Agriculture Robotics, (b) Soil Management and Monitoring (c) Predictive Analytics [14]. This could enrich information availability, farmers, and make informed choices, decisions, and actions regarding crop selection, farm practices, resource deployment, investment in crop management, identifying procurement place, price, *etc.*, resulting in uncertainty for-profits losses [15]. This AI intervention can boost the social and economic well-being of farmers within the medium to long run. Considering the above facts, it is concluded that the food demand increases further as farmers' aspirations will continue to grow to possess access to better technology and data, which may help them own better crop management, yield, and ultimately better income. Any device that adapts to data needs to make fair use of machine learning [16, 17].

Genetic Programming (GP) [18-22] is the type of engineering that has been adopted here and is especially desirable for this work as it can create complete programs from a mix of functions. Many authors have shown that first can be a GP 'engine' with an image processing and analytical library. Read history section items and then categorize them [46, 47]. This single system is trained for a variety of grading tasks. Moreover, studies are presented that show the results that various groups of operators integrate into the solution. It has been shown that form alone generates more minor than the use of shape and colour. Genetic programming (GP) was applied to an honest variety of vision and image processing tasks. It is essential to identify a body of providers who carry out tasks useful for solving the situation and a price feature that can decide how well a program resolves the matter [48]. A Random Programs population is then created and assessed using the value function; best-performing programs are combined to provide a brand-new population of programs with imitation replication and mutation. The tactic continues until a solution is found to fix the issue or transfer a cap to generations. The feature collection includes image processing operators for vision problems, while the value function typically computes the average square error between processed pixels and training data [23].

The primary use of GP to identify military targets in infrared images [24] was a recognizable computer vision challenge. A GP generated solution has been used as the classification step of a multiphase automatic recognition system, which uses mathematical combinations of these features and a conditional test to take some 20 features as input and issue a target/non-target classification. A 2000-example training set was used, and a test set of 7,000 was used to assess output. It was found that the GP solution outperformed multi-layer perception, with lower calculation, higher genuinely positive, and lower false-positive rates. A GP solution was also developed to represent rectangular image areas with simplified features and standard deviations. The latter was thus found to be simpler than the 20-feature solution. This course is followed by several subsequent attempts by GP to develop vision systems, which provide both image processing operators and classification operators to the GP 'driver' and run them until a solution has been achieved. Activities and heating cause rapid temperature shifts, which tend to be at a loss in the last 50 million years of every global temperature increase [25].

Atmospheric CO_2 levels have significantly risen over the last two centuries to a present level of more than 385 $\mu mol.mol^{-1}$ [53], rising from approximately 270 $\mu mol.mol^{-1}$ in 1750. In the light of the even harder forcing of methane, ozone, and aesthetic gasses, certain combined ambient gas levels are now predicted to be above 550$\mu mol.mol^{-1}$ by 2050 due to a rise in atmospheric CO_2. Greenhouse gases are rising, contributing to heating, and average annual warming rises from three to five cubic meters over the next 50–100 years. While models vary significantly in their local climate change predictions, they can agree with their forecasts of increased heat waves, tropical cyclones, floods, and sustained drought. There is a possibility that our planet's agricultural regions will suffer differentially. For example, average hemisphere surface temperatures are expected to rise by 2050 from 2–3 percent and at the maximum level by 6.5 percent at best. Because of the increased temperatures, projections for the western us include earlier snowmelt, resulting in reduced ice and decreased water storage within the spring [26]. Climate models tend to simplify observed crop responses to global climate change variables at both plot and field levels, reducing the degree of confidence in regional and global projections. Although climate models differ in their forecasts of the severity of temperature increases, plaster, and other climate variables, there is a consensus that changes will significantly impact future agricultural production on the atmospheric CO_2 level, the rise in the environmental temperatures, and regional changes in annual precipitation. Their genetic programming for early flotation and rapid senescence in response to fret is crucial for abiotic stress tolerance of annual crop plants. While this trend to survival in nature is accurate, the impact on crop productivity can be devastating. To resolve this genetic programming by expressing a cytokinin-biosynthesis gene-mediated under the influence of drought stress-inducible proponent, a drastic rise in plant productivity under conditions of drought stress has recently been shown [54]. Elucidating and controlling the epigenetic mechanisms that regulate the transition from vegetative to reproductive phases and early flowering during stress could positively affect plant productivity under stress. Because programmed death (PCD) is assumed to be activated by different abiotic conditions and enhanced ROS accumulation, as a component of annual plants' genetic programming, suppressing abiotic stress-induced PCD could also end within the identical enhancement of yield under stress. Although suppressing senescence and PCD during stress might sound counterproductive, annual plants may need mechanisms to resist far greater stresses than previously thought. Still, they either do not activate these mechanisms or use them just for a short period needed to return up with seeds during stress-induced early flowering and senescence. SYPRIA is an example of integrated land-change science that supports the fundamental utility of the driving-forces conceptualization of LUCC and global environmental change. It also addresses theoretical and methodological needs in human-environment modelling, LUCC, and geographic informatics. It does so by combining genetic programming, cellular models, and agent-based models during a GIS-based simulation framework. These techniques combined offer the simplest way to take an individual position actor with decision-making.

Analog that incorporates learning over time. They also afford the modeler the analytical tractability necessary to include spatial and temporal interdependencies between agents and their environment through movement and better process at a spatially local scale while simultaneously allowing examination of their net effects at larger scales. SYPRIA is one in every form of effort that links ABM and cellular models to leverage these advantages in examining LUCC but remains the sole one to our knowledge that uses genetic programs as a choice-making analog. Outstanding questions on complexity-based methods like ABM, cellular models, and genetic programming remain, however, particularly concerning standardizing implementations; building better theories of their underlying mechanics; crafting calibration, verification, and validation regimes specific to those techniques; and closely examining the role of those methods in constructing theories of natural, human, and human-environment systems [55]. India could see a farming revolution if AI systems can advise farmers on best practices. However, such a futuristic scenario incorporates a formidable challenge of scaling it up to hide the whole value chain with factors like capacity expansion and price reduction in mind. The role of AI is evolving in three main categories (a) Agriculture Robotics, (b) Soil Management and Monitoring (c) Predictive Analytics. This could enrich information availability, farmers, and make informed choices, decisions, and actions regarding crop selection, farm practices, resource deployment, investment in crop management, identifying procurement place, price, *etc.*, resulting in uncertainty for profits or losses. This AI intervention can boost the social and economic well-being of farmers within the medium to long run. Considering the above facts, it is concluded that moving forward, the food demand further as an aspiration of farmers will continue to grow to possess access to better technology and data, which may help them own better crop management, yield, and ultimately better income. Therefore, it becomes imperative to review the previous studies on AI in agriculture, its scope, application, and impact and how it is useful in the Indian context. Accordingly, define the way forward for successful adoption of such quite innovative technological interventions. This may pave how profitable and sustainable agriculture practices in India may transform the country's agricultural sector [27].

2. USAGE OF ARTIFICIAL INTELLIGENCE IN AGRICULTURE

The significant growth within the farming sector in developed nations is attributed to adopting AI-based expert systems. This implies that there are several benefits related to AI-based systems in agriculture.

Therefore, there's have to understand the varied benefits of such expert systems supported AI within agriculture by reviewing previous studies' findings. Some researchers have highlighted that making informed decisions with data and Communication Technology (ICT) helps farmers across the worth chain, promoting efficient production and commodity trade. The employment of deep learning techniques in Indian agriculture practices helps the farmers to create accurate crop yield assessments and predict the general production with more precision.

Moreover, with machine learning, farmers can classify and forecast farming yields, implement adequate food grading systems, and use the farming space more efficiently. It also enables the farmers to realize better learning, manage farm activities, and maintain supply chain processes adequately. Hence, it is said that thanks to various applications of AI like machine learning, deep learning, *etc.*, the farmers can gain more significant benefits thanks to increased farming productivity and fewer use of resources, which has increased income levels and promoted social and economic well-being. AI, which may be a boon for farmers and at the same time will be a doom for the agriculture workers. These findings are very critical in developing an underdeveloped economy like India. Climate-Smart Agriculture (CSA) is an AI-based scientific tool that wants to enhance the agricultural process by ensuring the accessibility of food resources under changed atmospheric conditions. It promotes effective resource management, provides farm-related technical learning to farmers, promotes genetic modifications in plants, ensures efficient land-use management, and performs crop relocation activities. It also helps raise the farmers' income levels by effectively increasing productivity and promoting positive global climate change adaptation strategies. The use of sensors was also incorporated within the expert system, referred to as EI–Embedded Intelligence, which incorporates smart farming, innovative crop management, smart irrigation, and smart greenhouse. A nation must include these practices for the inclusive growth of agriculture. It takes into consideration the scenario of Indian Agriculture to enhance the farm management of grape growers. It came out with a system predicting disease incidence in grapes. Often, the grape farmers were facing substantial crop losses within the absence of the correct information. Mobile-based recommendation systems and expert Systems are AI farming applications that are content, knowledge, and hybrid-based and use filtering methods to collect and evaluate the information associated with users. Farmers in Odisha, India, utilized the system, and it helped them extend their productivity by recommending seeds, producing disease-resistant crops, and advanced agricultural practices. As a result, farm productivity increased because of the adoption of those innovative technologies, which enhanced farmer's income. AI offers numerous opportunities to the agriculture sector by managing yields, monitoring crop health, automating the irrigation process, and identifying desired agricultural inputs, *etc.* The comprehensive literature review validates that AI, with its analytical excellence and algorithms, effectively translates captured data to information useful for agriculture and makes a massive impact on agriculture's sustainability, productivity, and prosperity. The review also specifies that there's an enormous divide in its implementation amongst developed and developing countries; thus, the advantages of this game-changing technology are still limited to a developing country like India, lack defined state policies associated with the adoption of AI, average infrastructure support, capability building of the system. Stakeholders are becoming an enormous challenge for its speedy rescale in developing and underdeveloped countries, like India. Agriculture is considered a fundamental pillar of the world's economy and satisfies one among the essential need of a person, *i.e.,* food. In most countries, it's considered the primary source of employment. Many countries like India still use the usual farming method; farmers are reluctant to use advanced technologies while farming due to the shortage of data, high cost, or the benefits of those technologies. Lack of information on soil types, yields, crops, weather, improper use of pesticides, problems in irrigation, wrong harvesting, and lack of data about market trends result in farmers' loss or additional cost. Lack of data in each stage of agriculture ends up in new problems or increases the old problems and adds value to farming. Growth within the population day by day also increases the pressure on the agriculture sectors. Overall losses within the agriculture processes ranging from crop selection to selling products are very high. As per the famous saying, "Information is that the Power," keeping track of data about the crops, environment, and market may help farmers require better decisions and alleviate agriculture problems.

Technologies like IoT, machine learning, deep learning, cloud computing, and edge computing may get information and process it. Application of computer vision, machine learning, IoT will help lift the assembly, improve the standard, and ultimately increase the farmers' profitability and associated domains. Precision learning in the field of agriculture is essential to boost the yield of harvesting. Machine learning (ML) and Deep Learning (DL) are the most recent emerging trends within the computer field. It has already been utilized in various domains like healthcare, cybercrime, biochemistry, robotics, metrology, banking sector, medicine, food, *etc.*, to resolve the researchers' complex problems. Deep learning algorithms are making machine learning more robust and accurate. Using automated machine learning (AutoML) can cut ML experts' demand to automate the ML pipeline with more accuracy.

While performing agriculture tasks, the following flowchart is followed by farmers:

Step 1: Selection of Crop

Step 2: Land Preparation

Step 3: Seed Sowing

Step 4: Irrigation

Step 5: Crop Maintenance

Step 6: Fertilizing

Step 7: Harvesting

Step 8: Post-Harvesting activities

In pre-harvesting tasks, farmers are focused on selecting crops, land preparation, seed sowing, irrigation, crop maintenance, and fertilizing. In yield estimation, the farmers do the activities like yield mapping and counting the number of fruits to predict the assembly and make the mandatory arrangements required at harvesting or post-harvesting. While harvesting, farmers are focused on the maturity of crops or fruits, market need, quality. Whereas in post-harvesting, farmers are focused on post-harvest storage and processing systems. Agriculture's key branches are

Agronomy, Horticulture, Forestry, Livestock, Fisheries, Agriculture Engineering, and Economics.

Pre-harvesting

Pre-harvesting parameters play a crucial role in the overall growth of crops/fruits. In pre-harvesting, machine learning is employed to capture the parameters of soil, seeds quality, fertilizer application, pruning, genetic and environmental conditions, and irrigation. Specializing in each component is vital to reduce the losses in production. Here we considered a few critical components within the pre-harvesting and the way neural networks; machine learning are employed to capture the parameters of every component.

In [5], a soil management survey is presented. The appliance of ML techniques for predication or identification of soil properties (estimation of soil temperature, soil drying, and moisture content) was reviewed. The categorization and estimation of the soil attributes help farmers minimize extra costs on fertilizers, cut the demand for soil analysis experts, increase profitability, and improve soil health. In [6], pH values and soil fertility indices classification and prediction model presented. In [7], as per the author, a significant indicator of soil fertility is pH values and Soil Organic matter (SOM). Thus, the author has predicted SOM and pH parameters in paddy soil. As soil moisture is usually related to variability in yield, in [9], the author has estimated the moisture content of soil using Auto-regressive error function (AREF) and machine learning algorithms. Seed germination is a significant factor for the quality of seed, which is an essential determining factor of yield and product quality. Seed germination rate calculation continues to be done manually with trained persons' assistance, which is not only a tiresome process but also liable to error. Thus, various machine learning and image recognition techniques are proposed by different authors to automate the method of seed sorting and calculation. Various computer vision, machine learning techniques, Convolution Neural Network (CNN) methods are presented. The author of develops an image recognition technique for seed sorting with high accuracy. In, the author has used a multilayer perceptron neural network model to improve the classification method of separating pepper seeds of high-quality from low-quality. In [28, 18], the author has used the deep neural network (DNN) model using CNN for an assessment of the number of seeds per pod in soybean [17] and sorting of haploid seeds based on shape, phenotypic expression, and therefore the embryo pose [18]. In [19], the author builds a model using CNN for plant seedlings classification into 12 species. The author of [20] has assessed computer vision's proficiency as an alternate to routine vigour tests to expedite the accurate seed physiological potential evolution. In [21], the author has used the image analysis technique, principal component analysis (PCA), to save lots of time and price of placing seeds in numerous clusters by reducing the features to be considered for clustering.

In [22] author has used machine learning (ML) techniques for efficient seed classification.

Pesticides and Disease Detection

In time, disease detection is the most vital task to avoid wasting crops. Most farmers assume the diseases and apply the pesticides on the crops equally. Some farmers regularly analyzing leaves or branches of the tree and identify the diseases. Both the activities are supported human experience, which is at risk of errors and risk. The decision of which pesticide and when to use it entirely depends on the variety of diseases and its stage. The application of random pesticides in random quantities on all the crops may harm crops and farmers. Precision agriculture helps farmers application of right pesticide at the right time at the right place. Many works combined pesticide prediction with the detection of the disease on plants [23]. In [24], the author elaborated very well about how diseases can raise crop losses individually and globally. He proposed three parts framework consisting of crop losses and their measurement, emphasizing hidden consequences, the multifaceted nature of crop losses, the character of risks involved and avenues to deal with them, and lastly, a geographic and crop-based structure. In [25], detailed studies about pesticides and their agriculture and bio-farming applications and their impact on the environment were presented. In [26], shortcomings of accessible DL models used for disease detections were discussed. The author built a unique model consisting of two-stage architecture Disease Net for disease classification, which achieved 93.67% training accuracy. In [27], the author explored the new approach using DL to spot plant diseases from individual lesions and spots rather than the leaf. In [28], a detailed review of DL models wants to envision various plant diseases was presented. The author suggests that advanced DL algorithms should be accustomed to increasing accuracy. In [28], the author used transfer learning using pre-trained models for feature extraction and further fine-tuning, and the performance of nine disease detection DL models was evaluated. The target of the study was to deploy a disease detection model into the android app. In [29], a CNN model was proposed to classify apple leaf diseases into Brown spot, Rust, Mosaic, and Alternaria leaf spot. A replacement dataset consisting of 13,689 images of diseased leaves, accustomed to training the novel architecture, supported AlexNet. For apple disease detection and classification in Kashmir Valley, another model called Fuzzy Rule-Based Approach for Disease Detection (FRADD) was proposed [30]. Though the model's accuracy is excellent, it considers only one disease referred to as scab and limited fruit types. In [31], the author proposed his model, DenseNet-16, to beat the restrictions of pre-trained models trained on the ImageNet dataset only. The proposed model is easy and effective as its dataset is employed for the training. This model will be employed in mobile devices due to its lightweight size. In [32], a model is presented to detect the citrus diseases using their physical parameters like hole structure (phenotypic nature), texture, colour, vectors, and morphology. As per the author, ANN performs better as compared to other algorithms for detection and classification. The result shows that the utilization of SVM with ANN helps in increasing disease detection and classification rate.

Harvesting

After taking care of parameters in a pre-harvesting stage like soil, seeds, weeds, *etc.*, when the fruits/vegetables are ready, then harvesting is the most vital stage. During this stage, the critical parameters that should be focused on are fruit/crop size, colour, firmness, taste, quality, maturity stage, market window, fruit detection, and harvesting classification. Careful and proper harvesting is directly correlated with profit. Within the survey, we found that auto-harvesting robots, machine learning, and deep learning techniques are achieving better results and reducing the losses in the harvesting stage. In [33], the authors presented a detailed survey on intelligent automatic fruit harvesting robots. The utilization of automatic robots in fields helps extend the assembly and ultimately profits of the farmers. In [34], authors developed a CNN model supported single shot detector (YOLO) algorithm for on-tree fruit detection. The training dataset was created by manually labelling 5000 images of pear and apple fruits. The result shows that the model achieved over 90% accuracy for on-tree fruit detection. In [35], two deep neural network models with different architectures were proposed to classify the fruits. The first model was built with six layers, while the second was fine-tuned visual geometry group-16 pre-trained DL model. In [36], a strawberry fruit detection system was developed supported DNN like Feature RetinaNet, Residual Neural Networks, and Pyramid Networks. The advantage of this technique was that it might be trained in an hour with fewer input images. A more accurate machine vision system was proposed in [37] to categorize the date fruit images per their various parameters. Transfer learning from two famous CNN models AlexNet and VGGNet, were accustomed build the three classification models to classify date fruit in line with their maturity stage, type, and whether they are harvestable or not.

Own dataset was created consisting of 8000 dates images of 5 verities of dates in several maturities and pre-maturity stages. To conduct the PA practices to skyrocket the yield and crop marketability before the harvest, authors in [38] developed a platform that chains up-to-date ML techniques, modern computer vision, and integrated software engineering practices to live yield-related phenotypes from ultra-large aerial imagery named as AirSurf. In [39], a harvesting robot was developed for autonomous harvesting, consisting of the low-priced gripper and a technique for detecting cutting-point. The study aimed to develop an autonomous harvester system that may harvest any crop with a peduncle instead of damaging its flesh. In [40], a replacement system consists of Single Shot MultiBox Detector (SSD), and a stereo camera was proposed for autonomous detection and harvesting of fruits. The experiment was conducted on a fruit tree called "Fuji." For accurately counting the fruits from the order of images, authors in [41] proposed a unique pipeline consisting of segmentation, 3D localization, and frame to border track.

Post- Harvesting

Post-harvesting is the last and most crucial area in agriculture that require more attention. After completing all stages ranging from yield-estimation to harvesting, post-harvesting negligence may spoil all the efforts and cause severe loss to farmers.

The subtasks we will consider during this stage are a) shelf-life of fruits and vegetables, b) post-harvest grading c) export [42]. Shows that every country has its standards for grading the fruit. In [42], an information manual with direction for "Post-harvest management of mango for quality and safety assurance" was presented. This was very insightful for all the stakeholders of the horticultural supply chain. Studies showed that wrong post-harvest handling methods could affect the standard and quantity of fruits, which increases the losses. 31% of losses, which are identified at the retail level, were caused by decay only. The opposite practices that add losses are poor harvesting, careless handling, and improper packaging and carriage conditions. the incorrect disease management during production causes the decay at high-level pre-harvest infections. The decays within the variety of anthracnose and stem-end rot are very commonly observed. A training manual for "handling fresh fruits, vegetables and root crops" for Grenada was presented by the author in [43], as an element of the "Agricultural Marketing Improvement" Project TCP/GRN/2901, which Grenada Government and FAO implemented. This project aimed to extend the profits for horticulture products and crop growers through a well-organized agricultural marketing system. This document provides a very sound study about all post-harvest stages with the way to minimize the losses in every stage. A model was developed using Python OpenCV and Tensorflow. The model achieved over 90% classification accuracy. In [44], a machine vision system for post-harvest tomato grading was proposed. The system works on RGB images given as input to the system. Own datasets were created by manually labelling the tomato images into four categories according to their defect, healthy, and ripeness parameters. Four different models were built to classify the image into one in every category with matching features. A total of 15 features were considered while making a choice. Results show that RBF-SVM performed well compared to others for category one, *i.e.*, healthy or defected, with 0.9709 detection accuracy. In [31], the author developed a system for banana (Musa acuminata AA Group 'Lakatan') classification using ML techniques supported tier-based. Internationale non-invasive tier-based technique was utilized in this study. ANN, SVM, and RF classifiers were wont to classify bananas into extra class, class I, class II and rejected classes. The result showed that the random-forest algorithm outperformed as compared to others with 94.2% accuracy. In [45], two hyper-spectral imaging technologies, long-wave near-infrared (LW-NIR) and short-wave near-infrared (SW-NIR) were studied and compared for early identification of Bruise of 'Pinggu' peaches, which cause a severe quality loss. An improved watershed segmentation algorithm was developed and tested on multispectral PC images during this study. The developed system comprises a roller, transporter, and sophistication conveyors joined with an inside cabin with a camera, load cell, and board units. The system classifies the apples on colour, size, and weight parameters and identifies terrible apples.

The system was able to categorize the dates into three classes (grade 1, 2, or 3) from the given RGB image as an input. A back-propagation algorithm was tested within the study, which showed 80% accuracy. Fruits and vegetables depend on their parameters like shape, size, texture, colour, and defects. Different methods should apply to classify the fruits and vegetables per their quality parameters like data collection, pre-processing of information, image segmentation, feature extraction, and eventually classification. The rise in the cost of cultivation, crop failures because of unpredictable diseases, loss of soil fertility, and labour shortage has a significant negative impact on agriculture. Increasing demand and absence of supply adversely affect the socio-economic status. Machine learning and computer science attain their importance to beat this strategy. Artificial intelligence is the intelligence exhibited by machines rather than humans or other animals. The action to maximize the success is dispensed by using the intelligent agents that perceive its environment. Artificial intelligence paves the way towards drones, robotics, and sensor-based technologies. Certain apps like plastics, ICRISAT sowing app, *etc.*, guide farmers throughout sowing, disease, pest management, harvesting, and produce. AI and Robots from picking fruits to harvesting plants. Various developed countries worldwide have developed machines or robots that may work with identical accuracy and care as a personality's, helping harvest apples, tomatoes, and other crops and increasing the harvest between 3-4%. It also interprets overtime syndrome for the soy fungal disease and prompts for the observation's placement and severity. Companies that help advance agriculture improve small farmers' standards and agriculture in the Indian atmosphere [46].

Intello Labs

Deep Learning is used for Analysing Images and provides advanced image detection or recognition that may easily observe faces, objects, flora fauna. Small "Our Image-based solutions provide insights on the crops' health during the growing period and its final harvested quality by the click of the photograph," the corporate publish on the website, which can help small farmers in scientific understanding of crop and its life cycle [47].

Microsoft India

AI-based Sowing App helps decide the right time to plant crops to avoid negative consequences of drought and unpredictable rainfall. Microsoft collaborated with International Crops Research Institute for Semi-Arid Tropics, developed a Sowing App-based machine learning &, to some extent, business intelligence. The application gives information to farmers about the optimal time and date to sow. It gives the good thing about reducing cost by eliminating the installation of sensors in farmer's field [48].

Gobasco is the Intelligent Agriculture Supply Chain. With its base within the North Indian states. This company is beneficial to farmers by performing Quality Maintaining Quality, Managing Credit Risk, and Agri-Mapping [49].

Gramophone Recognition of image for Soil-based research. Its base is within the state of Madhya Pradesh (India). It claims to have the ability of image classification and soil-based science to assist farmers [50].

AI-Based Machines in Agriculture

Drones have the potential to deal with significant challenges in agriculture. It gives a high-tech makeover in agriculture. It is used throughout the life cycle of the crop. The crop will be viewed by near-infrared, and visible radiation drone carried tools and devices that can help track changes, monitor plants' health, and respond to farmers about the diseases. Planting and spraying are quicker with drones than traditional machinery. The drone is one platform that permits the sphere to be sensed multiple times throughout the season for identifying the perfect timing for in-season fertilizer application. Piloted agricultural aircraft like unmanned aerial vehicles are remotely controlled for crop production. Robotics may be a new trend in agriculture. It performs various agricultural operations autonomously, such as spraying, weed control, fruit picking, and managing individual plants in novel ways. See and spray is a robot developed by blue river technology for efficient weed management. It utilizes sensors that detect weeds, the type of weeds, and the suitable herbicides that are sprayed. Robots are employed in lawns to chop the grass (Demeter). The higher quality products are sensed by machines (colour, weight, density, ripeness, size, shape). More than 90% of the fruits were detected to reap by the robot. Moreover, the robot could harvest fruit in 16s.

Wireless Sensor Network of devices may communicate the information gathered from a monitored field through wireless links. Various sensor nodes are placed in the field for monitoring the operations. Sensor-based irrigation scheduling may be done in step with the sensor data. The moisture percentage is going to be available in the smartphones of farmers automatically through message [51].

3. MOBILE APPS FOR PERFORMING AGRICULTURAL TASKS

Some mobile applications for performing tasks like disease detection, advising, checking the quality of air, soil, *etc.*, have been discussed in this section.

Plantix

Berlin-based set out to detect the defects and nutrient deficiencies. This app uses images to detect the diseases, and then a diagnosis of the plant's health is provided. It's initially launched within the Indian regional languages of Telugu and Hindi. Thirty crops and offers prescriptions for over 120 crop diseases [52].

Prospera

This Israeli based startup was founded in 2014. It guides the farmers by collecting their information, like soil/water sensors and aerial images. The Prospera device is often utilized in greenhouses also [53].

The Sowing App

Microsoft, in partnership with ICRISAT, developed a sowing app. It uses computing and crop modelling tools to provide farmers customized real-time advisories. It helps to define optimal sowing timings. Customized messages will be sent to the farmers that advise them on-farm operations to hold out [54].

Smart Greenhouses

Smart greenhouses manipulate the environmental parameters thru manual intervention or proportional control mechanisms. A sensible greenhouse can be designed with the internet of things; this format intelligently displays video units.

Even though machine learning has vast opportunities, there still exists an absence of familiarity with machines. A lot of data is required to coach the machines for precise predictions, but it is tough to induce the temporal data. To explore the enormous scope of AI in agriculture, applications must be more robust. The solutions must become cheaper so the technology will reach the masses. The answer is more affordable in the open-source platform; the best challenge is to make the solutions have a higher penetration among the farmers [55].

Deep Learning Overview

Deep Learning is the fast-growing branch of AI and plays a pivotal role in AI applications. Application of DL methods dramatically improved the ends up in computer vision, image, speech, video and audio processing, object detection, object classification [56]. DL's fundamental components are neural network consisting of multiple layers, which progressively extracts the feature in each layer from raw input. The various available DL architectures which are very fashionable are deep neural network (DNN), Convolutional Neural Network (CNN), Long Short Term Memory (LSTM)/Gated Recurrent Unit (GRU) Network, Deep Belief Network (DBF), Recurrent Neural Network (RNN), Auto-Encoder (AE), Restricted Boltzmann Machine (RBM), Deep Stacking Network (DSN), Generative Adversarial Networks (GANs). Out of that, CNN and RNN are two basic and most typically used approaches [57]. From the surveyed literature, we observed that CNN approach was utilized by maximum researchers either for classification or for prediction. CNN models performed well on image datasets. The CNN model consists of convolution layers, pooling layers, and activation functions arranged together to create the architecture. The CNN models' performance depends on the labelled input dataset's size, the number of layers utilized in the architecture, and training duration (epochs. Building a brand-new model from scratch is time-consuming needs high-end hardware support. Dataset plays a crucial role in building a highly accurate model. The more clean and equally distributed the input dataset, the more accuracy you may achieve. To beat the issues of your time required for training, high-end hardware requirement, and an enormous dataset, "Transfer Learning" is employed. Transfer learning helps to create accurate models in less time. CNN model layers are categorized into two parts: feature extraction layers and classification layers. Feature extraction layers are called convolution layers, which are comprised of convolution layers and pooling layers. Classification layers are composed of fully connected layers. Per supported this fact, and you'll be able to apply transfer learning in the following scenarios: a) train the whole model: use the pre-trained model and train it on own dataset b) fixed convolution layers: take a pre-trained model, freeze the feature-extraction layers and modify classification layers as per your need c) Fine-tune the ConvNet: use the pre-trained model and freeze few layers of convolution rather than all and retrain the model on your dataset. Deep learning technology is becoming mature day by day. The survey shows that the use of CNN in agriculture is extensive, and it is also getting remarkable results. By exploiting depth, other structure, and hardware support, the CNN's training capacity and accuracy are significantly improved. Still, there are challenges like dataset creation, the time required for training and testing, hardware support, deployment of huge models on small devices like boards or android phones, user awareness. Internet of Things (IoT) systems combined with machine learning provide a beneficial solution to enhance farming gains [58]. Real-time parameters of the farms are gathered using IoT, and machine learning algorithms employ the collected data either to predict or for recommendations to farmers for improvements in farming. The survey also observed that Single-Shot Convolution Neural YOLO (You only look once) could be a state-of-the-art, real-time object detection system that must be used for detection localization to extend the classification accuracy.

CONCLUDING REMARKS

Innovative farming practices are developed using artificial intelligence to reduce cultivation, lose farmers, and supply them with high yields. Crop production could also be done better and cheaper by using artificial intelligence-based technologies. Such technologies will reduce labour efforts and guide farmers throughout the crop cycle. The study highlights that AI-based farm advisory systems play an immense role in solving the farmers' problems by enabling them to require proactive decisions on their respective farms. AI has been widely used practice in developed nations, and farmers have also gained dividends. The employment of deep learning techniques in Indian agriculture helps the farmers form accurate crop yield assessments and predict general production with more precision. It promotes effective resource management, provides farm-related technical learning to farmers, promotes genetic modifications in plants, ensures efficient land-use management, and performs crop relocation activities. AI will be appropriate and influential in the agriculture sector because it optimizes resource use and efficiency. Adopting AI is useful in agriculture or can bring industrial revolution and explosion in agriculture to feed day by day, developing the world's human population.

CONSENT OF PUBLICATION

Not applicable.

CONFLICT OF INTEREST

The author declares no conflict of interest, financial or otherwise.

ACKNOWLEDGEMENTS

Declared none.

REFERENCES

[1]   T. Bera, A. Das, J. Sil, and A.K. Das, "A survey on rice plant disease identification using image processing and data mining techniques", In: *Emerging Technologies in Data Mining and Information Security*. Springer: Singapore, 2019, pp. 365-376.
[http://dx.doi.org/10.1007/978-981-13-1501-5_31]

[2]   V. Dharmaraj, and C. Vijayanand, "Artificial intelligence (AI) in agriculture", *Int. J. Curr. Microbiol. Appl. Sci.,* vol. 7, no. 12, pp. 2122-2128, 2018.
[http://dx.doi.org/10.20546/ijcmas.2018.712.241]

[3]   M. Mangla, R. Akhare, and S. Ambarkar, "Context-Aware Automation Based Energy Conservation Techniques for IoT Ecosystem", In: *Energy Conservation for IoT Devices*. Springer: Singapore, 2019, pp. 129-153.
[http://dx.doi.org/10.1007/978-981-13-7399-2_6]

[4]   S. Potluri, M. Mangla, S. Satpathy, and S.N. Mohanty, "Detection and Prevention Mechanisms for DDoS Attack in Cloud Computing Environment", *2020 11th International Conference on Computing, Communication and Networking Technologies (ICCCNT),* pp. 1-6, 2020.
[http://dx.doi.org/10.1109/ICCCNT49239.2020.9225396]

[5]   S. S. J. Singh, "A Review on Usage and Expected Benefits of Artificial Intelligence in Agriculture Sector",

[6]   A. Giri, D.R.R. Saxena, P. Saini, and D.S. Rawte, "Role of artificial intelligence in advancement of agriculture", *Int. J. Chem. Stud.,* vol. 8, no. 2, pp. 375-380, 2020.
[http://dx.doi.org/10.22271/chemi.2020.v8.i2f.8796]

[7]   A. Joshi, S.S. Thejeshwar, and K. Khed, *AI Enabled Smart Fusion Platform Architecture For Agriculture*.
.https://www.researchgate.net/profile/Abhay_Joshi9/publication/344208535_AI_Enabled_Smart_Fusi on_Platform_Architecture_For_Agriculture/links/5f5bb9b0299bf1d43cfaf544/AI-Enabled-Sma-t-Fusion-Platform-Architecture-For-Agriculture.pdf

[8]   *The World Factbook — Central Intelligence Agency*.www.CIA.gov

[9]   S.K. Goyal, J.P Rai, and S. Kumar, *Indian Agriculture And Farmers – Problems And Reforms*. Indian Agriculture and Farmers, 2016.

[10]   I. K. Arah, H. Amaglo, E. K. Kumah, and H. Ofori, "Preharvest and postharvest factors affecting the quality and shelf life of harvested tomatoes: A mini review", *Int. J. Agron,* 2015.
[http://dx.doi.org/10.1155/2015/478041]

[11]   M.S. Suchithra, and M.L. Pai, "Improving the prediction accuracy of soil nutrient classification by optimizing extreme learning machine parameters", *Inf. Process. Agric.,* vol. 7, no. 1, pp. 72-82, 2020.
[http://dx.doi.org/10.1016/j.inpa.2019.05.003]

[12]   H. Bhardwaj, and P. Dashore, "A novel genetic programming approach to control bloat using crossover and mutation with intelligence technique", *2015 International Conference on Computer, Communication and Control (IC4),* pp. 1-6, 2015.
[http://dx.doi.org/10.1109/IC4.2015.7375619]

[13]   H. Bhardwaj, P. Tomar, A. Sakalle, and W. Ibrahim, "EEG-based personality prediction using fast Fourier transform and deeplstm model", *Comput. Intell. Neurosci.,* vol. 2021, pp. 1-10, 2021. [http://dx.doi.org/10.1155/2021/6524858] [PMID: 34603433]

[14]   H. Bhardwaj, P. Tomar, A. Sakalle, and U. Sharma, "Principles and Foundations of Artificial Intelligence and Internet of Things Technology", In: *Artificial Intelligence to Solve Pervasive Internet of Things Issues* Academic Press, 2021, pp. 377-392. [http://dx.doi.org/10.1016/B978-0-12-818576-6.00020-4]

[15]   R.K. Prange, "Pre-harvest, harvest and post-harvest strategies for organic production of fruits and vegetables", In: *Acta Hortic* vol. 933. , 2012, pp. 43-50. [http://dx.doi.org/10.17660/ActaHortic.2012.933.3]

[16]   K. Liakos, P. Busato, D. Moshou, S. Pearson, and D. Bochtis, "Machine learning in agriculture: A review", *Sensors (Basel),* vol. 18, no. 8, p. 2674, 2018. [http://dx.doi.org/10.3390/s18082674] [PMID: 30110960]

[17]   V. Anand Thoutam, A. Srivastava, T. Badal, V. Kumar Mishra, G.R. Sinha, A. Sakalle, H. Bhardwaj, and M. Raj, "Yoga Pose Estimation and Feedback Generation Using Deep Learning", *Comput. Intell. Neurosci.,* vol. 2022, pp. 1-12, 2022. [http://dx.doi.org/10.1155/2022/4311350] [PMID: 35371230]

[18]   Taranjeet Singh, and Krishna Kumar, "A Review on PDIS (Plant Disease Identification Systems)", *International Journal Of Engineering Research & Technology (Ijert) Encadems,* vol. 8, no. 10, 2020.

[19]   H. Bhardwaj, P. Tomar, A. Sakalle, M. Sakalle, R. Asthana, A. Bhardwaj, and W. Ibrahim, "Personality Prediction with Hybrid Genetic Programming using Portable EEG Device", *Computational Intelligence and Neuroscience,* 2022. [http://dx.doi.org/10.1155/2022/4867630]

[20]   V. Meshram, K. Patil, and D. Hanchate, "Applications of machine learning in agriculture domain: A state-of-art survey", *Machine learning (ML),* vol. 29, no. 8, pp. 5319-5343, 2020.

[21]   D.P.C. Peters, H.M. Savoy, G.A. Ramirez, and H. Huang, "AI Recommender System With ML for Agricultural Research", *IT Prof.,* vol. 22, no. 3, pp. 30-32, 2020. [http://dx.doi.org/10.1109/MITP.2020.2986125]

[22]   A. Sakalle, P. Tomar, H. Bhardwaj, and M. Alim, "A Modified LSTM Framework for Analyzing COVID-19 Effect on Emotion and Mental Health during Pandemic Using the EEG Signals", *Journal of Healthcare Engineering,* 2022. [http://dx.doi.org/10.1155/2022/8412430]

[23]   A. Bhardwaj, Aditi Sakalle, H. Chouhan, and H. Bhardwaj, "Controlling the problem of bloating using stepwise crossover and double mutation technique", *Advanced Computing: An International Journal,* vol. 2, no. 6, pp. 59-68, 2011. [http://dx.doi.org/10.5121/acij.2011.2606]

[24]   H. Bhardwaj, P. Tomar, A. Sakalle, and A. Bhardwaj, "Classification of extraversion and introversion personality trait using electroencephalogram signals", In: *International Conference on Artificial Intelligence and Sustainable Computing* Springer: Cham, 2021, pp. 31-39. [http://dx.doi.org/10.1007/978-3-030-82322-1_3]

[25]   A. Sakalle, P. Tomar, H. Bhardwaj, and A. Bhardwaj, "Emotion recognition using portable eeg device", In: *International Conference on Artificial Intelligence and Sustainable Computing* Springer: Cham, 2021, pp. 17-30.

[26]   N.R. Navadia, G. Kaur, H. Bhardwaj, T. Singh, A. Sakalle, D. Acharya, and A. Bhardwaj, "Applications of Cloud-Based Internet of Things", In: *Integration and Implementation of the Internet of Things Through Cloud Computing.* IGI Global, 2021, pp. 65-84. [http://dx.doi.org/10.4018/978-1-7998-6981-8.ch004]

[27]   H. Bhardwaj, P. Tomar, A. Sakalle, D. Acharya, T. Badal, and A. Bhardwaj, "A DeepLSTM Model

for Personality Traits Classification Using EEG Signals", *J. Inst. Electron. Telecommun. Eng.,* pp. 1-9, 2021.

[28]   A. Sakalle, P. Tomar, H. Bhardwaj, A. Iqbal, M. Sakalle, A. Bhardwaj, and W. Ibrahim, "Genetic Programming-Based Feature Selection for Emotion Classification Using EEG Signal", *Journal of Healthcare Engineering,* 2022.
[http://dx.doi.org/10.1155/2022/8362091]

[29]   A. Sakalle, P. Tomar, H. Bhardwaj, D. Acharya, and A. Bhardwaj, "An Analysis of Machine Learning Algorithm for the Classification of Emotion Recognition", In: *Soft Computing for Problem Solving.* Springer: Singapore, 2021, pp. 399-408.
[http://dx.doi.org/10.1007/978-981-16-2712-5_33]

[30]   N.R. Navadia, G. Kaur, H. Bhardwaj, A. Sakalle, Y. Singh, and T. Singh, "A Critical Survey of Autonomous Vehicles", In: *Cyber-Physical, IoT, and Autonomous Systems in Industry 4.0* CRC Press, 2021, pp. 235-254.
[http://dx.doi.org/10.1201/9781003146711-15]

[31]   A. Bhardwaj, and A. Tiwari, "A novel genetic programming based classifier design using a new constructive crossover operator with a local search technique", In: *International conference on intelligent computing* Springer: Berlin, Heidelberg, 2013, pp. 86-95.
[http://dx.doi.org/10.1007/978-3-642-39479-9_11]

[32]   F. Kurtulmuş, "Classification of pepper seeds using machine vision based on neural network", *Int J Agric & Biol Eng.,* vol. 9, no. 1, pp. 51-62, 2016.
[http://dx.doi.org/10.3965/j.ijabe.20160901.1790]

[33]   S. Savary, "Crop losses due to diseases and their implications for global food production losses and food security", *Springer Science+ Business Media B.V. & International Society for Plant Pathology 201.*
[http://dx.doi.org/10.1007/s12571-012-0200-5]

[34]   I.Y. Pandya, "Pesticides and Their Applications in Agriculture", *Asian Journal of Applied Science and Technology,* vol. 2, no. 2, pp. 894-900, 2018. [AJAST].

[35]   A. Marko, "Solving Current Limitations of Deep Learning Based Approaches for Plant Disease Detection", *Symmetry,* vol. 29, no. 8, pp. 5319-5343, 2020.
[http://dx.doi.org/10.3390/sym11070939]

[36]   S. Deokar, M. Mangla, and R. Akhare, "A Secure Fog Computing Architecture for Continuous Health Monitoring", In: *Fog Computing for Healthcare 4.0 Environments.* Springer: Champp. 269-290.
[http://dx.doi.org/10.1007/978-3-030-46197-3_11]

[37]   N. Sharma, S. Yadav, M. Mangla, A. Mohanty, and S.N. Mohanty, "Multivariate Analysis of COVID-19 on Stock, Commodity & Purchase Manager Indices: A Global Perspective",
[http://dx.doi.org/10.21203/rs.3.rs-68388/v1]

[38]   J. Dev, M. Mangla, N. Sharma, and V. Wadhwa, "A Heterogeneous Ensemble Forecasting Model for Disease Prediction", In: *New Generation Computing (NGCO)* vol. 39. Springer, 2021, no. 3-4, pp. 701-715.

[39]   M. Mangla, N. Sharma, S. Yadav, V. Mehta, D. Kakkar, and P. Kandukuri, "Multivariate Economic Analysis of the Government Policies and COVID'19 on Financial Sector", In: *International Journal of Computer Applications in Technology. Inderscience* vol. 66. , 2022, no. 3-4, pp. 294-302.

[40]   D. Sharma, S. Singh, and M. Mittal, "Trust Models in Grid Computing: A Review", *Recent Pat. Eng.,* vol. 13, no. 2, pp. 94-100, 2019.
[http://dx.doi.org/10.2174/1872212112666180427143757]

[41]   V. Tulshyan, D. Sharma, and M. Mittal, "An Eye on the Future of COVID-19: Prediction of Likely Positive Cases and Fatality in India over a 30-Day Horizon Using the Prophet Model", *Disaster Med. Public Health Prep.,* pp. 1-7, 2020.

[PMID: 33203489]

[42]   V. Joshi, M.S. Adhikari, R. Patel, R. Singh, and A. Gehlot, *Industrial Automation: Learn the current and leading-edge research on SCADA security.* BPB Publications, 2019.

[43]   A. Bhardwaj, A. Tiwari, D. Chandarana, and D. Babel, "A genetically optimized neural network for classification of breast cancer disease", *7th International Conference on Biomedical Engineering and Informatics,* pp. 693-698, 2014.
[http://dx.doi.org/10.1109/BMEI.2014.7002862]

[44]   A. Purohit, A. Bhardwaj, A. Tiwari, and N.S. Choudhari, "Removing code bloating in crossover operation in genetic programming", In: *2011 International Conference on Recent Trends in Information Technology (ICRTIT)* IEEE, 2011, pp. 1126-1130.
[http://dx.doi.org/10.1109/ICRTIT.2011.5972430]

[45]   D. Acharya, S. Goel, R. Asthana, and A. Bhardwaj, "A novel fitness function in genetic programming to handle unbalanced emotion recognition data", *Pattern Recognit. Lett.,* vol. 133, pp. 272-279, 2020.
[http://dx.doi.org/10.1016/j.patrec.2020.03.005]

[46]   A. Bhardwaj, and A. Tiwari, "Performance improvement in genetic programming using modified crossover and node mutation", *Proceedings of the 15th annual conference companion on Genetic and evolutionary computation,* pp. 1721-1722, 2013.
[http://dx.doi.org/10.1145/2464576.2480787]

[47]   A. Kumar, N. Sinha, and A. Bhardwaj, "A novel fitness function in genetic programming for medical data classification", *J. Biomed. Inform.,* vol. 112, 2020.103623
[http://dx.doi.org/10.1016/j.jbi.2020.103623] [PMID: 33197613]

[48]   S. Tiwari, S. Goel, and A. Bhardwaj, "Machine Learning approach for the classification of EEG signals of multiple imagery tasks", *2020 11th International Conference on Computing, Communication and Networking Technologies (ICCCNT),* pp. 1-7, 2020.
[http://dx.doi.org/10.1109/ICCCNT49239.2020.9225291]

[49]   D. Devarriya, C. Gulati, V. Mansharamani, A. Sakalle, and A. Bhardwaj, "Unbalanced breast cancer data classification using novel fitness functions in genetic programming", *Expert Syst. Appl.,* vol. 140, 2020.112866
[http://dx.doi.org/10.1016/j.eswa.2019.112866]

[50]   A. Bhardwaj, A. Tiwari, M.V. Varma, and M.R. Krishna, "Classification of EEG signals using a novel genetic programming approach", *Proceedings of the Companion Publication of the 2014 Annual Conference on Genetic and Evolutionary Computation,* pp. 1297-1304, 2014.
[http://dx.doi.org/10.1145/2598394.2609851]

[51]   M. Yang, D. Xu, S. Chen, H. Li, and Z. Shi, "Evaluation of machine learning approaches to predict soil organic matter and pH using vis-NIR spectra", *Sensors (Basel),* vol. 19, no. 2, p. 263, 2019.
[http://dx.doi.org/10.3390/s19020263] [PMID: 30641879]

[52]   A. Morellos, "Machine learning based prediction of soil total nitrogen, organic carbon and moisture content by using VIS-NIR spectroscopy, Biosyst. Eng., vol. 152, pp. 104–116, 2016", *International Journal of Advanced Science and Technology,* vol. 29, no. 8, pp. 5319-5343, 2020.

[53]   A. Bhardwaj, A. Tiwari, H. Bhardwaj, and A. Bhardwaj, "A genetically optimized neural network model for multi-class classification", *Expert Syst. Appl.,* vol. 60, pp. 211-221, 2016.
[http://dx.doi.org/10.1016/j.eswa.2016.04.036]

[54]   U. Sharma, P. Tomar, H. Bhardwaj, and A. Sakalle, "Artificial Intelligence and Its Implications in Education", In: *Impact of AI Technologies on Teaching, Learning, and Research in Higher Education.* IGI Global, 2020, pp. 222-235.

[55]   A. Sakalle, P. Tomar, H. Bhardwaj, and U. Sharma, "Impact and Latest Trends of Intelligent Learning With Artificial Intelligence", In: *Impact of AI Technologies on Teaching, Learning, and Research in Higher Education.* IGI Global, 2020, pp. 172-189.

[56]   Harshit Bhardwaj, Pradeep Tomar, Aditi Sakalle, and Uttam Sharma, "Artificial Intelligence and Its Applications in Agriculture with the Future of Smart Agriculture Techniques", *Artificial Intelligence and IoT-Based Technologies for Sustainable Farming and Smart Agriculture,* pp. 25-39, .
[http://dx.doi.org/10.4018/978-1-7998-1722-2.ch002]

[57]   T. Singh, "A Survey on Intelligent Techniques for Disease Recognition in Agricultural Crops", *SSRN,* 2020p. 3616700.
[http://dx.doi.org/10.2139/ssrn.3616700]

[58]   T. Singh, K. Kumar, and S.S. Bedi, "A Review on Artificial Intelligence Techniques for Disease Recognition in Plants", In: *IOP Conference Series: Materials Science and Engineering* vol. 1022. IOP Publishing, 2021, p. 012032.
[http://dx.doi.org/10.1088/1757-899X/1022/1/012032]

SUBJECT INDEX

A

Abiotic 185, 186
    stress tolerance 185
    suppressing 186
Activities 54, 76
    decision-making 54
    visualization 76
Acute renal dysfunctioning 77
Adaptive production processes scheduling
        problems 11
Adoption 16, 59, 181, 183, 187, 188
    industrial 16
Aesthetic gasses 185
Agents 7, 8, 16, 17, 186
    autonomous 17
Agile methodology 97
Agricultural aircraft 195
Agriculture 182, 183, 184, 186, 188
    emergency 183
    processes 188
    production 182
    Robotics 184, 186
Agriculture's 188, 189
    key branches 189
    sustainability 188
AI-based machines in agriculture 195
Algorithms 6, 7, 8, 9, 10, 11, 12, 17, 18, 19,
        111, 116, 126, 163, 164, 171, 173, 174,
        175, 176, 192, 194
    back-propagation 194
    machine-learning 10, 11
Anaconda distribution 98
    of python 98
Analysis, medical 79
Analytical tractability 186
Analyzing pneumonia 77
ANN methods 112, 114
Ant colony optimization (ACO) 159, 170
APIs, free cryptocurrency 95
Application 95, 197
    of DL methods 197

programming interfaces 95
Applications 67, 191
    bio-farming 191
    complicated 67
Approaches 113, 140, 163, 165, 168
    cluster-based 113
    complementary 140
    corpus-based 163, 165
    lexicon-based 163, 165, 168
Architecture 3, 4, 17, 56, 58, 61, 70, 96, 100,
        101, 167, 192, 197
    business's 3
    heterarchical control 17
    service-oriented 61
Areas, medical care 59
Artificial 4, 9, 13, 14, 15, 69, 70, 111, 112,
        114, 115, 192, 194
    neural networks (ANNs) 4, 9, 13, 14, 15,
        69, 70, 111, 112, 114, 115, 192, 194
    neurons 69
Artificial intelligence 1, 3, 5, 53, 67, 68, 71,
        74, 75, 78, 111, 181, 182, 183, 194
    for software testing association (AISTA)
        111
    techniques 74
Attacks 29, 72, 73, 163
    panic 29
    poisoning 72
    privacy violation 73
    terrorist 163
Automated 183
    data analytics 183
    reasoning 183
Automatic 11, 185
    recognition system 185
    scheduling systems 11
Automation process 34
Automobile companies 30
Autonomous 15, 61, 193
    harvester system 193
    modeling techniques 15
    system reconfiguration 61

S

Sarcasm nature 163
SARS-CoV-2 67, 74, 131
  coronavirus 67
Scale evaluation method 166
Seed(s) 186, 188, 190, 191, 192
  germination 190
  haploid 190
Self-organized 13, 62
  clustering algorithms 13
  manufacturing system 62
Sensor(s) 14, 25, 27, 30, 37, 41, 44, 45, 50,
    51, 53, 57, 188, 195, 196
  convergence 14
  data 196
  intelligent 41, 53
Sentiment 166, 169
  lexica technique 169
  polarities 166
Services 25, 26, 31, 33, 56, 167
  healthcare 26
  integrated 56
  teleconsultation 33
  telemedicine 33
  traffic police 31
  web 167
  web-bases national teleconsultation 33
Signals 7, 15, 69
  numerical feedback 7
SLT implementation 9
Software 27, 43, 56, 58, 96, 99, 109, 110, 111,
    113, 114, 116, 123, 124, 125, 126, 127,
    192
  as-a-service 58
  cloud 27
  defect predictive development (SDPD) 116
  development life cycle (SDLC) 110, 111
  engineering 124, 126
  fault prediction techniques 114
  integrated 192
  social 43
  testing 110, 116, 123
  test-effective 113

  transform 111
Software applications 46, 93
  traditional 93
  vertical 46
Software quality 109, 110, 111, 116, 123, 125,
    126
  assurance process 109
Soil 183, 184, 186, 190, 192, 194, 195, 196
  based research 195
  drying 190
  fertility 190, 194
  management 183, 184, 186
  moisture 190
  paddy 190
Statistical 8, 9, 20, 136, 166
  estimation problem 136
  feature selection methods 166
  learning theory (SLT) 8, 9, 20
Strawberry fruit detection system 192
Structural risk minimization (SRM) 141
Structure 2, 5, 15, 18, 19, 51, 61, 102, 131,
    163, 198
  medical 61
Sugar level, blood 28
Supply chain 27, 187
  operations 27
  processes 187
Support vector 8, 9, 10, 12, 131, 141, 146,
    151, 153, 155, 159, 161, 164, 165, 168,
    169, 192
  classification (SVC) 141
  machines (SVM) 8, 9, 10, 12, 141, 146,
    151, 153, 155, 159, 161, 164, 165, 168,
    192
  regression (SVR) 131, 141, 169
Symbolic regression 113
Systems 3, 15, 16, 43, 56, 61, 62, 71, 72, 73,
    88, 95, 101, 111, 177, 188, 194
  autonomous 43
  holonic 16
  hybrid 15
  mechanical 61

www.ingramcontent.com/pod-product-compliance
Lightning Source LLC
Chambersburg PA
CBHW050837220326
41598CB00006B/383